JAPAN'S QUIET LEADERSHIP

RESHAPING THE INDO-PACIFIC

MIREYA SOLÍS

Brookings Institution Press
Washington, D.C.

Published by Brookings Institution Press
1775 Massachusetts Avenue, NW
Washington, DC 20036
www.brookings.edu/bipress

Co-published by Rowman & Littlefield
An imprint of The Rowman & Littlefield Publishing Group, Inc.
4501 Forbes Boulevard, Suite 200, Lanham, Maryland 20706
www.rowman.com

86-90 Paul Street, London EC2A 4NE

The Brookings Institution is a nonprofit organization devoted to research, education, and publication on important issues of domestic and foreign policy. Its principal purpose is to bring the highest quality independent research and analysis to bear on current and emerging policy problems.

British Library Cataloguing in Publication Information Available

Library of Congress Cataloging-in-Publication Data
Names: Solís, Mireya, author.
Title: Japan's quiet leadership : reshaping the Indo-Pacific / Mireya Solis.
Description: Washington, DC : Brookings Institution Press, 2023. | Includes bibliographical references and index.
Identifiers: LCCN 2023008224 (print) | LCCN 2023008225 (ebook) | ISBN 9780815740261 (cloth) | ISBN 9780815739975 (paperback) | ISBN 9780815739982 (ebook)
Subjects: LCSH: Political leadership--Japan. | Geopolitics--Japan. | Globalization--Japan. | Japan--Politics and government. | Japan--Economic aspects.
Classification: LCC JQ1683 .S65 2023 (print) | LCC JQ1683 (ebook) | DDC 320.952–dc23/eng/20230417
LC record available at https://lccn.loc.gov/2023008224
LC ebook record available at https://lccn.loc.gov/2023008225

*To my mother Mireya
and
To Joan and Ed*

Contents

Note on Japanese Names

Japanese names mentioned in the main text follow the Japanese convention of family name followed by given name. Endnotes follow the Western convention of given name followed by family name to provide consistency among references.

Introduction

Moving Past the Narrative of Stagnation

Thirty years ago, the world was fixated on Japan. The country appeared to be an unstoppable economic juggernaut, in which a savvy developmental state had nurtured and propelled Japanese companies that were capturing ever larger shares of the world's export markets. Japan's rise was not without friction—charges of Japanese mercantilism and of security freeriding dominated U.S.-Japan relations in the heady 1980s. The period of high growth came to an end, however, and the stock market and housing bubbles burst in the early 1990s, producing sharp economic contraction and protracted deflation, thus robbing a generation of young Japanese of the economic and social opportunities that their forebears had enjoyed. Population ageing and decline, an ossified political system that appeared incapable of change, and the inability of Japanese leaders to adapt to the harsh realities of the post–Cold War era completed the picture of Japan's inexorable decline. As Japan became a model of what not to do, it ceased to capture the public's imagination.

The image of Japanese stagnation is pervasive yet inaccurate, for it glosses over the profound currents of change in Japan's economy and politics as well as the marked transformation in the country's international role. Popular perceptions of Japan still gravitate toward depictions of a country experiencing economic stasis, political indecisiveness, and passivity in foreign affairs. The reality points to a different and more nuanced state of affairs. Today, Japan offers both positive and negative lessons for how other developed nations can cope with similar economic and demographic challenges: financial crises, secular stagnation, and a shrinking working-age population.[1] While Japan's more successful adjustment to economic globalization provides clues for countries where a populist backlash has intensified protectionist pressures, the country still struggles with advancing immigration reforms and attracting global talent.

Japan is no longer the perennial underperformer among industrialized nations, as it has made headway in breaking the deflationary inertia and experienced average GDP per capita growth in the past decade that tracks with its G7 peers. Additionally, many Japanese firms operate at the technological frontier and occupy central nodes in critical supply chains. In contrast to many other liberal democracies, Japan has been spared a populist surge espousing nativism, illiberalism, and economic nationalism. Japan's social and political stability has enabled a more proactive foreign policy, especially in the last decade, including leadership in international trade and its blueprint for a Free and Open Indo-Pacific (FOIP) at a time of waning multilateralism, rekindled geopolitical rivalry, and pandemic disruption.

Undoubtedly, Japan faces profound challenges at home and abroad. Income inequality has grown, while real wages remain stagnant. The ranks of non-regular workers, who are deprived of the same opportunities for career advancement and economic security as traditional employees, have increased. The Japanese government has been late to lay out strategies to advance green, digital, and human capital transformations. Japan has not been gripped by political polarization, nor has it had populist demagogues unraveling national politics, but the country faces significant challenges to revitalizing its democracy. The political and administrative reforms of the 1990s and 2000s succeeded in strengthening the policymaking authority of the prime minister but did not develop a competitive multiparty system. Hence, traditional channels to keep elected officials accountable and responsive to public demands have weakened, and voter apathy has grown. Abroad, Japan's geopolitical space is more constrained due to a more unpredictable America, a more assertive China, and a more dangerous North Korea. In the aftermath of Russia's invasion of Ukraine and China's increased coerciveness toward Taiwan, the fear of a great power war is on the rise.

Japan lives in an increasingly dangerous neighborhood but still operates with strict conditions on the use of hard power.

A MORE CONSEQUENTIAL JAPAN

The narratives of Japan moving on an inexorable trajectory—rise or decline—are easily dismissed. The stark reality of a nation confronted with stern demographic trends, slow economic growth, and security threats posed by the significant military buildup of potential adversaries just beyond its borders cannot be denied. It is the recognition of Japan's mixed track record and diminishing relative capabilities that points to the more interesting puzzle at the heart of this book: Why has Japan emerged from the "lost decades" to become more relevant to the world and more consequential to the new geopolitics of the Indo-Pacific region? This book finds answers to this question in both Japan's own transformation and dramatic changes to the international order. Regarding the former, three main factors are of utmost significance: Japan's resilience against populism, with greater social cohesion, and democratic stability than many of its Western counterparts; the emergence of political executive leadership facilitated by institutional reforms, coupled with periods of deft political management; and a grand strategy centered on a connectivity push to rewire lines of economic and security cooperation in the Indo-Pacific. Japan's proactive foreign role was spurred by the current geopolitical moment. At a time when assertive powers are using force or coercion to change the status quo, economic nationalism festers, and long-term U.S. leadership is less predictable, Japan has become a more vocal champion of liberal international norms.

Whereas in the past Japan was passive on economic rulemaking and downplayed a regional political role, today Tokyo is an important architect in the emerging structures of economic and security cooperation in the Indo-Pacific. Under the broad frame of the Free and Open Indo-Pacific, Japan has deployed an economic engagement strategy comprising mega trade deals, quality infrastructure investment, and digital governance initiatives. This was done in tandem with proactive security diplomacy that included capacity-building to patrol the seas in Southeast Asia; the cultivation of new security partnerships with regional and extra-regional actors; and the consolidation of cooperation among the maritime democracies of the United States, India, Australia, and Japan (known as the Quad). It hinged as well on a deepened alliance with the

United States, characterized by closer coordination on regional contingency planning and Japan's reinterpretation of constitutional strictures to allow limited collective self-defense.

Japan has emerged as a central partner for the United States in areas that Washington has identified as top priorities for its own diplomacy: consolidating and renewing its role as an Indo-Pacific power and addressing the multifaceted China challenge. While the United States has abandoned trade liberalization and only recently put forward an untested approach to regional economic cooperation (the Indo-Pacific Economic Framework), Japan led in the creation of the Comprehensive and Progressive Trans-Pacific Partnership agreement after the United States' abrupt withdrawal from the original trade deal. Japan's leadership has facilitated the dissemination of economic standards in the digital economy and disciplines for state-owned enterprises that the United States endorses. Japan's robust funding of big-ticket infrastructure projects helps ease overdependence by developing Asia on China. Japanese firms enjoy strong international competitiveness in advanced materials and emerging technologies, and government and industry have experience hedging against China's economic coercion. Hence, competitiveness in advanced technologies as well as supply chain resilience have become important points of coordination in U.S.-Japan relations. Japan's 2022 national security strategy and Tokyo's push for greater defense spending and new weapons systems will influence the division of labor between both countries, as well as their coordinated efforts at regional deterrence.

China figures prominently in Japan's geopolitical awakening. After decades of investing in economic engagement to repair ties with Beijing since the 1972 normalization of relations, and later reaping the benefits of China's partial opening to become factory to the world, Japan's top security threat is China's military buildup and its expansive territorial claims made with disregard for international law. Throughout the twenty-first century, economic integration between China and Japan continued apace, but political relations fluctuated sharply between attempts at practical cooperation and deep tensions over Chinese economic coercion and pressure tactics used to claim the Senkaku Islands. Much of Japan's broader diplomacy has been articulated with China in mind. On the economic front, as China rolled out its Belt and Road Initiative, Tokyo has sought to avoid Japan becoming a legacy power in the realms of development aid and infrastructure finance. On the security front, Japan has endeavored to prevent Chinese regional primacy at the expense of its security guarantor, the United States. But Tokyo has not defined the contest with China in the Indo-Pacific and elsewhere in zero-sum terms. The search for a pragmatic balance between competition and cooperation continues.

Japan's more capable statecraft faces challenges that grow by the day. Border closures in response to the COVID-19 pandemic, intensified state rivalry, and the weaponization of economic interdependence test the core objective of Japan's successful diplomatic push: to become a network power through a connectivity strategy. Preserving Asia's long peace and reconciling economic integration with economic security are the critical tasks of today and tomorrow. Domestic politics are also in flux after a period of stable leadership. Abe Shinzo presided over the country's longest premiership in Japanese history, stepped down in the middle of an unprecedented pandemic in 2020, and was tragically shot and killed in July 2022 in a country where gun violence is practically nonexistent. While the nation reckons with Abe's hefty and complex legacy, his successors must retain the faith of voters, maintain party unity, and deliver on plans for economic revitalization and sustained foreign policy activism. At home and abroad, the country is at a critical juncture, but there have been other moments of exigency in the past. Dismissing Japan was premature before and will likely be so again.

This book offers a bird's-eye view of the past three decades of Japan's economic and political evolution, including its experience with globalization, the impact and recalibration of its of economic statecraft, and the array of geopolitical challenges that have triggered a gradual but substantial shift in Japan's security profile. In doing so, it aims to tell the story of a changing, imperfect, and more consequential Japan.

NOTES

1. Other keen observers of Japan's trajectory have also pointed to Japan's position at the forefront of manifold policy challenges other nations presently or will eventually confront. For instance, Phillip Lipscy uses the term "harbinger state" and Noah Sneider uses "frontline state" to capture this dynamic. See Phillip Lipscy, "Japan: The Harbinger State," *Journal of Japanese Studies* 24, no. 1 (December 23, 2022): 1–18, https://doi.org/10.1017/S1468109922000329; and Noah Sneider, "A Country That Is on the Front Line," *The Economist*, December 7, 2021, https://www.economist.com/special-report/2021/12/07/a-country-that-is-on-the-front-line.

SECTION 1

Globalization

CHAPTER 1

Stability amid Economic Globalization

The image of mercantilist Japan ducking globalization is well entrenched, but it has become increasingly inaccurate. In fact, Japan's globalization sped up starting in the mid-1990s. The country caught up to the United States in the aftermath of the Global Financial Crisis (GFC) of 2008. While high-income countries experienced stalled globalization in the wake of the GFC, Japan doubled down on globalization in the years thereafter. To be sure, Japan's integration into the world economy has been uneven. Bastions of protectionism in agriculture and services plus a defensive stance toward foreign capital delayed liberalization, but meaningful change has reached these remnants of Japanese insularity. Moreover, contrary to the myth that Japan has kept globalization at bay, the country has intensely experienced the offshoring of production that has proved toxic to the politics of the West, and it has felt more deeply than the United States the effects of China's emergence as an export powerhouse. But Japan has not experienced the anti-globalization back-lash that has consumed other industrialized nations, pointing to the need for a better understanding of how it adjusted to economic integration.

The globalization of the world economy has not been uniform across all nations, nor has it been a smooth, incremental process. Rather, it has advanced in fits and starts. At least twice in the twenty-first century, globalization has been besieged by systemic stressors, leading many to question whether the benefits of interconnectedness justify the risks of contagion or manipulation. Much can be learned from a country's globalization trajectory by assessing its responses to such crises: the

GFC of 2008, and the increasing securitization of globalization from 2018 onward due to strategic competition between the great powers, COVID-19 pandemic lockdowns from 2020, and war in Europe sparked by the invasion of Ukraine by Russia in February 2022. Being buffeted by the crises of globalization, Japan has aimed to boost its resilience to adverse shocks, but it has also not given in to nationalist temptations, knowing that its prosperity and international influence depend on its connection to the outside world.

GLOBALIZING JAPAN

By far, the most comprehensive measurement of globalization is the KOF Globalisation Index compiled by the KOF Swiss Economic Institute. In its latest version, it provides panel data for over two hundred countries for close to half a century (1970–2019). It works from the definition of globalization as a "process that erodes national boundaries, integrates national economies, cultures, technologies and governance, and produces complex relations of mutual interdependence."[1] Its economic globalization index captures trade, investment, and financial integration with measurements of de facto flows and activities and de jure domestic policies and international agreements. Viewed through this comprehensive lens, Japan's economic globalization is a story of convergence and resilience.

The evolution of Japan's economic globalization compared to other industrialized nations, its neighbors in East Asia, and other giants of the world economy (e.g., the United States, China, and Germany) can be gleaned from Figure 1.1. A key takeaway from this graph is that Japan has globalized to the point of matching and even surpassing the United States. In 1970, Japan's economic interdependence with the world ranked far lower than all other reference countries in the graph, except China. Between the mid-1980s and early 2000s, the U.S.-Japan economic globalization gap expanded, given the faster clip at which the United States integrated into the world economy. But this trend was reversed in the aftermath of the GFC. The subsequent Great Recession brought about a flattening of globalization's advance in Western industrialized countries, while China did not recover its globalization momentum of prior decades and its appetite for economic liberalization waned. Among the peer nations in this figure, only Japan doubled down on globalization in the post-GFC world.

Figure 1.1. Economic globalization index

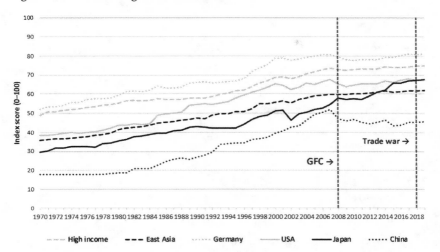

Source: Savina Gygli, Florian Haelg, Niklas Potrafke, and Jan-Egbert Sturm, "The KOF Globalisation Index—Revisited," *Review of International Organizations* 14, no. 3 (2019): 543–74, https://kof.ethz.ch/en/forecasts-and-indicators/indicators/kof-globalisation-index.html.

Japan's reputation as an incorrigible mercantilist is based on the enduring power of its non-tariff barriers. Even though Japan has had the lowest average tariffs among industrialized countries since the early 1970s, a host of discriminatory government regulations and exclusionary business practices have been deemed responsible for keeping foreign goods and companies at bay. And yet, a U.S.-Japan comparison of trade liberalization (factoring in tariffs, non-tariff barriers, and participation in trade agreements) shows significant change in Japan. Figure 1.2 shows that throughout the 1970s, Japan's trade policy regime was very restrictive—some incremental changes took place in the 1980s, but liberalization accelerated after the establishment of the World Trade Organization (WTO) in the mid-1990s. By 2019, Japan had caught up with the United States, reflecting the sharply different choices made in recent years by Washington (unilateral tariffs) and Tokyo (mega-trade agreements).[2]

Japan's trade integration (as measured by share of GDP of exports and imports of goods and services) increased to 36.7 percent in 2018, according to a WTO report that also noted that Japan's trade agreements have brought about significant liberalization by doubling the number of duty-free tariff lines to 40.5 percent.[3] There is still a large gap in the openness

Figure 1.2. De jure trade globalization

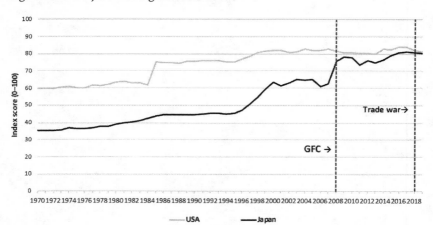

Source: Savina Gygli, Florian Haelg, Niklas Potrafke, and Jan-Egbert Sturm, "The KOF Globalisation Index—Revisited," *Review of International Organizations* 14, no. 3 (2019): 543–74, https://kof.ethz.ch/en/forecasts-and-indicators/indicators/kof-globalisation-index.html.

of manufacturing (where the simple average tariff is 3.5 percent) and agriculture (17.9 percent), but trade agreements have made a dent in the traditionally sheltered sectors of farming and services. For example, due to Japan's participation in the Trans-Pacific Partnership (TPP), the share of imported products never subject to tariff elimination was halved from 10 percent to 5 percent, including some tariff reductions on the five "sacred commodities" (rice, wheat, beef and poultry, dairy, and sugar).[4] By increasing the number of non-financial subsectors receiving national treatment from 26 to 85, Japan greatly improved its commitments to services liberalization in the TPP compared to its commitments in the previously negotiated General Agreement on Trade in Services (GATS).[5]

In one important dimension of globalization, the ability to attract foreign investors, Japan has badly struggled. Among its industrialized nation peers, in 2020 Japan ranked at the bottom in terms of the stock of inward foreign direct investment (FDI) as a percentage of GDP at 5 percent, compared to a 56 percent average for Organization for Economic Co-operation and Development (OECD) countries and 59 percent for the United States.[6] But Japan has made strides in increasing FDI, and the barriers to inward direct investment have shifted in important ways. The stock of inward FDI to GDP was a meager 0.63 percent in 1995, which means that Japan has done a better job attracting investment in a period characterized by prolonged deflation and population decline than during its high-growth era. Profound regulatory change helps explain this peculiar outcome. In its heyday, the Japanese developmental state used its broad regulatory powers (with a rigorous screening mechanism and wide discretion to reject investments deemed harmful to the national economy) to keep foreign multinationals at bay in order to nurture infant industries. But the Japanese government overhauled its foreign investment regime and converged to the more liberalized standards of the West (see Chapter 9)—so much so that in 2017, the OECD estimated that regulations on inward FDI were more onerous in the United States than in Japan.[7]

From restriction, the Japanese government shifted to outright promotion of inward FDI since the mid-2000s with the hope of spurring growth and innovation in an economy that had markedly slowed down. But clearly this has not been enough for Japan to become a magnet for FDI. Some formidable barriers remain. Richard Katz points to the resistance of corporate Japan to foreign purchases of domestic firms. While mergers and acquisitions represent the brunt of foreign investment cases in high-income economies (80 percent), they are much rarer in Japan (18 percent).[8] A survey of foreign companies in Japan underscores other barriers to investment, primarily the high cost of business (e.g., taxes, labor, and real estate) and difficulty in recruiting personnel.[9]

In sharp contrast, Japanese companies have been a driving force of globalization through investments overseas. In 1960, Japan represented a mere 0.8 percent of worldwide outward investment stock, but by 1990, its share had grown to 13 percent.[10] Today, Japan's outward FDI stock ranks fourth at $1.98 trillion, after the United States ($9.81 trillion), China ($2.58 trillion), and the United Kingdom ($2.16 trillion). In terms of outward FDI stock as a percentage of GDP, Japan at 40.2 percent is close to the United States at 42.7 percent, while China is far behind at 14.8 percent.[11] Japan stands out in the central role its manufacturing sector has played in its international investment activities (representing 41 percent of outward FDI stock in 2020) compared to the UK (16.5 percent) and the U.S. (15.5 percent).[12] The internationalization of Japanese industrial production is striking and was spurred by the major appreciation of the yen in the mid-1980s. Japanese companies responded to the loss of export competitiveness with a sustained wave of direct investment abroad. They reconfigured their operations by fragmenting and spreading across borders the different stages of the production process, giving birth to global supply chains that have transformed international production and the nature of international trade. The outward globalization push, in turn, transformed Japan.

ADJUSTING TO ECONOMIC GLOBALIZATION

The hardships of factory workers due to the overseas migration of industry and the avalanche of imported goods produced by cheap foreign labor has been a potent source of populist discontent in the industrialized West. Japan has experienced with peculiar intensity these globalization forces, offshoring a significant share of its manufacturing base and witnessing a steep rise of imports from developing countries, notably China. Concerns over deindustrialization and China as a competitive threat have been recurrent topics of discussion in Japanese media and academic circles, and yet Japan has not experienced an outright anti-globalization backlash.[13] Indeed, one of the most notable aspects of the politics of globalization in Japan is that sheltered sectors (e.g., agriculture) have fiercely resisted liberalization, while those more exposed to international competition (e.g., manufacturing) have not, even though Japanese corporations have embraced international production and welcomed imports from China. When it comes to the economic globalization forces credited with fueling populism and social discontent elsewhere—offshoring and import competition from low-wage economies—Japan's experience has been decidedly different.

Outsourcing Is Not a Political Minefield in Japan

The internationalization of Japanese manufacturing has been profound. Although the Japanese economy first caught the world's attention on the strength of its export drive, since the onset of the twenty-first century, more Japanese branded products have been produced overseas than domestically.[14] This transformation was decades in the making. The first Japanese investment projects in the 1960s and 1970s sought to remedy Japan's deficiencies: the dearth of natural resources and rising domestic costs as wages increased and energy prices spiked in the aftermath of oil shocks. But the visible hand of the United States had much to do with the vertiginous pace of Japanese direct investments abroad since the mid-1980s. Concerned with the rise of protectionism in the United

States (with the imposition of "voluntary" export restraints on Japanese autos), Japanese firms responded by shifting assembly production to the United States. American economic diplomacy had an even broader effect on the internationalization of Japanese manufacturing when it delivered a coordinated effort to appreciate the value of the yen vis-à-vis the dollar through the Plaza Accord (1985).

Japanese manufacturers responded to the doubling in value of the yen with an unprecedented rush to shift manufacturing overseas. Other bouts of yen appreciation (in the mid-1990s and in the post-GFC years) were also followed by an uptick in Japanese overseas investment. The annual value of Japanese overseas investment went from $3.6 billion in 1983 to $34.2 billion in 1988, and it reached $73.5 billion in 2007 and $258.3 billion in 2019 before the COVID-19 pandemic hit.[15] Importantly, over time, Japanese companies diverted a higher share of their manufacturing activities to other parts of East Asia, effectively knitting the region together through production networks. Hence, the centrality of the United States as a trading partner and a destination for Japanese investment receded, while Asia—and China in particular—gained prominence in Japan's international economic activities. Facing growing competition from East Asian producers, Japanese companies moved up in the value chain, specializing in advanced materials and sophisticated production machinery, manifesting in, as Ulrike Schaede puts it, the "technological pivot of the Asian supply chain."[16]

In spearheading the global value chain (GVC) revolution, Japanese companies also delivered profound changes to the domestic political economy. Prior to the Plaza Accord, Japanese industry had not emphasized production abroad. The overseas production ratio (Japanese companies' share of manufacturing undertaken in their factories abroad) was just shy of 3 percent in 1985. But currency fluctuations and the technological push to fragment production across national borders soon changed that. In a decade, the overseas production ratio tripled to 10 percent in 1996, and peaked from 2015 to 2018 at 25 percent. The overseas production ratio was 46.9 percent for transportation equipment, 29.2 percent for general purpose machinery, and 27.8 percent for information and communications electronic equipment in 2018.[17] The globalization of industry also saw a marked increase of import penetration in manufacturing, from 9 percent in 1990 to 19 percent in 2012, which was particularly acute in textiles and electrical machinery, with import penetrations of 50 percent and 21 percent, respectively.[18]

Despite the sizable relocation of manufacturing capacity abroad, off-shoring has not become a rallying point for unions and workers to decry globalization, as has often happened in other industrialized nations. In Japan, several factors account for the muted opposition to the relocation of industry abroad. Overseas investment activities have been critical to sustaining the competitiveness of Japanese companies, especially as the domestic market contracts due to population decline, and many Japanese companies have developed niche core technologies that position them at the heart of complex supply chains. Several studies have found a positive correlation between foreign production by Japanese companies and a boost in their R&D capabilities at headquarters and the creation of domestic jobs.[19] The positive relationship between outward direct investment, higher value-added operations, and domestic employment is not unique to Japan; it is a pattern that applies to the United States as well.[20] The difference lies in the labor adjustment practices of each country, with a much stronger emphasis on employment security and hence the absence of mass layoffs in Japan's case.

Despite the brisk increase in the overseas production ratio, the unemployment rate in Japan has only hovered between 2.5 percent and 5 percent (see Figure 1.3). Faced with structural decline, low growth, and technological change and globalization, Japanese companies have gone to great lengths to avoid job termination for their regular employees given the severe legal hurdles for dismissals. Firms seeking layoffs must clear a high bar, not only showing that job cuts are unavoidable, but also that they have pursued other cost-reducing measures, including the reduction of executive pay, reallocation of personnel among subsidiaries, reduction of work hours, and the negotiation of voluntary early retirement.[21] Increasingly, however, the brunt of the adjustment burden has fallen on the growing ranks of non-regular workers, mostly female and part-time employees, as discussed in Chapter 4.

The Missing China Trade Shock

Critics of globalization posit that the integration of millions of unskilled workers into the world economy has undercut the middle class in industrialized nations. In this view, the sharp increase in imports from low-wage economies resulted in a wave of factory closures and the contraction of manufacturing employment in the developed world. The empirical record points to a positive-sum dynamic, with most countries

Figure 1.3. Overseas production ratio (manufacturing industries) and national unemployment rate (1985–2019)

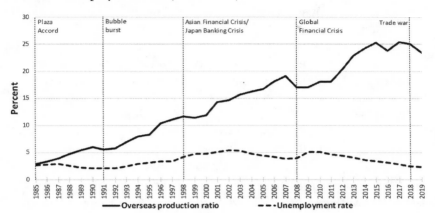

Sources: Overseas production ratio data from Ministry of Economy, Trade and Industry, "Survey on Overseas Business Activities," 2017, 2008, 2006, http://www. meti.go.jp/english/statistics/tyo/kaigaizi/index.html, and Ministry of Finance, "Financial Statements Statistics of Corporations by Industry," https://www.mof. go.jp/pri/reference/ssc/results/index.htm; unemployment rate data from OECD, "Unemployment Rate (Indicator)," https://data.oecd.org/unemp/unemployment-rate.htm.

raising their living standards as globalization increased.[22] But the question of the distributional consequences of economic liberalization within a country remains a potent force for populist mobilization.

Japan has not remained impervious to the dramatic takeoff of emerging economies in the twenty-first century, but it also has not been gripped by a national debate on jobs lost to China as it rose to become an export powerhouse. The contrast with the United States, where the discussions over the "China trade shock" figured prominently in the 2016 presidential campaigns, could not be starker.[23] Trade skepticism was a fixture of the U.S. presidential campaign debates and not a single candidate supported the recently inked Trans-Pacific Partnership trade agreement.[24]

Taniguchi Mina documents how Japan has experienced intensely the new realities of international trade and manufacturing: imports from developing countries tripled between 1995 and 2007, the country has run a steady trade deficit with China, manufacturing plants in Japan decreased from 435,000 in 1990 to 224,000 in 2010, and the share of manufacturing employment contracted from 22 percent to 14 percent in that same period. The crucial difference, as she demonstrates, is the labor outcomes of trade with China. Taniguchi found that Japanese prefectures that import more intensively from China experienced *growth* in industrial employment, especially if those imports were intermediate products.[25]

In fact, there are critical differences in the trading relationships that the United States and Japan have crafted with China. As Naka Rei and Fukagawa Yukiko point out, Japan rapidly increased its imports from China following China's WTO accession in 2001, and imports from China have since occupied a larger share of total imports in Japan than in the United States. The globalization of China clearly impacted Japan. But there are stark differences on the export side. Namely, China is a larger export market for Japan (21.6 percent of total exports) than for the United States (10.5 percent), and more importantly, Japan exports a much larger share of intermediate products (64.6 percent) than the United States (40.8 percent) in trade flows with China.[26]

It matters greatly that component trade is at the heart of Japan-China economic relations. Cutting-edge research on advanced economies has found that once value chain trade is factored in, the negative impact of imports on manufacturing employment is significantly diminished, though regional disparities may persist.[27] Intra- and inter-industry linkages are key in that inexpensive inputs will increase the competitiveness of downstream sectors and foster job creation. For instance, Jakubik and Stolzenburg estimate that the loss of U.S. manufacturing jobs due to Chinese imports is one-third less than the initial China shock studies once value chain effects are taken into account.[28]

An important reason why the China trade shock missed Japan is that the two Asian nations integrated more deeply through production sharing in GVCs, which made the distributional consequences of trade less divisive.

NAVIGATING TWENTY-FIRST-CENTURY GLOBALIZATION CRISES

The Global Financial Crisis

The 2008 Global Financial Crisis was a crisis of globalization in two profound ways. First, it underscored the deep interdependence tying the fates of countries across the world together. While the boom of crisscrossing capital flows created many growth opportunities, with it came vulnerabilities. As these risks were exposed, a fractious debate ensued on where to place blame for the meltdown: Was it an Asian savings glut enabling the low-interest rate environment behind the consumption/ debt binge in the West, or an outright regulatory failure in the country at the heart of the world financial system, with an American real estate bubble and toxic subprime assets that spread across markets? The common thread in this debate, however, was the deep awareness of interconnectedness, especially in lean times. In contrast to past episodes of financial turbulence confined to a single country or region, this time the world economy seized up in the worst downturn since the Great Depression.[29]

It was globalization that brought the GFC to the shores of Japan. And when it hit, it hit with a vengeance. At the onset of the GFC, Japan was spared. Coming out of its own banking crisis a decade earlier, authorities had tightened financial regulations and Japanese banks were very cautious, limiting their exposure to subprime financial products. But Japan's deep integration into the world economy left it exposed to a reversal of capital flows with the Lehman shock (foreign investors held one-fifth of Tokyo Stock Exchange listings)[30] and a collapse in exports as demand in industrial countries plummeted. At its nadir in February 2009, the value of Japanese exports was just half of what it had been a year before, and that year's GDP contraction at −6.3 percent was the worst ever for postwar Japan, and the worst among advanced industrialized nations. Globalization shook Japan.

The Great Recession was a child of globalization in one more way: the dissemination of policy ideas on how to respond to financial crises in industrialized nations. The lessons of Japan's own financial crisis traveled and provided an important roadmap to Western countries as they stared into the abyss of a systemic shock in 2008. Lessons eventually learned by Japan in the 1990s and applied swiftly by others during the GFC included recapitalization of the financial sector, large-scale fiscal stimulus, and zero-interest rates plus monetary easing.[31] Throughout, however, Japan operated with a double handicap. As aptly described by Lipscy and Takinami, one was the "first-mover disadvantage." Japan muddled through its response to the burst of the bubble in 1990, the ensuing banking crisis, and the dismantlement of its "convoy system" of financial regulation.[32] Effective policy measures were thereby delayed at great cost to the Japanese economy and society. Katada Saori identifies Japan's other liability: "financial crisis fatigue." Japan came to the

fight for restarting growth during the Great Recession already weary
due to fiscal constraints (public debt to GDP had soared to over 200 percent), interest rates already at zero percent, and unresponsive economic
agents (businesses and consumers), dulled to stimulus measures that had
spanned years.[33]

Hence, Japan's recovery from the GFC was slower than that of the
United States, but drawing a direct comparison is difficult because of
the jolt of the March 11, 2011, "triple disaster" in northeastern Japan
(earthquake, tsunami, and nuclear accident). In the short span of three
years, Japan experienced frontal assaults to its outward-led economic
model, including a demand shock courtesy of the GFC, a supply shock
due to damage dealt to production networks in disaster-afflicted areas,
and an energy shock due to the shutdown of nuclear reactors nationwide in the aftermath of 3/11. And yet, when it came to the social costs
of the Great Recession, the outcomes between the United States and
Japan were reversed. Peak unemployment rates reached 10 percent in the
United States, but only 5 percent in Japan, and even by 2014 the U.S.
unemployment rate was above the precrisis level with a much higher
proportion of long-term unemployment. Japan outperformed the United
States on both scores.[34]

Most notably, Japan deepened its outward integration during the
postcrisis era in contrast to the "slowbalization" experienced elsewhere, with a sharp contraction of capital flows and the stagnation of
supply chain trade.[35] Cross-border capital flows dropped from 22.5
percent of GDP in 2007 to 6.1 percent in 2016. The retrenchment of
western European banks was most dramatic, as these banks reduced
foreign claims by 45 percent in this period. In contrast, Japanese banks
expanded 1.5 times their foreign assets to a total of $1.476 trillion.[36]

Contrary to the experience of other countries, which saw their degree
of participation in GVCs stall after the 2008 GFC, Japanese companies
intensified their reliance on regional production networks. The GVC
Participation Index, which measures forward and backward production
linkages, shows deeper integration for Japan and retreat or slowdown
for China and the United States.[37] Moreover, the severe trade shocks
Japan experienced did not affect the consistent level of support for trade
among the Japanese public, but American free trade sentiment did take
a hit during the Great Recession (Figure 1.4).

Figure 1.4. Percent of respondents who think trade is a good thing

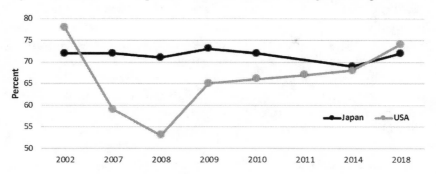

Sources: Pew Research Center, "Global Trends and Attitudes Survey," 2002, 2008, 2014, 2018, https://www.pewglobal.org/datasets/2018; Pew Research Center, "Pew Global Attitudes & Trends Question Database," https://www.pewresearch. org/global/question-search/?qid=1011&cntIDs=&stdIDs=.

Security-First Globalization[38]

Japan's outward economic integration proved resilient to the first systemic crisis of globalization in the twenty-first century. Today, international economic integration faces a very different, yet powerful, set of counterforces. Rather than an abrupt onset of crisis attributable to a primary trigger (toxic financial assets in the West) with cascading spillover effects, this time the crisis of globalization is slow churning, with attacks coming from all sides. These disparate forces converge to increase the risks of economic interdependence and have similar international and domestic repercussions. Specifically, increasing friction in the world economy has prompted louder assertions from governments of their right to regulate and interdict international economic transactions by invoking the national interest.

U.S.-China strategic rivalry is reshaping globalization. The optimism of an earlier age that deep ties of economic interdependence would produce well-balanced gains, provide an anchor for the bilateral relationship, and pave the way for China to emerge as a responsible stakeholder has faded. Washington has grown skeptical of its past engagement as China has doubled down on market-distorting policies to achieve self-reliance in high-tech sectors, and the WTO has proved unsuccessful in disciplining Chinese state capitalism. The souring of U.S.-China ties has intensified with the ability of China to use its economic might to finance a major military buildup and its leverage over others through acts of economic coercion. The impact of this fallout has been widely felt through the 2018 onset of a trade war and a constant tightening of national security controls over economic flows.

The COVID-19 pandemic further strained economic globalization. The global public health crisis underscored the severe limits of international cooperation, as evidenced by the quick imposition of export bans on medical supplies and vaccine nationalism. Production shutdowns and depressed economic activity wrought havoc on tightly coordinated "just-in-time" supply chains, while calls to re-shore international production grew louder. Russia's invasion of Ukraine in 2022 further triggered global food shortages and an oil price hike that dampened growth and made the operation costs of far-flung supply chains more onerous. The imposition of unprecedented sanctions (financial, trade, and export controls) by the United States and its allies on Russia and its leadership underscores the increasing use of economic interdependence as a tool of statecraft.

Despite these headwinds, there is no evidence that globalization is dying. Rather, it is adapting to a new risk environment. Propelled by the digital shift, the ratio of services trade to global GDP continues to grow,[39] and globalization is a solution to many problems of the current era, from vaccine development to alleviating domestic shortages through international trade. Wholesale decoupling of the two largest economies in the world is not a cost that either the United States or China wants to pay (yet), but trade and technology restrictions are encouraging fragmentation of supply chains in targeted high-tech sectors. Hedging against mounting risks and unpredictable rules of the road is a much larger consideration for global supply chains, which until recently placed a greater emphasis on efficiency. The coming age of globalization will also redraw the state-market boundary, as governments award themselves more authority to control (regulation) and promote (industrial policy) trade, investment, and technology flows.

The securitization of globalization is likely to exert a more profound impact on Japan than the GFC did. The forces previously described have already given rise to a comprehensive effort to develop an economic security toolkit (see Chapter 10). While there are many risk factors at play, a recalibration of relations with China will figure prominently in Japan's globalization rethink. A 2022 Japan Cabinet Office report tackled the question of the risk posed by overreliance on imports from China. Through a comparison with the United States and Germany, it found Japan had an elevated exposure.[40] As Figure 1.5 shows, Japan had the largest number of imported commodities where supply is highly concentrated to only a few locations: 2,305 compared to 1,719 for the United States and 990 for Germany. Within this set of imported products, China played an outsized role as top supplier of Japanese imports (39 percent), and a significant but lesser role for American (25 percent) and German (13 percent) imports. The extreme geographical concentration of imports to a single source, the government report warned, makes it difficult to find alternative suppliers, compromising resilience.

But the private sector will also have a vote on the future economic relationship with China. As Figure 1.6 shows, there is an awareness of the growing risks attached to supply chains routed through China, and as many as 41 percent of companies participating in the Japan Center for Economic Research (JCER) survey expect a smaller role for China as a production hub. But when asked about the importance of the Chinese market, 67 percent of respondents expected it to continue or grow in importance in the future. Evidently, corporate Japan is not willing to renounce the Chinese market.

Figure 1.5. Overdependence on China: Comparison of Germany, U.S., and Japan (number of goods with supplier concentration/China's import share)

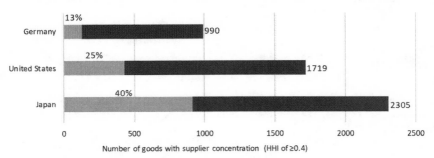

Note: The Herfindahl-Hirschman Index measures the geographical concentration of imports and takes a value of 0 to 1. The goods counted in this figure scored 0.4 and above (high supplier concentration). Percentages show the share of products where China is the top supplier.

Source: "世界経済の潮流 2021年 II—中国の経済成長と貿易構造の変化" [2021 World Economic Trends II: China's Economic Growth and Trading System Changes], White Paper (Tokyo: Cabinet Office of Japan, February 3, 2022), 60, https://www5.cao.go.jp/j-j/sekai_chouryuu/sa21-02/sa21.html.

Figure 1.6. Future dependence on China

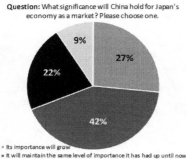

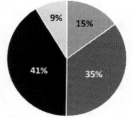

Question: What significance will China hold for Japan's economy as a market? Please choose one.

- Its importance will grow
- It will maintain the same level of importance it has had up until now
- Its importance will diminish
- I don't know

Question: What significance will China hold for Japan's economy as a hub for production? Please choose one.

- Its importance will grow
- It will maintain the same level of importance it has had up until now
- Its importance will diminish
- I don't know

Note: This survey was conducted on July 14–16, 2020, and respondents included 3,000 full-time employees over 20 years of age from publicly listed Japanese companies located in Japan.

Source: "「ポストコロナ時代の米中関係と日本」上場企業3000人調査" [U.S.-China Relations and Japan in the Post-COVID-19 Era: Survey of 3,000 Public Company Employees], Japan Center for Economic Research (JCER), September 2020, https://www.jcer.or.jp/ jcer_download_log.php?f=eyJwb3N0X2lkIjo2ODQyMSwiZmlsZZ V9wb3N0X2lkIjoiNjg0MjIifQ ==&post_id=68421&file_post_id=68422.

NOTES

1. Savina Gygli et al., "The KOF Globalisation Index—Revisited," *The Review of International Organizations* 14 (2019): 543–74.

2. Mireya Solís, "Reinventing the Trading Nation: Japan, the United States, and the Future of Asia-Pacific Trade," *The New Geopolitics Series*, The Brookings Institution, Washington, DC, November 2019, www.brookings.edu/research/reinventing-the-trading-nation-japan-the-united-states-and-the-future-of-asia-pacific-trade/.

3. World Trade Organization (WTO) Secretariat, "Trade Policy Review, Japan," WT/TPR/S/397, January 22, 2020, www.wto.org/english/tratop_e/tpr_e/s397_e.pdf.

4. Mireya Solís, *Dilemmas of a Trading Nation: Japan and the United States in the Evolving Asia-Pacific Order* (Washington, DC: Brookings Institution Press, 2017).

5. Gary Clyde Hufbauer, "Liberalization of Services Trade," in *Assessing the Trans-Pacific Partnership, Volume 1: Market Access and Sectoral issues* (81–90), Peterson Institute for International Economics (PIIE) Briefing 16–1, February 2016, www.piie.com/publications/piie-briefings/assessing-trans-pacific-partnership-volume-1-market-access-and-sectoral. The 2018 OECD Services Trade Restrictiveness Index—measuring barriers to services trade in 22 sectors

for 45 countries—further corroborates the progress Japan has made. Japan has more sectors (20) scoring below the average level of restriction than the United States (15). In contrast, China is far more restrictive, with only one sector (architecture) below the average restrictiveness level. See the index's 2022 China report: www.oecd.org/trade/topics/services-trade/documents/oecd-stri-country -note-china.pdf.

6. See OECD, "FDI Stocks," 2022, https://data.oecd.org/fdi/fdi-stocks.htm #indicator-chart.

7. The OECD's FDI Regulatory Restrictiveness Index measures foreign equity caps; screening or approval mechanisms; restrictions on employment of foreign personnel in management positions; and restrictions on operations such as branching, land ownership, and capital repatriation. The year 2017 was chosen for a comparison because since then there has been a move toward re-regulation across the industrialized world for national security purposes (discussed in Chapter 9). The percentage score that year for Japan was 0.052 and 0.089 for the United States. See OECD, "FDI Restrictiveness," 2022, https:// data.oecd.org/fdi/fdi-restrictiveness.htm.

8. Richard Katz, "Why Nobody Invests in Japan: Tokyo's Failure to Welcome Foreign Capital Is Wobbling Its Economy," *Foreign Affairs*, October 13, 2021, https://www.foreignaffairs.com/articles/japan/2021-10-13/why-nobody -invests-japan.

9. Japan External Trade Organization, "JETRO Invest Japan Report 2021," December 2021, www.jetro.go.jp/en/invest/investment_environment/ijre/ report2021/.

10. Mireya Solís, *Banking on Multinationals: Public Credit and the Export of Japanese Sunset Industries* (Stanford: Stanford University Press, 2004), 39.

11. See United Nations Conference on Trade and Development (UNCTAD), "Country Fact Sheet: Japan," *World Investment Report 2022*, 2022, https:// unctad.org/system/files/non-official-document/wir_fs_jp_en.pdf.

12. See OECD, "Outward FDI Stocks by Industry," 2022, https://data.oecd .org/fdi/outward-fdi-stocks-by-industry.htm.

13. For the debates on deindustrialization, or "hollowing out," in Japan, see Chiohiko Minotani, ed., 産業空洞化：日本のマクロ経済 [Industrial Hollowing Out: Japan's Macroeconomics] (Tokyo: Taga Shuppan, 1996). On competition with low-cost China (the so-called "China syndrome"), see Chi-Hung Kwan, "Japan's 'China Syndrome' Dissipating as Exports to China Surge," Research Institute of Economy, Trade and Industry (RIETI), March 1, 2004, www.rieti .go.jp/en/china/04030101.html.

14. Ulrike Schaede notes that for the first time in 1999, foreign production of Japanese companies surpassed exports. See Schaede, *The Business Reinvention of Japan: How to Make Sense of the New Japan and Why It Matters* (Stanford: Stanford University Press, 2008), 142.

15. All figures are from the Japan External Trade Organization (JETRO): www.jetro.go.jp/en/reports/statistics.html.

16. Schaede, *The Business Reinvention of Japan*.

17. See Ministry of Economy, Trade and Industry (METI), "Summary of the 49th Basic Survey on Overseas Business Activities," July 2019, www.meti.go.jp /english/statistics/tyo/kaigaizi/pdf/h2c412je.pdf.

18. Mitsuyo Ando and Fukunari Kimura, "Job Creation and Destruction at the Levels of Intra-Firm Sections, Firms, and Industries in Globalization: The Case of Japanese Manufacturing Firms," *RIETI Discussion Paper Series*, 17-E-100, July 2017, 16, www.rieti.go.jp/jp/publications/dp/17e100.pdf.

19. Using a comprehensive data set of Japanese firms with manufacturing activities in East Asia for the period 1998–2003, Ando and Kimura (2007, 3–4) show that overseas investment activities made a significant difference to domestic employment outcomes. Firms that expanded into East Asia for the first time briskly increased their domestic payroll (by 9 percent), while those that folded operations in the region reduced domestic employment (by 10 percent). Other studies have shown that Japanese firms investing abroad have reduced their manufacturing divisions in Japan, but in turn they increased R&D expenditures, services divisions, and employee training in their domestic operations. See Mitsuyo Ando and Fukunari Kimura, "Can Offshoring Create Domestic Jobs? Evidence from Japanese Data," Centre for Economic Policy Research, *Policy Insight* 16 (December 2007); and METI, *White Paper on International Economy and Trade*, Tokyo, 2012, 478–79, https://www.meti.go.jp/english/ report/data/gWT2012fe.html.

20. Gary Clyde Hufbauer et al., *Outward Direct Investment and U.S. Exports, Jobs, and R&D: Implications for U.S. Policy* (Washington, DC: Peterson Institute for International Economics, 2013).

21. Squire Patton Boggs, "Three Ways to Dismiss Employees in Japan," Employment Law Worldview, March 29, 2016, https://www .employmentlawworldview.com/three-ways-to-dismiss-employees-in-japan/.

22. Douglas A. Irwin, "Globalization Has Helped Raise Incomes Almost Everywhere since the 1980s," Peterson Institute for International Economics, June 29, 2022, www.piie.com/research/piie-charts/globalization-has-helped -raise-incomes-almost-everywhere-1980s.

23. In a set of very influential academic papers, David Autor and colleagues found that regions in the United States importing most intensively from China faced the highest labor adjustment costs, estimating that a quarter of manufacturing jobs lost during the 2000s were lost due to import competition with China. See David H. Autor, David Dorn, and Gordon H. Hanson, "The China Shock: Learning From Labor Market Adjustment to Large Changes in Trade," Working Paper 21906, National Bureau of Economic Research (NBER), Cambridge, MA, January 2016, www.nber.org/papers/w21906.

24. Mireya Solís, *Dilemmas of a Trading Nation: Japan and the United States in the Evolving Asia-Pacific Order.*

25. Mina Taniguchi, "The Effect of an Increase in Imports from China on Local Labor Markets in Japan," *Journal of Japanese and International Economies* 51 (March 2019): 1–18.

26. Rei Naka and Yukiko Fukagawa, "Globalism at a Crossroads: Rising Protectionism and What It Means for East Asia," *Japan Spotlight*, Special Article 2 (May–June 2017): 53–58, www.jef.or.jp/journal/pdf/213th_Special _Article_02.pdf. Figures are for 2014.

27. Marc Bacchetta and Victor Stolzenburg, "Trade, Value Chains and Labor Markets in Advanced Economies," in *Global Value Chain Development Report, 2019: Technological Innovation, Supply Chain Trade and Workers in a Globalized World*, WTO, 2019, https://www.worldbank.org/en/topic/trade/ publication/global-value-chain-development-report-2019.

28. Adam Jakubik and Victor Stolzenburg, "The 'China Shock' Revisited: Insights from Value Added Trade Flows," WTO Working Paper, ERSD-2018-10, Geneva, October 26, 2018, https://www.wto.org/english/res_e /reser_e/ersd201810_e.pdf.

29. Jean-Yves Huwart and Loïc Verdier, "The 2008 Financial Crisis—A Crisis of Globalisation?" in *Economic Globalisation: Origins and Consequences*, OECD Insights (Paris: OECD Publishing, 2013): 126–43.

30. Uwe Vollmer and Ralf Bebenroth, "The Financial Crisis in Japan: Causes and Policy Reactions by the Bank of Japan," *The European Journal of Comparative Economics* 9, no. 1 (2012): 51–77.

31. Phillip Y. Lipscy and Hirofumi Takinami, "The Politics of Financial Crisis Response in Japan and the United States," *Japanese Journal of Political Science* 14, no. 3 (2013): 321–53.

32. Prizing stability over growth, Japanese regulators ensured that the main financial players moved in tandem with and at the speed of the weakest institutions, and orchestrated bank rescues at times of distress, thereby contributing to moral hazard.

33. Saori Katada, "Financial Crisis Fatigue? Politics behind Japan's Post-Global Financial Crisis Economic Contraction," *Japanese Journal of Political Science* 14, no. 2 (June 2013): 223–42.

34. Jun Saito, "Recovery from a Crisis: U.S. and Japan," Japan Center for Economic Research, May 7, 2014, https://www.jcer.or.jp/english/recovery-from -a-crisis-us-and-japan.

35. "Slowbalisation: The Steam Has Gone Out of Globalization," *The Economist*, January 24, 2019, www.economist.com/leaders/2019/01/24/the-steam -has-gone-out-of-globalisation.

36. Susan Lund et al., "The New Dynamics of Financial Globalization," McKinsey Global Institute, McKinsey & Company, August 2017, www .mckinsey.com/industries/financial-services/our-insights/the-new-dynamics-of -financial-globalization.

37. Xin Li, Bo Meng, and Zhi Wang, "Recent Patterns of Global Production and GVC Participation," in *Global Value Chain Development Report 2019: Technological Innovation, Supply Chain Trade, and Workers in a Globalized World* (Geneva: World Trade Organization, 2019). The GVC Participation Index scores for Japan, China, and the United States were graciously provided by Li and his co-authors. Japan's forward participation score in 2010 was 7.6

percent of GDP and it increased to 8.3 percent in 2017. China's score decreased from 10.6 percent to 8.1 percent and for the United States from 6.0 percent to 5.6 percent. Japan's backward participation score in 2010 was 7.5 percent to final goods production and it grew to 9.1 percent. China's score dropped from 13.7 percent to 9.1 percent and for the United States from 6.4 percent to 6.1 percent.

38. See "Reinventing Globalisation," *The Economist*, June 18, 2022, www.economist.com/leaders/2022/06/16/the-tricky-restructuring-of-global-supply-chains.

39. Pascal Lamy and Nicolas Kohler-Suzuki, "Deglobalization Is Not Inevitable," *Foreign Affairs*, June 8, 2022, www.foreignaffairs.com/articles/world/2022-06-09/deglobalization-not-inevitable.

40. Japan Cabinet Office, "中国の経済成長と貿易構造の変化" [Growth of the Chinese Economy and Changes to the Structure of Trade], February 2022, www5.cao.go.jp/j-j/sekai_chouryuu/sa21-02/index-pdf.html.

CHAPTER 2

Foreign Workers in Japan

BREAKING TABOOS, CLOSING BORDERS

In the post–World War II era, Japan adopted highly restrictive immigration policies, awarding citizenship based on blood ties, emphasizing the merits of ethnic homogeneity, and resorting to side channels for the arrival of needed foreign workers. Japan's insularity is most entrenched in its immigration policy, but the country is changing, albeit slowly and haltingly. A significant transformation in the composition of the non-Japanese community has taken place over the last three decades, reflecting both the nation's historical legacies and its most pressing policy challenges. Several generations of ethnic Korean permanent residents (commonly called *Zainichi*, or residents in Japan) made strides in securing social policy benefits, and with rising rates of naturalization, their share of the foreign resident population decreased markedly. The number of incoming foreign workers (ethnic Japanese from Brazil and trainees in the Technical Intern Training Program from developing Asia) rapidly increased when the Japanese government opened immigration side doors from the 1990s onward. With the onset of the Global Financial Crisis (GFC), many Brazilian-Japanese returned to Brazil, and in the ensuing decade the size of the foreign resident population tripled, in large part due to the expansion of the technical intern program.

However, due to the government's refusal to acknowledge the de facto guest worker program and offer commensurate labor protections and integration support, its approach to immigration proved an ineffective solution for the intensifying labor crunch. A taboo was broken with the revision of the Immigration Control Act that took effect in 2019, which for the first time created a visa program for manual workers, and for a subset of them opened the road to long-term settlement. Japan's liberalization of its immigration regime took place at a time when many industrialized countries were moving in the opposite direction. As such, the country bucked the trend observed in many advanced industrialized nations of xenophobia upending established political systems and immigration regimes and becoming more restrictive.

The COVID-19 pandemic conjured new questions about Japan's ability to stay the course, however. For over two years, the government imposed strict border controls preventing the arrival of foreign non-residents. The loosening of entry restrictions in spring 2022 by Prime Minister Kishida Fumio's administration offered a glimmer of hope, for Japan's ability to recommit to greater openness is key to securing its economic future.

POSTWAR IMMIGRATION REGIME

Japan's migration history casts a long shadow over its more contemporary experiences. The country's first bout of large cross-border movements of people involved outflows. Japanese farmers and laborers seeking a better economic future crossed the Pacific and established large overseas communities in countries like Brazil, Peru, and Mexico.[1] Japan's imperial past generated sizable immigration flows of colonial subjects as well—voluntary arrivals, but also forced relocations as labor shortages intensified with the war effort. At the end of World War II, there were more than two million Koreans in Japan and thousands of Chinese and Taiwanese.[2] These individuals were abruptly stripped of their Japanese nationality in 1947 and, finding themselves relabeled as "foreigners" with meager prospects in war-ravaged Japan, many returned to their countries of origin. But many others remained. The multigenerational community of Zainichi Korean residents provided the most indelible imprint on Japan's immigration experience.[3] Decades later, another echo from the past left its mark on contemporary Japanese immigration policy: an invitation to Japanese descendants in Latin America (often referred to as *Nikkeijin*, to denote their shared ethnicity) to come work in Japan and ameliorate the country's labor crunch.

In the postwar era, Japan embarked on an immigration policy regime that formally aspired to autarky and rested on the myth of a nation with no migration past and complete ethnic homogeneity. The Immigration Control and Refugee Recognition Act of 1952 embraced a narrow definition of Japanese nationality based exclusively on blood ties, with no provisions for birthright. The law banned unskilled workers from entering the country and allowed only temporary visas to new arrivals. Japanese officials insisted that the country did not have an "immigration policy," but rather a "foreigner policy."[4] The government denied foreign residents access to important social benefits such as national health and pension plans, public sector employment, and public housing and established high hurdles for naturalization. In addition to the formal requirements of renouncing prior nationality, adopting a Japanese name, and demonstrating economic self-sufficiency and cultural assimilation, Japanese officials employed broad discretion over naturalization cases.[5] Furthermore, Japan maintained by and large a closed-door policy for refugees, with very strict criteria to determine harm from persecution,[6] which resulted in refugee acceptance rates below 1 percent, a very low level by international standards.[7]

PATCHWORK REFORMS: IMPERFECT INTEGRATION AND SIDE DOORS

Japan's restrictive approach to immigration was all-encompassing but not impervious to change. Figure 2.1 tracks the evolution of the regulatory regime and shows an upward trajectory toward openness starting in the 1980s.[8] An important shift took place in the mid-1980s when the government extended to foreign residents social policy benefits such as health insurance, pension plans, and childcare allowances, both to comply with human rights conventions and to respond to growing demands from the Zainichi community.[9]

The 1990 revision to the Immigration Act brought about significant changes, less because of the explicit endorsement of skilled migration and more due to the unofficial opening of entry channels for manual workers. A new long-term resident visa category was established to enable Japanese descendants up to the third generation to work in Japan, with a renewable visa and family reunification rights. The revised law also systematized a trainee program that ostensibly sought to transfer skills to developing countries in Asia, but primarily served industries

Figure 2.1. Japan's immigration regime

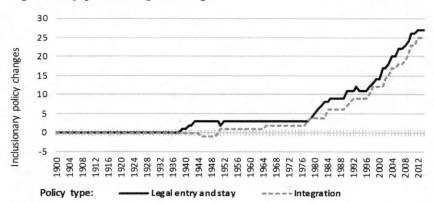

Sources: *DEMIG Policy, version 1.3, online edition*, International Migration Institute, University of Oxford; Sarah W. Goodman and T. Pepinsky, "The Exclusionary Foundations of Embedded Liberalism," paper presented at the 2019 IPES Conference Program, San Diego, California, November 2019.

and small firms in Japan in finding increasingly scarce labor. As Michael Strausz explains, Japan opted for side doors for low-skilled migration that would fall short of labor demand because the business community was unable to persuade politicians and bureaucrats, who feared social instability, to allow for a more open immigration policy.[10]

Nevertheless, the immigration experience in Japan diversified and transformed. With rising rates of naturalization and marriage to Japanese nationals, the share of Zainichi among foreign residents decreased to just 15 percent of the foreign population in Japan.[11] With the new visa status, the number of Nikkeijin in Japan exploded from 2,135 in 1986 to 154,650 in 1993, and the boom in arrivals quickly exposed the facile assumptions of immigration officials that ethnicity would allow smooth assimilation. The wave of Nikkeijin immigrants revealed the deep shortcomings of bringing in foreign workers without sufficient integration support from the national government, leaving local governments scrambling to devise policies to facilitate adjustment to life in Japan. When the economic contraction in 2008 idled many factories, the national government not only subsidized voluntary repatriation of Nikkeijin, but also adopted emergency support measures for foreign residents, including training, housing, and children's education.[12]

The gap between rhetoric and reality in the Technical Intern Training Program generated many problems as well. Admitted for nonrenewable periods of three years, the trainees could not bring along family members, were not awarded protections under employment laws, and could not switch to an internship with a different company. Complaints mounted of employers confiscating passports and demanding extra work or underpaying. It was not until 2009 that the government finally extended the protections of the Labor Standards Act to technical interns. By 2016, there were far more trainees working in Japan than Nikkeijin, at 211,108 and 132,669, respectively.[13]

Official rhetoric notwithstanding, Japan's immigration regime resulted in larger flows of unskilled compared to skilled workers.[14] The effort to include skilled nurse quotas in trade agreements with Indonesia, the Philippines, and Vietnam yielded modest results. Facing opposition from Japan's Nursing Association, the Japanese government introduced stringent certification requirements that resulted in a mere trickle of nurses into the country despite the dire needs of an ageing Japanese population. The call for global talent, especially in the information and communications technology (ICT) sector, went largely unheeded. The 2012 introduction of a point-based immigration system for the highly skilled, offering a fast track to permanent residency, could not quite overcome powerful disincentives such as insufficient portability of pension plans, the lack of English use in the office, and traditional management practices such as seniority promotion.[15] Keenly aware that it was falling behind in the search for global talent, the government in 2017 offered the possibility of applying for permanent residence at the record speed of one year to professionals scoring above 80 points.[16] The goal was to increase the number of high-skilled professionals from 8,515 in 2017 to 20,000 in 2022,[17] a mere fraction of the 1.5 million foreign workers in Japan.

The gradual relaxation of strict entry restrictions, the extension of safety net benefits to foreign residents, and the visible shift in the composition of non-Japanese living in the country did not generate major swings in public opinion, nor did these changes register widely in national politics. In postwar Japan, immigration policy has not been an emblematic issue for the major parties. Immigration has not been used as a rallying cry to build party identity nor to mobilize the public for an advantage at the ballot box. This low political saliency is partly due to low immigration levels and foreign workers arriving through informal channels, but also because, as Jeff Kingston puts it, "no party has embraced xenophobia."[18] There were two main exceptions, when immigration policies did figure prominently in debates among the national parties. One was failed attempts in the National Diet to award local voting rights to foreign residents in the 2000s, and the second was Japan's own reckoning with its need for foreign blue-collar workers a decade later (see next section). At the Diet, it was the ruling party's coalition partner, Komeito (linked to the Buddhist sect Soka Gakkai) that repeatedly championed the move to let permanent residents vote in local elections, probably motivated by its large number of rank-and-file members within the Zainichi community. The ruling Liberal Democratic Party (LDP) did not support the move and the initiative faltered, with no change in national policy.[19]

But the more interesting battlelines—between the advocacy for greater integration support and the rejection of ethnic minorities—were drawn at the subnational level. Once again, it was the local governments which pushed for a more expansive definition of rights (this time, political rights), and in the absence of Diet action, several municipalities have introduced foreign resident assemblies and local referenda, giving some voice to noncitizens in local affairs since the 1990s.[20] The emergence of nativist far-right movements in the mid-2000s was a significant development, since they broke away from the traditional embrace of imperial Japan's rhetoric of Pan-Asianism, instead choosing to target minorities and recruit netizens to partake in street demonstrations.[21] One such movement, the Zaikokutai, trained its ire on ethnic Koreans, accusing them of possessing special privileges and fostering hostility toward the Zainichi community; but their extreme views did not transfer to mainstream public opinion (discussed later). The Diet sought to take some action with the 2016 passage of the Anti-Hate Speech Law, but the adopted bill did not ban or penalize hate speech. Again, it was the local governments that took the initiative further: in 2019, the Kawasaki Municipal Assembly attached criminal penalties to hate speech and discriminatory actions.[22]

THE FRONT DOOR OPENS TO FOREIGN WORKERS

Immigration policy headlined Diet debates in 2018, when the government for the first time acknowledged that policy changes were needed to bring in manual workers. The ban on low-skilled labor was no longer sustainable for several reasons. First, the gap between rhetoric and reality had become too obvious. The ranks of foreign workers in Japan tripled, from under half a million to a million and a half, in the decade after the GFC (see Figure 2.2).[23] In urban centers, the presence of non-Japanese staff in the service sector (convenience stores, restaurants, hotels) had become ubiquitous. Many of them were exchange students with visas that allow for part-time work. And in the countryside, where the graying of the farming population has been acutely felt, there was a heavy reliance on work from foreign trainees. For example, in Ibaraki Prefecture in the late 2010s, one in three young agricultural workers were foreign born.[24]

At the same time, unofficial side channels for unskilled immigration (for the Nikkeijin and the trainees) were problematic due to a lack of support measures for adjustment to life in Japan and subpar labor protections. Additionally, these side channels did not solve the ever-growing labor shortages, which were especially acute in nursing, agriculture, and construction. The government estimated labor shortfalls of 780,000 to 930,000 in the construction sector and of 550,000 in nursing and elder care by 2025. In agriculture, the labor shortfall was expected to be in the range of 46,000 to 103,000.[25] Immigration policy appeared both shallow (by failing to acknowledge the de facto role of lower-skilled foreign workers in Japan's society and economy) and ineffectual (by relying on unofficial channels that failed to close yawning labor gaps).

The revised Immigration Act, which went into effect in 2019, broke new ground in several ways. First, it made way for the arrival of manual workers at the medium-skill level in fourteen different industries

Figure 2.2. Number of foreign workers in Japan (2008–2021)

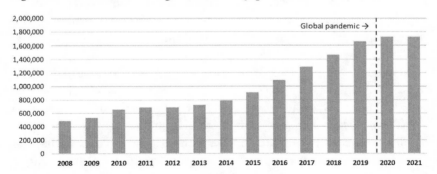

Source: "外国人雇用状況の届出状況について" [About the State of the Job Market for Foreigners] (Tokyo: Ministry of Health, Labour and Welfare, 2008–2021), https://www.mhlw.go.jp/stf/seisakunitsuite/bunya/koyou_roudou/koyou/gaikoku-jin/gaikokujin-koyou/06.html.

besieged by labor shortages. The revised law established two new visa categories. One is for workers at a lower skill level, who can transition from the existing trainee program to work in Japan for up to an additional five years but do not enjoy family reunification privileges. The second visa category applies to workers at a higher skill level in specialized sectors such as construction and shipbuilding, with the possibility of being accompanied by immediate family members. For both sets of foreign workers, there is freedom to change employers and wages must be on par with industry standards. Before arriving in Japan, workers in these visa categories must demonstrate some level of competency in the Japanese language and must be tested for their industry-specific skills.

Second, the revised legal framework for the first time recognized the need for the central government to create a nationwide system of integration support measures. It called for the creation of one hundred one-stop centers to provide multilingual assistance to help the new arrivals adjust to life in Japan, and an upgraded Immigration Services Agency with the added mandate of improving the living and working environments of foreign workers.[26] Third, while the government was adamant that the revisions amounted to only a guest worker program and did not constitute an opening of borders to immigration, workers of the higher skill set can renew their three-year visas indefinitely, making long-term settlement possible[27] and possibly creating an opening for permanent residency.[28]

The 2019 immigration reforms were grounded in Japan's past practices in several key ways. The government remained in charge of allocating the flow of foreign workers to designated economic sectors, and it capped the number of arrivals to 345,000 for the next five years. Instead of overhauling the controversial Technical Intern Training Program, the new bill chose to expand upon it, including adding some provisions to prevent employer abuse. The proposed reforms generated heated debate in the Diet (and an occasional physical altercation),[29] as opposition parties complained about the potential for abuse (e.g., the reinforcement of the trainee system rather than more regular employment, and noneligible dependents receiving medical attention in Japan), the inadequacy of the adjustment supports offered, and insufficient information and time for debate in the Diet. Revealingly, opposition to the revised bill did not question the premise of the policy change: Japan's dire need for manual workers. Nor was there visible backlash from the public to the explicit recognition that foreign-born workers at all skill levels are essential to Japan's future. For example, a December 2018 poll by Nippon TV showed more people in support (46 percent) than in opposition (39 percent) to the increase of foreign manual workers.[30]

In fact, an international comparison of public views on immigration does not reveal the Japanese public as particularly skeptical or defensive. In a March 2019 Pew Research Center survey, 59 percent of Japanese respondents endorsed the statement that "immigrants make the country stronger," above the 18-country median of 56 percent. The Japanese public led other surveyed countries in its belief in the willingness of immigrants to integrate socially and culturally (at 75 percent compared to the median of 45 percent). Half of Japanese respondents did not attribute an increase in crime to migrants, and 60 percent did not associate them with an increased risk of terrorism.[31] Other surveys have not found widespread intolerance of foreigners. Kage Rieko and her co-authors found that 60 percent of survey participants in Japan had a positive view of immigration for either economic or cultural reasons.[32] These findings are interesting because they come at a time when foreigners working in Japan are no longer an invisible community—their ranks have increased rapidly—and the country has officially opened the front door to manual workers from abroad.

While the number of foreign workers saw swift growth in 2019, the utilization of the new government visas had a sluggish start with only 1,621 visa holders out of the anticipated 47,000. As Deborah Milly points out, the shortfall likely reflected the time needed to set up the infrastructure to test and certify workers in their home countries. During that first year, Japan negotiated agreements with twelve Asian countries. But just as the program's mechanics had been established, the arrival of COVID-19 effectively put it on hold. The government resorted to tight border controls to manage the ensuing pandemic, curtailing the arrival of all foreign nationals in Japan (workers, international students, and tourists). Hence, the number of foreign workers post-pandemic exhibited negligible annual growth (0.2 percent in 2021) compared to the brisk increase of years prior (a 13–14 percent increase in 2018 and 2019).

A CLOSED NATION ONCE AGAIN? COVID-19 AND JAPAN

The onset of the novel coronavirus pandemic in late 2019 upended the world with mass casualties (over six million as of April 2022, according to the World Health Organization), a severe economic downturn, and the inability of the international community to effectively coordinate a response to the health crisis and vaccinate large swaths of the global population. Governments of all types have struggled in their efforts to save lives, protect livelihoods, and keep faith with the public.

Two and a half years into the pandemic and experiencing a seventh wave of infections from a virus that continues to mutate rapidly, the outcomes of Japan's handling of the COVID-19 emergency are robust. By mid-2022, Japan had the lowest per capita COVID-19-attributable deaths (246 per million people) among OECD member nations.[33] The vast majority of Japan's population is vaccinated (76 percent have received at least two shots of two-dose vaccines, and 60 percent a booster as of June 2022).[34] The early approach suggested by Japanese epidemiologists to handle a novel airborne virus proved prescient and easy to communicate to the public, through the slogan "Avoid the three C's" (closed spaces, crowded spaces, and close-contact settings).[35] Japan evaded the harsh lockdowns adopted by other nations, most poignantly China. Lacking the constitutional authority to impose mandatory restrictions on personal mobility with police enforcement, the Japanese government declared numerous states of emergency that called for restricted hours of operation for businesses and curtailed large-scale events, all while relying entirely on voluntary compliance. Masking among the population has been nearly universal (it was a common practice prior to the COVID-19 pandemic) and it has not become a divisive social issue as it has in the United States.

While Japan's results at this stage of the pandemic are sound, there have been obstacles and mistakes along the way that have taken a toll on the public's confidence. A premature "Go-To Travel" campaign in 2020 that sought to revive domestic tourism had to be scrapped when infections began to climb. The slow rollout of the vaccination program (because the government required its own clinical trials for the newly developed mRNA vaccines rather than relying on trials conducted by the United States and others), just as Prime Minister Suga Yoshihide's administration moved forward with a spectator-free Olympic Games in summer 2021, created much public anxiety and dissatisfaction. Even though the Olympics were managed safely, disapproval of the decision to host the games played an important role in Suga's downfall just one year into his tenure. As Yves Tiberghien has noted, the Japanese public has been very reactive to any uptick in COVID-19 cases, placing strong constraints on Japanese leaders.[36]

Prime Minister Kishida, who succeeded Suga in fall 2021, was quick to reinstate stiff cross-border travel restrictions that November when the more infectious Omicron-variant wave first loomed on the horizon. The public endorsed the move to tighten restrictions, which largely precluded the arrival of foreigners into Japan (there was 90 percent approval in some opinion polls).[37] To be sure, border closures in the pandemic era have been common. By some estimates, 189 countries, comprising 63 percent of the world's population, shut their borders to mitigate virus transmission in 2020.[38] But Japan's border measures stand out in two important ways. First, Japan has maintained the most severe and longest-lasting border controls among the G7 countries. Other industrialized countries loosened restrictions on foreign travel much earlier. Second, the Japanese government used citizenship status, not public health science, in making determinations on entry authorization.[39]

At the recommendation of the Ministry of Justice, the Government of Japan decided to invoke the Immigration Control Act to impose an entry ban on foreigners traveling from countries with high infection rates as of February 1, 2020. The Asia-Pacific Initiative's investigative report on the government's response to COVID-19 characterized this as "an extremely unusual step in that it was not targeted at particular individuals but all foreigners who had stayed in certain countries or regions."[40] The National Security Council expanded the list of restricted countries to 146 by July 2020 and refused reentry to permanent residents traveling from the listed countries. The government cited insufficient quarantine testing capacity at ports of entry as the reason for such measures, but this set Japan apart, since it is common practice to treat long-term residents and nationals alike. As testing capacity increased, the government authorized the phased-in arrival of long-term residents with reentry permits starting in late July 2020,[41] but the near ban on foreign nonresidents continued for nearly two more years.

Foreign nationals with plans to work, conduct business, visit family, or carry out research in Japan were therefore placed in limbo, hurting Japan's economic interests and hindering its ties to the world. Facing strong business pressure and international backlash, the Kishida administration began to loosen border restrictions in March 2022 by extending work, study, and research visas and pledging to accept by the end of May all foreign students whose arrival in Japan had been suspended.[42]

The protracted border closures based on citizenship status proved to be the Achilles' heel of Japan's pandemic response. They are especially counterproductive in light of new estimates presented at a symposium hosted by the Japan International Cooperation Agency that showed that a fourfold increase in the foreign worker population to 6.74 million by 2040 will be required for the country to sustain a 1.24 percent GDP yearly growth rate.[43] The demand for foreign manual workers will be particularly acute in manufacturing (1.55 million), wholesale and retail (1.04 million), and construction (500,000), with most of these workers expected to come from Southeast and South Asia (and nearly one-third from Vietnam alone). Competition to entice these workers will be stiff, as sending nations are also undergoing demographic changes and enjoying higher living standards.[44]

Better integration supports and more attractive visa programs will be critical. Since short-term work stays are not enticing, the Japanese government appeared ready in fall 2021 to entertain indefinite renewals for all manual workers' visas in fourteen designated sectors.[45] The Omicron variant put those plans on hold as the government once again shut the door to non-Japanese. The loosening of the border restrictions is not only a welcomed development, it is imperative if Japan is to move past a dynamic of embracing bolder change and openly welcoming foreign manual workers, only to subsequently impose overzealous pandemic restrictions on international mobility that defeat crucial longer-term goals.

NOTES

1. Japanese emigration started in 1899 but was concentrated into two distinct waves: 1923–1941 and 1953–1973. See Apichai W. Shipper, *Fighting for Foreigners: Immigration and Its Impact on Japanese Democracy* (Ithaca, NY: Cornell University Press, 2008), 38.

2. Mike Douglass and Glenda S. Roberts, *Japan and Global Migration: Foreign Workers and the Advent of a Multicultural Society* (New York: Routledge, 2000), 6.

3. Erin Aeran Chung, *Immigration and Citizenship in Japan* (New York: Cambridge University Press, 2010).

4. Ayako Komine, "A Closed Immigration Country: Revisiting Japan as a Negative Case," *International Migration* 56, no. 5 (2018): 106–22.

5. Between 1970 and 2005, naturalization rates per 100,000 foreigners were 887 in Japan, which was slightly above Germany at 840 but much below the United States at 5,146. See Thomas Janoski, *The Ironies of Citizenship: Natu-*

ralization and Integration in Industrialized Countries (Cambridge, UK: Cambridge University Press, 2010), 17.

6. Saburo Takizawa, "Japan's Refugee Policy: Issues and Outlook," *Japan's Contribution to International Peace and Security Series*, Japan Institute for International Affairs, Tokyo, March 2018, https://www2.jiia.or.jp/en/pdf/digital_library/peace/Saburo_Takizawa-Japan_s_Refugee_Policy_Issues_and_Outlook.pdf.

7. In 2019, Japan granted asylum to 44 applicants, an acceptance rate of 0.4 percent in contrast to Germany's 25.9 percent and the United States' 29.6 percent. See Daisuke Akimoto, "Japan's Changing Immigration and Refugee Policy," *The Diplomat*, March 12, 2021, https://thediplomat.com/2021/03/japans-changing-immigration-and-refugee-policy/. The most recent and significant change is Japan welcoming close to 2,000 Ukrainians as "evacuees" in the months after Russia's 2022 invasion, providing them with temporary visas, free housing, and other support. And in March 2023 the Japanese Cabinet approved the creation of a new system in its immigration law to offer people escaping from conflicts protections similar to those given to refugees. The new measure still requires Diet approval. See "Japan's Cabinet Approves Draft Revisions to Immigration Law," *NHK World*, March 7, 2023, https://www3.nhk.or.jp/nhkworld/en/news/20230307_13/.

8. The figure uses the Determinants of International Migration (DEMIG) database and replicates the methodology of Goodman and Pepinsky in scoring regulatory changes. It shows the orientation of Japanese immigration policy (liberalization vs. restriction) but does not measure which regulatory changes are more consequential. It is a helpful "direction of travel" indicator. See International Migration Institute, *DEMIG Policy, Version 1.3, online edition*, University of Oxford, United Kingdom, 2015; and Sara Wallace Goodman and Thomas Pepinsky, "The Exclusionary Foundations of Embedded Liberalism," draft paper presented at the 2019 IPES Conference Program, San Diego, CA, November 2019, https://www.internationalpoliticaleconomysociety.org/sites/default/files/paper-uploads/2019-11-15-23_58_03-pepinsky@cornell.edu.pdf.

9. Hawon Jang, "The Special Permanent Residents in Japan: Zainichi Korean," *The Yale Review of International Studies*, January 2019, http://yris.yira.org/comments/2873#_ftn14.

10. Michael Strausz, *Help (Not) Wanted: Immigration Politics in Japan* (Albany: State University of New York Press, 2019).

11. David Green, "As Its Population Ages, Japan Quietly Turns to Immigration," Migration Policy Institute, March 28, 2017, www.migrationpolicy.org/article/its-population-ages-japan-quietly-turns-immigration.

12. Deborah J. Milly, *New Policies for New Residents: Immigrants, Advocacy, and Governance in Japan and Beyond* (Ithaca, NY: Cornell University Press, 2014, 65, 174.

13. Yunchen Tian, "Workers by Any Other Name: Comparing Co-ethnics and 'Interns' as Labor Migrants to Japan," *Journal of Ethnic and Migration Studies* 45, no. 9 (2019): 1496–514.

14. Komine, "A Closed Immigration Country," 106–22.

15. Nana Oishi, "Redefining the 'Highly Skilled': The Points-Based System for Highly Skilled Foreign Professionals in Japan," *Asian and Pacific Migration Journal* 23, no. 4 (2014): 421–50.

16. Japan ranked twenty-ninth in the 2018 International Institute for Management Development (IMD) World Talent Ranking. See Mitsuru Obe, "Japan to Asia: Give Us Your Young, Your Skilled, Your Eager Workers," *Nikkei Asia*, January 1, 2019, https://asia.nikkei.com/Spotlight/Asia-Insight/Japan-to-Asia-Give-us-your-young-your-skilled-your-eager-workers.

17. Kazuaki Nagata, "With Fast-Track Permanent Residency Rule, Japan Looks to Shed Its Closed Image," *The Japan Times*, January 4, 2018, www.japantimes.co.jp/news/2018/01/04/national/fast-track-permanent-residency-rule-japan-looks-shed-closed-image/.

18. Cited in Mitsuru Obe, "Famous for Its Resistance to Immigration, Japan Opens Its Doors," *Nikkei Asia*, May 30, 2018, https://asia.nikkei.com/Spotlight/The-Big-Story/Famous-for-its-resistance-to-immigration-Japan-opens-its-doors. Far-right groups in postwar Japan did not form political parties to advance their causes but engaged in street activism and formed links with individual conservative politicians. See Nathaniel Smith, "Vigilante Video: Digital Populism and Anxious Anonymity among Japan's New Netizens," *Critical Asian Voices* 52, no. 1 (2020): 67–86.

19. Michael Strausz, "Japanese Conservatism and the Integration of Foreign Residents," *Japanese Journal of Political Science* 11, no. 2 (2010): 245–64.

20. Michael Orlando Sharpe, "What Can the United States and Japan Learn from Each Other's Immigration Policies?" in *Expert Voices on Japan: Security, Economic, Social, and Foreign Policy Recommendations*, ed. Arthur Alexander, U.S.-Japan Network for the Future Cohort IV (Washington, DC: The Maureen and Mike Mansfield Foundation, 2018), 139–56, https://mansfieldfdn.org/wp-content/uploads/2018/06/Expert_Voices-FINAL.pdf.

21. Nathaniel Smith, "Fights on the Right: Social Citizenship, Ethnicity, and Postwar Cohorts of the Japanese Activist Right," *Social Science Japan Journal* 21, no. 2 (Summer 2018): 261–83.

22. See "Kawasaki Enacts Japan's First Bill Punishing Hate Speech," *The Japan Times*, December 12, 2019, www.japantimes.co.jp/news/2019/12/12/national/crime-legal/kawasaki-first-japan-bill-punishing-hate-speech/.

23. This was a decade of rapid change in other ways. Between 2007 and 2017, there was a 70 percent increase in the number of permanent residents, and 124,000 applications for naturalization were approved (representing 22 percent of all naturalizations since 1952). See Deborah J. Milly, "Japan's Labor Migration Reforms: Breaking with the Past?" Migration Policy Institute, February 20, 2020, www.migrationpolicy.org/article/japan-labor-migration-reforms-breaking-past.

24. Yuko Aizawa, "Opening the Door to Incoming Workers," *NHK Newsline*, February 27, 2019, https://www3.nhk.or.jp/nhkworld/en/news/backstories/383/.

25. Figures reported in "Japan to Ease Language Requirements for Unskilled Foreign Workers," *Nikkei Asia*, May 29, 2018, https://asia.nikkei.com/Economy/Japan-to-ease-language-requirements-for-unskilled-foreign-workers.

26. See "Bureau Head Shoko Sasaki to Lead Upgraded Immigration Agency When It Launches April 1," *The Japan Times*, March 28, 2019, www.japantimes.co.jp/news/2019/03/28/national/bureau-head-shoko-sasaki-lead-upgraded-immigration-agency-launches-april-1/.

27. Jiyeon Song, "The Political Dynamics of Japan's Immigration Policies during the Abe Government," *Pacific Focus* 35, no. 3 (December 2020): 613–40.

28. Milly, "Japan's Labor Migration Reforms."

29. See "Japan Enacts Divisive Foreign Worker Bill to Ease Labor Shortage," *Nikkei Asia*, December 8, 2018, https://asia.nikkei.com/Spotlight/Japan-immigration/Japan-enacts-divisive-foreign-worker-bill-to-ease-labor-shortage.

30. Nippon TV, "定例世論調査：2018年12月" [Regular Public Opinion Poll: December 2018], www.ntv.co.jp/yoron/tnvmcctideuawq3h.html.

31. See Anna Gonzalez-Barrera and Phillip Conor, "Around the World, More Say Immigrants Are a Strength han a Burden," Pew Research Center, March 14, 2019, www.pewresearch.org/global/2019/03/14/around-the-world-more-say-immigrants-are-a-strength-than-a-burden/.

32. Rieko Kage, Frances M. Rosenbluth, and Seiki Tanaka, "Varieties of Public Attitudes toward Immigration: Evidence from Survey Experiments in Japan," *Political Research Quarterly* 75, no. 1 (2022): 216–30.

33. Kanoko Matsuyama and James Mayger, "How Japan Achieved One of the Lowest COVID Death Rates," *Bloomberg*, June 17, 2022, www.bloomberg.com/news/articles/2022-06-17/how-japan-achieved-one-of-the-world-s-lowest-covid-death-rates.

34. See Statista, "Coronavirus Disease (COVID-19) Vaccination Rate in Japan as of June 6, 2022," www.statista.com/statistics/1239927/japan-covid-19-vaccination-rate/.

35. Adapted from the Ministry of Health, Labour and Welfare's Japanese version of the slogan: "「三つの密を避けましょう！１．換気が悪い密閉空間２．多数が集まる密集場所３．間近会話や発声をする密接場面」."

36. Yves Tiberghien, "Panel 1: Japan's Domestic Politics and the Economy," webinar, Japan in 2022, Brookings Institution and the Japan-America Society of Washington, DC, January 18, 2022, www.brookings.edu/events/japan-in-2022/.

37. Isabel Reynolds, "Xenophobia Spills into Japan's COVID Era Debate on Immigration," *Bloomberg*, December 26, 2021, www.bloomberg.com/news/articles/2021-12-26/xenophobia-spills-into-japan-s-covid-era-debate-on-immigration.

38. See Mary A. Shiraef, "Closed Borders, Travel Bans and Halted Immigration: 5 Ways COVID-19 Changed How—and Where—People Move around the World," *The Conversation*, March 18, 2021, https://theconversation.com

/closed-borders-travel-bans-and-halted-immigration-5-ways-covid-19-changed
-how-and-where-people-move-around-the-world-157040.

39. "U.S.-Japan Community Urges Government of Japan to Relax Border
Closure," NichiBei Connect, January 19, 2022, https://www.nichibeiconnect
.com/u-s-japan-community-comes-together-to-express-concerns-to-goverment
-of-japan/.

40. Asia-Pacific Initiative (API), "Border Control (Resumption of International Travel)," in *The Independent Investigation Commission on the Japanese
Government's Response to COVID-19*, Tokyo, January 8, 2021, 13, https://
apinitiative.org/en/project/covid19/.

41. Ibid., 15–16.

42. See "Japan Looks to Accept Most Foreign Students Waiting to Enter by
End of May," *The Japan Times*, March 9, 2022, www.japantimes.co.jp/news
/2022/03/09/national/higher-entry-cap-foreign-students/.

43. See 価値総合研究所 [Value Management Institute, Inc.], "2030/40 年
の外国人との共生社会の実現に向けた調査研究," [Research Survey for the
2030/40 Implementation of a Society Inclusive of Foreign Residents], presented
at JICA 緒方研究所主催シンポジウム 2030/40 年の外国人との共生社会の実現に
向けて [The 2030/40 Implementation of a Society Inclusive of Foreign Residents
Symposium, hosted by the JICA Ogata Research Institute], Tokyo, February
3, 2022, www.jica.go.jp/jica-ri/ja/news/event/tfpeil0000002f5m-att/20220203
_01.pdf.

44. See Mitsuru Obe, "Japan to Require Four Times More Foreign Workers,
Study Says," *Nikkei Asia*, February 3, 2022, https://asia.nikkei.com/Spotlight
/Japan-immigration/Japan-to-require-four-times-more-foreign-workers-study
-says.

45. "In Major Shift, Japan Looks to Allow More Foreign Workers to Stay Indefinitely," *The Japan Times*, November 8, 2021, www.japantimes.co.jp/news
/2021/11/18/national/japan-indefinite-visas/.

SECTION 2

Economics

CHAPTER 3

What Went Wrong (and Right) during Japan's Lost Decades?

For the past thirty years, Japan's economy has underwhelmed. Japan was long hailed for its dramatic reconstruction in the aftermath of World War II's devastation, its economic takeoff as it developed a succession of highly competitive industries capturing overseas markets, and its deft dealing with crises that touched on its most serious vulnerabilities, such as the 1970s oil shocks. But Japan's signal achievement in the postwar era was the creation of an affluent middle-class society. The last quarter century, however, has seen many reversals. Since the burst of the bubble economy in the early 1990s, Japan has been saddled with low growth and stubborn deflation. Successive Japanese administrations have endeavored—mostly unsuccessfully—to find a path back to sustained growth. Adverse demographic trends, including a rapidly ageing and contracting population, have made this challenge all the more daunting. Economic recessions have had social consequences, such as a swift increase in income inequality.[1]

And yet, Japan's performance over the past quarter century has not been a linear trend of economic decline and ossification of the economic system. Bursts of growth, corporate renewal, policy experimentation, and recovery from major external shocks and natural disasters have also been a part of the Japanese experience. Japan's socioeconomic record over the last three decades tells many stories, from the disheartening examples of demographic contraction, economic policy malpractice, and the rise of the gap society, to the inspiring ones of adaptability of core institutions of Japanese capitalism, economic reform crusades, and

resilient social cohesion. Meta-narratives are in fact a poor fit for Japan—
not only the already debunked image of an unstoppable economic juggernaut, but also the still enduring impression of an inert Japan.

A WINDING ROAD: JAPAN'S ECONOMIC PERFORMANCE

The Japanese economy's trials and achievements can be garnered from
Figure 3.1. The comedown in the early 1990s was indeed abrupt, with a
plunge in real estate and stock prices as the bubble burst and the economy entered a recession. Many assumed that Japan had experienced a
temporary setback, but this proved wishful thinking as the gravity of the
banking crisis came into focus as the years passed. A poorly timed consumption tax hike in 1997 and the bankruptcy of large financial firms
for the first time in postwar history produced an even larger recession
and prompted the onset of protracted deflation. Under the administration of Prime Minister Koizumi Junichiro in the first half of the 2000s,
Japan saw a return to growth, especially after reining in its nonperforming loans problem, but the recovery was short lived. Japan's GDP took
a nosedive when the 2008 Global Financial Crisis dried up overseas
demand for Japanese exports and the V-shaped recovery was cut short
by the triple disaster of March 11, 2011. A powerful earthquake and
tsunami devastated Japan and resulted in great loss of life, with close
to twenty thousand reported casualties. The ensuing nuclear accident
in Fukushima Prefecture forced Japan to rebalance its energy mix away
from nuclear power and further stalled economic recovery.

Prime Minister Abe Shinzo's reform program produced the longest
economic expansion of the postwar era and finally put an end to the
fifteen-year deflationary streak. But the economic recovery was fragile, with a contraction that followed when the consumption tax was
increased in 2014 and again in 2019. The external economic environment also became more challenging. There was a marked turn with
the onset of the U.S.-China trade war in 2018, involving a tit-for-tat
imposition of tariffs and a deceleration of international trade flows. The
global COVID-19 pandemic in 2020 delivered twin demand and supply shocks that resulted in a sharp contraction of the world economy
that year. Prospects for recovery were clouded by recurring waves of a
rapidly mutating virus, China's "zero COVID" policies and consequent
harsh lockdowns, and the outbreak of Russia's war in Ukraine that put
enormous pressure on food and oil prices.

Figure 3.1. Real GDP growth, core inflation, and unemployment rates in Japan

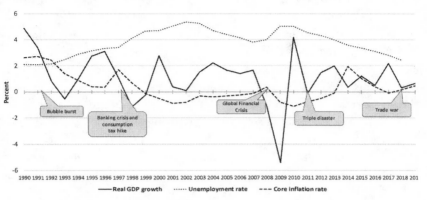

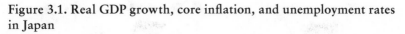

Sources: GDP data from OECD.Stat, "Gross Domestic Product (GDP), Growth Rate," https://stats.oecd.org; unemployment data from OECD, "Unemployment Rate," https://data.oecd.org/unemp/unemployment-rate.htm; and inflation data from OECD.Stat, "Consumer Price Indices (CPis): Consumer Prices—Annual Inflation," https://stats.oecd.org.

Two additional important trends complete this overview of Japan's economic performance during the low-growth era. First, despite the severe economic shocks experienced on several occasions, joblessness has not been rampant. Japan's peak unemployment rate of 5.4 percent would be the envy of many industrialized nations. Second, Japan's growth performance in the 2010s ranked well compared to its G7 peers in terms of GDP per capita. The average annual growth per person was a meager 0.4 percent for Japan during the 2000s, compared to an average of 1.0 percent for the rest of the G7. However, in the Abenomics period, the average GDP per capita annual growth for Japan of 1.3 percent was slightly above the rest of the G7 at 1.2 percent.[2]

Headline figures on growth, inflation, and employment rates contextualize Japan's experience, but they are just a prelude to the more interesting set of questions addressed in this and the following chapters. Why couldn't Japan bounce back after the bubble burst like it had when confronted with other serious economic setbacks? What difference has political leadership made to economic reform prospects? How does the middle-class society fare when there is low growth and stagnant wages? And what are the prospects for the digital, green, and human capital transformations that have gained prominence in the post-Abenomics period?

LOST 1990S: THE BUBBLE AND THE BANKING CRISIS

The 1990s were indeed a lost decade for Japan. The seeds of the asset bubble were planted in the heady 1980s. During that decade, Japanese companies captured large market shares abroad, leading to American and Japanese governments squaring off in heated trade negotiations as the Americans sought to level the playing field and gain access to the Japanese market. The sharp appreciation of the yen that followed the 1985 Plaza Accord brought about yet another demonstration of the might of Japanese capital. The manufacturing sector roused a wave of overseas investments to relocate its factories abroad, while corporate Japan collected "trophy" real estate, such as the Rockefeller Center in New York. Concerned about the impact of yen appreciation on the economy, the Bank of Japan (BOJ) loosened interest rates to spur economic activity, resulting in the Japanese economy growing at a robust 4 percent in the second half of the 1980s.[3] The sense of invincibility was fueled by the boom in stock and real estate prices. The Nikkei 225 index rose from close to 10,000 yen in 1984 to 38,916 yen at its peak in December 1989, and real estate prices soared at the close of the decade.[4]

But the asset price boom was a mirage made possible by false certainties that real estate prices would only go up—as they had throughout the postwar era—and that the explosive credit boom would leave no casualties since the government was expected to step in to prevent financial instability.[5] Such intervention had been a long-established practice when Japanese financial markets were heavily regulated. To this end, the government implemented a "convoy" system of keeping banks moving at the same pace and stepped in to organize rescues when needed. The moral hazard became more acute as deregulation and internationalization permitted large firms to tap into alternative sources of finance. Banks searched for new clients and increased their exposure to the real estate market. In 1990, when the BOJ increased interest rates to puncture the asset price bubble, it got more than it bargained for when stocks plummeted and real estate values sank (the Nikkei swiftly fell by half and land prices by a third). The economy nosedived, and corporations and households saw their wealth abruptly diminish. But a reckoning with the enormity of economic malaise was not forthcoming.

Banks were reluctant to acknowledge the disrepair of their balance sheets and preferred to keep credit lines open to unprofitable firms to avoid loan defaults. These so-called "zombie" firms became deadweights on the economy, dragging down productivity levels and preventing the churning of the economy by exiting the market.[6] Zombie banks also emerged as government officials injected capital to avoid bankruptcies but did not force weak banks to restructure. Some problems could not be plastered over, however. In the mid-1990s, the government disbursed 658 billion yen in a bailout package to fourteen financial firms specializing in housing loans. The rescue amounts were modest but, facing intense public outcry, market participants and government officials opted to keep the lid on the much larger nonbanking loan problem.[7]

Regulatory forbearance left the Japanese economy in a fragile state. Encouraged by early signs of potential recovery, Prime Minister Hashimoto Ryutaro's administration went forward with the consumption tax increase in April 1997. Contrary to the government's expectation that a post-tax hike downturn would be temporary, economic activity remained depressed. More bad news arrived in summer of that year when Japanese exports suffered with the onset of the Asian Financial Crisis. By fall, Japan had a full-blown banking crisis on its hands when in the space of a few months prominent securities firms and banks went under. The convoy system was officially defunct. Politicians extracted their pound of flesh from the Ministry of Finance by removing a core area of its jurisdiction, banking oversight, to a newly minted Financial Supervisory Agency (FSA). Some mortally wounded banks like the Long-Term Credit Bank were nationalized, but the larger task of cleaning up troubled loan portfolios across the board remained undone. Japan entered an era of protracted deflation.

Why couldn't Japan recover from a speculative bubble? And why did it stall for so long, only making the economic malaise more acute? As Hoshi and Kashyap observe, Japan had long left behind the high-growth years as it finished its catch-up process, and the ageing of the population began to lower the potential for growth.[8] But these long-term changes did not mean that Japan was preordained to lose a decade. Policy failures in a number of critical areas better account for Japan's dismal performance.

Three costly mistakes stand out. First, there was a sin of omission in tackling early and decisively the nonperforming loans. The inaction resulted not just from lack of political will to deal with the fallout of unpopular bailout packages. There was a lack of recognition that tighter financial supervision and mechanisms to restructure failed financial institutions were sorely needed, since deregulation and internationalization had increased the risks of unsound lending and speculative bubbles.

Second, the BOJ was too timid in its handling of the situation. It clung to conventional monetary policy, remained stubbornly focused on inflation concerns, and was half-hearted about stimulating the economy. For instance, its 1999 experiment with zero interest rate policy was short lived, and it pursued only moderate quantitative easing between 2001 and 2003.[9]

Third, macroeconomic and fiscal policy frequently worked at cross-purposes. Whether the Japanese government effectively delivered Keynesian stimulus or spent less than advertised or directed funds to low-productivity public works has been hotly debated. But as Kuttner and his co-authors point out, macroeconomic coordination to tackle the economic downturn was lacking, with bouts of expansionary monetary policy coinciding with fiscal consolidation, and vice versa.[10]

KOIZUMI'S RECOVERY: LASTING AND EPHEMERAL REFORMS

At the onset of the twenty-first century, Japan's economic fortunes took a turn with the arrival of Koizumi Junichiro as prime minister in spring 2001. Over his five-plus years at the helm, Koizumi shook up Japanese politics, starting with his surprise rise to the party presidency as he elicited the support of rank-and-file members to overcome reticent legislators, and culminating in 2005 with his sacking of prominent Diet members from his party as he made good on his vow to crush the "forces of resistance" to his reform policies. Koizumi injected new life into Japanese politics and policymaking. He showed the way in connecting directly with urban voters through a savvy media campaign to build support for his reform program, and he challenged the grip of iron triangles on policymaking by empowering prime-minister-appointed councils to take the lead on priority policies.

But Koizumi did not remake Japanese politics, nor did key planks of his economic reforms stand the test of time. His legacy of top-down charismatic leadership was soon upended when his chosen successor, Abe Shinzo, readmitted Koizumi's foes to the party, and the levers of executive leadership remained untouched as Japan entered a period of back-to-back short-tenured prime ministers. Koizumi's record on economic reforms is mixed. On the positive side of the ledger, his tenure demonstrated that with the right policy mix (and a favorable external environment), Japan could return to growth. The banking reforms that enabled Japan to get out from under a mountain of nonperforming loans were critical to this endeavor. Koizumi's pet policy—the privatization of the postal system that would curtail the government's access to the vast pool of postal savings that had funded the pork-barrel state—was largely subverted after he left office. His brand of "no growth without pain" led to a backlash against his policies of fiscal tightening and labor deregulation.

As long as the malaise of the banking system was left unaddressed, Japan could only hope to limp along. Unhealthy balance sheets meant that Japanese banks were motivated both to keep zombie firms afloat to avoid a costly reckoning and to restrain lending elsewhere, producing a credit crunch that held the economy back. Decisive action to clean up the banking sector materialized when Prime Minister Koizumi appointed Takenaka Heizo, a Keio University professor and Koizumi's point man for economic reform, as minister of the FSA. With political backing from the top, Takenaka finally compelled Japanese banks to restructure their operations with increased transparency of balance sheets; disposal of bad loans; and, if needed, capital injections from the government and the replacement of bank management leadership. The results were dramatic. By 2005, the number of nonperforming loans in the Japanese banking system was halved.[11]

Restoring the banking industry to health remains a signal accomplishment of Koizumi's leadership. But the prime minister himself set his sights on his pet project to build his legacy. The privatization of postal savings was an ambitious project, putting on notice the traditional clientelist state by taking away the privileges of postmasters (a core support group of Koizumi's party) and curbing the vast flow of postal savings to government financial institutions that politicians had increasingly directed to favored constituencies.[12] The politics of postal privatization yielded the highest drama of the Koizumi era with the snap election of 2005 called, and won, by Koizumi to secure approval of his reform bill. But the actual outcome was a compromise, dividing postal services into four different entities and putting off until the future actual government divestiture. And the privatization plans themselves were put on hold when the opposing Democratic Party of Japan, upon winning control of the government in the 2009 election, put a moratorium on sales of Japan Post companies.[13]

In an effort to diminish the hold of vested interests over economic policies, Koizumi shifted policymaking dynamics by pushing signature initiatives through newly empowered bodies such as the Council for Economic and Fiscal Policy. This was a novel exercise in executive-led reform, but the efforts to close the spigot of postal savings and to discipline the array of public financial corporations (in highway construction, for instance) were reduced by formidable opposition. Koizumi did have another card to play in his quest to tame the pork-barrel state: cutting back spending on public works.[14] The belt-tightening measures went further by capping social security expenditures and pushing local governments to be more financially self-reliant. Many localities struggled to make this transition, which contributed to the backlash against a reform effort delivered with a strong dose of austerity. Koizumi's neoliberal push extended to labor market reform by aiming to give corporations flexibility in adapting to leaner times. The 2003 Worker Dispatch Law made it easier to rely on short-term contract labor, even in the manufacturing sector, which further contributed to socioeconomic disparities in the Japanese workforce.

Income inequality did not arrive at Japan's doorstep due to Koizumi's reforms, but the prime minister's penchant for fiscal retrenchment and deregulation did put the question of the gap society front and center in the public debate.[15] Future reformers would henceforth have to contend with the public's disquiet over the idea that the price for greater competitiveness could be discarded social protections. Hand-wringing over how to navigate the tradeoffs of structural reform receded to the background. Crisis management was the central concern in light of the Global Financial Crisis and the 3/11 triple disaster, but the government appeared kneecapped by a carousel of short-tenured prime ministers. When Abe reinvented himself as economic reformer in his bid for a second chance at the highest political office, the question of whether he could go beyond an unequal recovery was never far from the public's mind.

NOTES

1. Mireya Solís, "Japan's Consolidated Democracy in an Era of Populist Turbulence," Policy Brief, The Brookings Institution, 2019, 6, https://www .brookings.edu/wp-content/uploads/2019/02/FP_20190227_japan_democracy _solis.pdf.

2. Author's calculations using World Bank data. See World Bank, "World Bank Open Data," https://data.worldbank.org/.

3. Takatoshi Ito and Takeo Hoshi, *The Japanese Economy*, 2nd ed. (Cambridge, MA: MIT Press, 2020), 166.

4. Ibid., 97, 166–67.

5. Keiichiro Kobayashi, "The Two 'Lost Decades' and Macroeconomics: Changing Economic Policies," in *Examining Japan's Lost Decades*, ed. Yoichi Funabashi and Barak Kushner, Routledge Contemporary Japan Series (New York: Routledge, 2015), 37–55.

6. Caballero et al. estimate that by 1996, close to 35 percent of firms could be categorized as zombies (i.e., they needed special support to stay afloat). The proportion was higher in the services sector. See Ricardo J. Caballero, Takeo Hoshi, and Anyl Kashyap, "Zombie Lending and Depressed Restructuring in Japan," *American Economic Review* 98, no. 5 (2008): 1943–77.

7. Takeo Hoshi and Anil Kashyap, "Why Did Japan Stop Growing?" National Institute for Research Advancement, Tokyo January 21, 2011, 27, www.nira.or.jp/pdf/1002english_report.pdf.

8. Ibid., 3.

9. Ito and Hoshi, *The Japanese Economy*, 541.

10. Kenneth Kuttner, Tokuo Iwaisako, and Adam Posen, "Monetary and Fiscal Policies during the Lost Decades," in *Examining Japan's Lost Decades*, ed. Yoichi Funabashi and Barak Kushner (New York: Routledge, 2015), 17–36.

11. Ito and Hoshi, *The Japanese Economy*, 136–37.

12. Kenji E. Kushida and Kay Shimizu, "The Politics of Syncretism in Japan's Political Economy: Finance and Postal Reforms," in *Syncretism: The Politics of Economic Restructuring and System Reform in Japan*, ed. Kenji E. Kushida, Kay Shimizu, and Jean C. Oi (Stanford: The Walter Shorenstein Asia-Pacific Research Center, Stanford University, 2013), 37–76.

13. Chul-Ju Kim and Michael C. Huang, "The Privatization of Japan Rail and Japan Post: Why, How, and Now," *Asian Development Bank Institute (ADBI) Working Paper Series*, no. 1039, 2019, www.econstor.eu/bitstream/10419/222806/1/1685187595.pdf.

14. Gregory W. Noble, "Koizumi's Complementary Coalition for (Mostly) Neoliberal Reform in Japan," in *Syncretism: The Politics of Economic Restructuring and System Reform in Japan*, ed. Kenji E. Kushida, Kay Shimizu, and Jean C. Oi (Stanford: The Walter Shorenstein Asia-Pacific Research Center, Stanford University, 2013), 115–46.

15. Yves Tiberghien, "Thirty Years of Neo-Liberal Reforms in Japan," in *The Great Transformation of Japanese Capitalism*, ed. Sebastien Lechevalier, The Nissan Institute/Routledge Japanese Studies Series (New York: Routledge, 2016), 26–55.

CHAPTER 4

Enter Abenomics

When Prime Minister Abe Shinzo returned to the highest office of the land at the end of 2012, the mandate from voters was to kickstart an economy sapped by protracted deflation and diminished economic opportunity. Abe obliged with a revitalization strategy known as "Abenomics" that pledged to go beyond previous efforts to return the economy to a sustained growth trajectory. The architects of Abenomics sought to learn from two central mistakes committed by previous administrations: letting protracted deflation take hold of the country and pairing austerity with structural reform to "revive" the Japanese economy.

Instead, Abenomics promised a three-pronged approach (known as the "three arrows"): robust monetary expansion to shake up inflationary expectations; flexible fiscal policy to stimulate the economy when needed and to repair public finances through long-term restraint; and productivity-enhancing reforms encouraging firms to invest and take risks, women to stay in the workforce, and declining sectors like agriculture to find niche growth opportunities. Hence, Abenomics set out to improve upon the Koizumi program in both policy prescriptions (with better macro-coordination and broader structural changes) and reform politics (avoiding charges of market fundamentalism).

Abenomics also had an international audience in mind. Promising to tackle the foundations of Japanese regulatory protectionism, Abe sought not only to persuade foreign investors to buy his Abenomics, but also to convince the American government and other participants in the

Trans-Pacific Partnership (TPP) trade negotiations that Japan was an asset rather than a liability in the advancement of the deal.

Abenomics delivered on its promise with the end of deflation and the onset of growth, but it fell short of its stated targets of 2 percent inflation and 2 percent real GDP increase. Moreover, the recovery was brittle (with deep contractions after tax hikes) and unequal (with a sharp contrast between booming stock markets and stagnant wages). The ability of the Abe administration to concurrently push structural reforms in corporate governance, female labor participation, and agricultural reforms are noteworthy, as is its ability to correct course with the adoption of workstyle labor reforms. But the fate of the Abenomics "third arrow" reveals much about Abe as a reformer, for he did not dismantle the bedrock of the socioeconomic regime—stakeholder capitalism, part-time farming, gender inequality, and a labor system privileging core workers. The changes he brought to Japan in the board room, the rural community, and the workplace were political compromises par excellence.

JAPAN'S REFLATIONIST TURN

As Abe's biographer Tobias Harris has pointed out, the embrace of reflationism was critical to Abe's political comeback in 2012, as he was able to transcend his public image as a security hawk to become a fervent proponent of economic revitalization.[1] Abe's embrace of a significant course correction for Japan's macroeconomic management reflected the growing frustrations in many policymaking circles with the Bank of Japan's (BOJ) stubborn refusal to deviate from orthodox monetary policy. Concerns abounded over the vicious economic cycle of protracted deflation: once the expectation sets in that prices will continue to fall, households postpone consumption and businesses cut back on investments, decisions that in turn prolong anemic growth.[2]

During the long stagnation, however, the leadership at the BOJ had diagnosed the problem of deflation differently. By attributing it to structural factors like demographic decline, the BOJ had ruled out monetary policy as the main tool to tackle the problem. The contrast with the proactive use of quantitative easing by other Western central banks to combat the 2008 Global Financial Crisis (GFC) was not only striking, but also resulted in significant yen appreciation, making the concerns over the direction of monetary policy more urgent. Both the Democratic Party of Japan (DPJ) and the Liberal Democratic Party (LDP) launched election manifestos for the December 2012 general election that embraced inflation targeting as a solution to the country's economic ills.[3]

Riding on a landslide victory, Abe went all in on a reflationist course. He cajoled the BOJ Governor Shirakawa Masaaki to adopt an agreement with the Government of Japan (GOJ) to combat deflation, and he used his power of appointment to handpick in Shirakawa's successor, a self-proclaimed reflationist named Kuroda Haruhiko. In spring 2013, the Kuroda "bazooka" was announced with the launch of a quantitative and qualitative easing (QQE) policy. With the aim of switching inflation expectations, the new monetary policy committed the GOJ to double the monetary base to achieve a 2 percent inflation rate in two years. The effects were noticeable right away. Even before the policy had been implemented, market expectations of a monetary regime change resulted in palpable yen depreciation to 102 yen to the dollar, and stock market gains with the Nikkei index rising above 15,500 yen.[4] Soon after the launch of QQE, Japan's inflation rate became positive and reached almost 1 percent.

The headwinds were strong, however. The fall of international oil prices and bouts of recession put downward pressure on oil prices in Japan during the Abe years. The BOJ doubled down on monetary easing and in 2014 expanded the rate of asset purchases to 80 trillion yen per year. A couple of years later, the BOJ waded into negative interest rates by charging a deposit fee to commercial banks. This move was followed by another qualitative shift (known as yield-curve control), targeting asset purchases to bring down long-term interest rates. The degree of monetary activism is reflected in the sharp expansion of the BOJ's balance sheet, which saw a 244 percent increase during Kuroda's tenure.[5]

The monetary easing experiment paid off in bringing Japan out of a prolonged deflationary spell, but it did not achieve the 2 percent target during the second Abe government, with the inflation rate in Japan averaging 0.4 percent.[6] The inability of a very accommodative monetary policy to achieve more decisive inflation outcomes has raised questions about the effectiveness of forward guidance in uprooting entrenched deflationary expectations. It has also increased concerns about the financial risk derived from a massive increase in the BOJ's balance sheet.

Abenomics, however, was much more than a reflationary strategy. This was merely the first "arrow" in its quiver. The economic reform program aimed to achieve greater macroeconomic coordination with a flexible fiscal policy (second arrow), and to increase potential growth through structural reforms (third arrow). The challenges in these two other parts of the economic reform program were also steep.

PUBLIC DEBT AND TAX FIGHTS

An aspiration of Abenomics was to improve macroeconomic management through better coordination of monetary and fiscal policies. A deft use of fiscal policy would entail expanding public expenditures to stimulate the economy at times of sluggish demand, then eventually tightening the fiscal leash in order to ameliorate strained public finances. Japan holds the dubious honor of recording the largest public debt to GDP ratio among developed nations at a whopping 234.5 percent in 2019.[7] The Abe administration rocketed out the gate with a strong dose of stimulus, securing a 13-trillion-yen supplementary package that, together with the aggressive monetary push, immediately improved the economic outlook. Yen depreciation, stock market gains, and an uptick in investment and consumption augured well for the launch of the revitalization strategy.

But the fiscal stimulus was short-lived. As economist Edward Lincoln pointed out, central government annual budgets (including supplementary packages) from 2013 to 2019 were smaller than those of the two years prior to the start of Abenomics, when disaster relief loomed large after the 2011 Tohoku earthquake, tsunami, and nuclear accident.[8] The central battle concerning Abenomics fiscal policy centered on the fight over fulfilling the pledge to raise the consumption tax, a promise Abe inherited from the previous administration of Prime Minister Noda Yoshihiko. The stakes went beyond a technocratic disagreement on the timing or pace of a tax hike to a question about Abe's political fortunes given the well-earned reputation of the consumption tax as "slayer of prime ministers," to borrow Tobias Harris's apt phrase.[9] With fragile domestic consumption, a tax increase risked reverting to stagnation with a price to pay in terms of public support, which Abe needed to advance his less popular priorities on constitutional and security policy reforms and to prevail in the next election.

Supporters of the tax increase (mostly housed in the Ministry of Finance) pointed to the need to repair an unsustainable fiscal situation and forecasted only a temporary dip in domestic demand with a tax hike implemented in two tranches. Such was the calculus that persuaded Abe to make the first move in raising the consumption tax in spring 2014 from 5 percent to 8 percent. The economic contraction, however, was steeper and more prolonged than the government had anticipated. Abe subsequently twice punted the decision to implement the second tranche, which called for increasing the consumption tax to 10 percent, and in so doing, he sidelined powerful politicians from the LDP's tax policy tribe who were urging faster steps toward fiscal consolidation. Abe called for a national election in winter 2014 with the explicit purpose of seeking a mandate from the public to delay the next consumption tax increase scheduled for the following year. After handily winning the election, a few months later Abe removed a powerful opponent: Noda Takeshi, head of the LDP's tax policy commission and a champion of fiscal consolidation.[10] Abe's grip over his party and the centrality he attached to controlling the fate of the consumption tax were evident.

As the Japanese economy appeared close to breaking the postwar record of 73 consecutive months of (moderate) expansion, Abe was finally ready to implement the second tranche of the tax hike in October 2019. To avoid a repeat of the 2014 fiasco, the Abe administration readied government stimulus measures, exempted fresh foods from the tax increase, and promised that some of the tax revenue would be directed to popular policies such as free preschool and higher education for underprivileged students. These measures notwithstanding, the economy once again seized up with an annualized –7.1 percent contraction in GDP in the last quarter of 2019.[11] There was no opportunity to test the theory of a V-shaped recovery since the onset of the COVID-19 pandemic sunk Japan into a recession in 2020.

In addressing the COVID-19 crisis, fiscal restraint gave way to major public spending packages. The Japanese government adopted three hefty supplementary budgets for the 2020 fiscal year with a combined value of 77.4 billion yen. At 106.6 trillion yen, the 2021 fiscal year budget broke new records and entailed an unprecedented level of public debt issuance at 112.55 trillion yen.[12] In a single year (2020), the ratio of government debt to GDP increased markedly to 257.8 percent.[13] The steep negative effects of the pandemic on the economy—depressed domestic consumption and business activities, frozen international tourism flows, and harsh lockdowns abroad disrupting supply chains—required a forceful government response. However, as economist Ito Takatoshi points out, concern remains over the eventual winding down of expenditures since, historically, welfare payments do not return to precrisis levels.[14]

High public debt has not produced the dreaded bond crisis; interest rates remain very low, and most debt is domestically held. Japan's past ability to avert financial instability has been attributed to a combination of three factors: restraint in social security expenditures, tax increases, and the BOJ's sharp uptake of government bonds.[15] But this challenge will be thornier in the post-COVID environment given the difficulty of winding down social security expenditures. As such, Abenomics' second arrow could not solve Japan's fundamental fiscal conundrum. Given the fragility of domestic consumption, attempts at fiscal consolidation put economic recovery at risk and periodic crises have compelled muscular public spending, further compromising the health of public finances.

THE POLITICS OF PRODUCTIVITY

Abating deflation and achieving fiscal balance, important objectives though they are, would not suffice in curing Japan's economic malaise. Structural change to unleash the forces of productivity and innovation has long been identified as a critical front in the economic revitalization quest. Hence, Abenomics' third arrow centered on a growth-oriented reform agenda that promised to cut through the prerogatives of vested interests; encourage firms to invest, innovate, and take risks; and lean on untapped human capital as Japan increasingly felt the rigors of demographic changes and a punishing labor crunch. In selling his recipe for economic revitalization, Prime Minister Abe portrayed himself as the "drill bit that would break through the bedrock of Japanese regulations."[16]

The goal was to boost the metabolism of Japanese capitalism by overcoming rigidities and bottlenecks to growth so that the country could take on a key challenge to its present and future prosperity: dwindling productivity. The performance gap between Japan and its industrialized peer countries has grown. In 2017, Japan's labor productivity was more than a quarter below the top half of Organization for Economic Co-operation and Development (OECD) countries, and within-sector and within-firm productivity differentials were starker in Japan that in the other advanced economies. Lagging labor productivity yields stagnant wages, thereby contributing to social inequality, but it also saps the country's vitality. As reported by the OECD, "With structurally falling labour inputs due to demographic ageing, productivity improvement remains Japan's *only* growth channel" (emphasis is mine).[17]

The government's 2013 growth strategy and its subsequent iterations advertised transformative change for Japan to secure openness, innovation, and competitiveness through a variety of reform efforts. A wide net was cast to include, among other goals, deregulation of the electricity market, faster deregulation within special economic zones, strengthened corporate governance, reform of the public pension fund, labor market reforms, participation in trade agreements, and attracting global talent. Yet, Abenomics' third arrow has frequently been cast as the weak link of the reform program because of the lack of prioritization of reform initiatives,[18] the uneasy mix of genuine deregulation efforts with old-style industrial policy ambitions,[19] and the absence of a vision for Japan's new growth model.[20] Despite these deficiencies, Abenomics did score some concrete wins in its first three years in areas such as corporate governance, female workforce participation, and agricultural reform.

Corporate Governance

Corporate governance reform was central to Abe's revitalization program for its anticipated effect in spurring business dynamism and attracting foreign investors. The low profitability of Japanese companies by international standards and the risk aversion that frequently characterized Japanese top management—for instance, hoarding vast amounts of cash holdings instead of investing in new businesses—were attributed to the decision-making structure of the Japanese enterprise.[21] In contrast to shareholder capitalism that prioritizes dividend gains and short-term profitability metrics, the traditional Japanese company gravitated to a stakeholder model with an emphasis on internal promotion of employees and close ties and coordination with related firms and suppliers cemented with cross-shareholding of stocks. On the positive side, this corporate model enabled long-term planning and offered employment stability to its regular employees. But the downside for corporate decision-making was also evident, namely, silent capital that shelters management and a board of insiders that presents challenges to increasing diversity, accountability, and transparency. [22]

Japan's business landscape has seen major changes over the past few decades with the demise of the main banking system, the erosion of cross-shareholdings, and the inflow of portfolio investment from abroad. But corporate governance did not move in tandem with these developments, nor did it prepare Japanese companies to increase profitability and take new risks. Abenomics aimed to shake up the governance of the Japanese firm with three major moves. The Stewardship Code of 2014 (which borrowed heavily from the UK Code) sought to make institutional investors more proactive in ensuring their investee companies maximized corporate value.[23] The reform of the Companies Act in 2015 sought to provide more choice to Japanese corporations regarding board organization by adding the alternative of an audit/supervisory committee. And the Corporate Governance Code of 2015 created the expectation that all companies would appoint at least two outside directors or would explain their reasons for not conforming with this guideline.

The reforms operated with a soft-law approach of "comply or explain," trying to use public shame or praise to bring change to the Japanese boardroom. A very successful initiative was the Tokyo Stock Exchange's (TSE) creation in 2014 of the JPX-Nikkei Index 400 for top-performing companies, which spurred firms to increase their returns on investment to join the listing. There was little coaxing of reluctant firms since there was no mandatory obligation to appoint outside directors, but peer pressure seemed to work. The share of TSE companies with two or more outside directors jumped from 22 percent in 2014 to 91.3 percent in 2018.[24]

The broader questions surrounding Abenomics' corporate governance agenda revolved around the assumptions behind the reform effort and the ability of the government, with the finite set of tools at its disposal, to induce broad changes in the direction of corporate governance. The reforms were inspired by a desire to move away from the traditional stakeholder model of the Japanese firm to give more voice to shareholders with the goal of increasing profitability and investment activity. But Steven Vogel is on the mark when he points to the weaknesses of shareholder capitalism to improve business performance (for example, the distorted incentive of tying executive compensation to stock valuation). A full-blown transition to shareholder sovereignty was never in the works, Vogel adds, due to the successful efforts of business interests in Japan to protect core elements of the stakeholder model (rejecting mandatory obligations to the board structure, maintaining defense mechanisms against hostile takeovers, and serving the interests of a broader set of constituencies).[25] The legal changes implemented, therefore, avoided hard legal commitments and had a more modest aim (nudging the appointment of independent directors), making it unlikely that they could deliver a major shift toward greater innovation or risk-taking in corporate decision-making.[26]

Japanese companies continued to accumulate the largest levels of cash holdings,[27] private domestic investment did not make a leap, and despite the direct entreaties of Prime Minister Abe to Japan, Inc. to raise wages as part of the campaign to boost consumption, hourly wages in Japan remained stagnant.

Womenomics

Addressing the crushing labor shortage resulting from adverse demographics (ageing and population decline due to a drop in the fertility rate) was also central to Abe's economic revitalization strategy. The government seized on a concept dubbed "Womenomics" to tap into a human capital source that had until then been underutilized. The female half of the population in Japan is highly educated, but its labor force participation remained low compared to males in Japan and females in other advanced industrialized nations. A critical problem was addressing a ubiquitous trait of the Japanese labor market. The so-called "M-curve" (which tracks female labor participation by age) reflected the marked drop-off of female employees from the workforce upon marriage or childbirth, only to return years later to part-time, lowly remunerated employment.

Japan paid a heavy price for lacking an environment that supports the careers of working mothers. The inability to balance work and family commitments meant that many women postponed or gave up on having children in order to pursue their professional goals, or felt compelled to abandon work when they started a family. Insufficient childcare, lopsided responsibilities at home (with very few men taking paternity leave or sharing more equitably in childrearing duties), plus a rigid working environment (that puts women on track early on for nonmanagerial work and expects long hours) denied many women the chance to achieve their full personal and professional potential. For the country as a whole, this meant lower fertility rates, a reduced labor supply, and wasted human capital, all in turn compounding national social and economic problems.

Expanded female employment was expected to generate a significant economic payoff. Kathy Matsui and her co-authors estimated that achieving gender parity in labor participation would raise Japan's GDP by 10 percent. But they also noted the benefits of greater diversity in increasing innovation and creativity as firms that achieve greater gender balance are more profitable.[28] Enhanced labor participation would also help to revive domestic consumption by raising the income levels of dual-earner families. In making the economic case for boosting female employment, Prime Minister Abe was not breaking new ground (previous administrations had identified these problems and attempted some solutions), but the novelty was employing Womenomics as a keystone of the conceptualization of the national growth strategy.[29]

The government laid out in 2013 and 2014 a number of objectives to achieve women's economic empowerment: increasing prime-aged female labor participation from 68 percent to 73 percent by 2020; expanding childcare capacity by 400,000 slots; increasing the percentage of men who took parental leave from 2.6 percent in 2011 to 13 percent by 2020; and boosting female representation in leadership positions across all fields in Japan to 30 percent by 2020.[30] A 2015 law called the Promotion of Women's Advancement in the Workplace followed. The bill mandated that firms with more than 300 employees were to publish information on their gender diversity outcomes, produce and disseminate corporate diversity plans, and appoint at least one female board member. To reward companies excelling in their diversity goals, the government created a certification program with a distinctive seal that could be stamped on their products.

Abe's Womenomics campaign yielded results in some important areas. Most notably, there was a marked increase in female labor participation and an expansion of childcare facilities. At 71 percent, female labor participation in Japan has surpassed that of the United States as of 2019. There has been some improvement in tackling the M-curve. Labor participation in the 25- to 44-year-old cohort grew from 71 percent in 2010 to 86 percent in 2020. Childcare capacity expanded by 27 percent between 2012 and 2018.[31] Nagase Nobuko has found that the increase in infant care facilities and some reduction of working hours for working mothers had a strong impact on labor participation rates.[32]

Nevertheless, Womenomics has fallen woefully short in securing meaningful gender equality. The male-female wage gap in Japan of 74 percent[33] continues to be severe, in large part because the increase in female employment is concentrated in nonregular work. Women hold more than 50 percent of part-time work jobs in Japan and as such they receive lower compensation, job security, and career mentoring. The female empowerment strategy has not delivered on quality employment opportunities, nor has it delivered on the reform of tax and social security provisions that penalize married women for increasing their earning power. Instead, the tax code continues to be wedded to an outdated single-earner household model. Although the growing number of female university graduates should increase the future ranks of female managers and professionals,[34] Abe's Womenomics fell short of all its targets for women in leadership positions and eventually had to abandon the goal of 30 percent female participation in leadership positions.

Figure 4.1 captures the two faces of Womenomics: marked improvement in female labor participation but little progress in addressing gender disparities. Japan ranks on the lower end of the World Economic Forum's gender gap index (120 out of 156 nations) and a decade of Womenomics did little to raise Japan's overall score. There is a sharp contrast between the very high marks Japan receives for its health and education outcomes and its mediocre scores for economic and political participation. While there are distinct gains in the economic opportunity metric, the backsliding of female political empowerment during the 2010s is of concern. In 2021, women only held 10 percent of parliamentary seats. Gender equality is still very much a work in progress in Japan.

Figure 4.1. The two faces of Womenomics

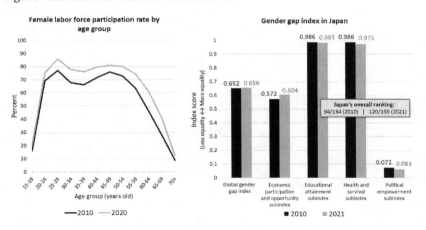

Sources: Government of Japan, e-Stat Portal Site of Official Statistics of Japan, https://www.e-stat.go.jp/en; "Global Gender Gap Report 2021," *Insight Report* (Geneva: World Economic Forum, March 30, 2021), https://weforum.org/reports/global-gender-gap-report-2021.

Agricultural Reform

Changing demographics have taken a toll on Japanese agriculture. A sharp decline in the rural population and the graying of farmers, whose average age is sixty-five years old, put the long-term sustainability of Japanese agriculture in question. But a flawed policy regime contributed significantly to the structural decline of farming. Production cutbacks, land restrictions, heavy subsidization, and tariff shelters sustained a politically powerful constituency (part-time rice farmers) but blunted the emergence of a competitive agricultural sector capable of attracting new generations of farmers and competing for international markets. Key planks of this agricultural regime included the set-aside program (which mandated the idling of some rice paddies) to increase producer prices, steep tariff walls (the ad valorem tariff for rice was 778 percent), hefty state subsidies, and bans on the acquisition of farmland for corporations seeking to launch commercial agriculture ventures. It was a system that discouraged innovation and productivity but was sustained by a political symbiosis: the farm vote for state protection.

Prime Minister Abe seized on agricultural modernization as a landmark initiative for his structural reform agenda. In this pursuit, he targeted the ultimate iron triangle: LDP politicians, agricultural cooperatives, and Agriculture Ministry bureaucrats.[35] A profound crisis in the countryside—most starkly depicted by the dearth of a new generation of farmers—provided a powerful motivation to introduce efficiency-driven reforms to brighten agriculture's future.[36] Moreover, as long as the agricultural lobby continued to exercise veto power over trade policy, Abe's efforts to join the TPP, both to bolster the credibility of its economy-wide reforms and to elevate Japan's international profile, would come to naught.[37]

Abenomics promised a rethink of past government policies to deliver an "agriculture on the offensive." Instead of letting the agricultural industry continue its decline, market-oriented reforms that centered on farmers—not the interests of the agricultural bureaucratic machinery—could increase competitiveness and open export opportunities for Japanese agriculture. In 2013, Prime Minister Abe cinched Japan's accession to the TPP by addressing both the offensive (export potential) and defensive (import protection) concerns of Japanese agriculture. On the latter, the pledge to reject full tariff elimination in five "sacred" commodities (rice, wheat, dairy, beef and pork, and sugar) became a mandate for Japanese trade negotiators, which resulted in Japan committing to eliminating only 81 percent of agricultural tariffs.[38] But the TPP move also demonstrated that the direction of trade policy now rested firmly in the Executive's hands, and not with the agricultural lobby.[39] That same year, the Abe administration trained its eye on another bastion of the farming policy regime: the set-aside program responsible for high producer prices that enabled part-time farming to survive. While the government's move appeared consequential—the plan was to phase out the set-aside policy in five years—it in fact launched production restrictions for cattle feed rice, mitigating the actual reach of the reform.[40]

In May 2014, Abe's reform campaign turned its attention to the power center of organized agriculture: the cooperative system itself. Known by its acronym "JA," the agricultural cooperative movement was a sprawling hierarchical organization that exerted top-down control over prefectural and local cooperatives and touched on all areas of agricultural production and distribution (including rice sales, machinery and fertilizer sales, banking, and insurance). At its apex, its political arm *JA Zenchu* mobilized the farmer vote and was a key voice in agricultural policy decisions. While JA's power had diminished over time due to demographic changes plus administrative and electoral reforms, it could still mobilize against politicians who threatened its core interests. For that reason, JA reform had been off-limits until Abe's Regulatory Reform Council proposed to strip JA Zenchu from the Agricultural Cooperative Law, to transition JA's mammoth marketing arm to a joint stock company (which would cause JA to lose its exemption from the Antimonopoly Act), and to relax centralized control over local cooperatives by enabling independent audits and decentralized finances.[41]

Backed by its allies in the LDP, JA pushed back and championed self-reform. The political compromise that emerged in the 2015 amendments to the Agricultural Cooperative Association Law stripped JA Zenchu's special status, gave the marketing arm the option (but not the obligation) to transition to a joint stock company, transferred the right to collect levies from the local units to prefectural (not central) chapters, and increased the influence of full-time farmers on local cooperatives.[42]

Undoubtedly, Abe went beyond his predecessors in weakening organized agriculture's hold over trade policy and shrinking important institutional and policy prerogatives of its lobbying arm. However, the much-vaunted productivity revolution did not occur. The government showered Japanese agriculture with hefty subsidies after signing the TPP (even though no major import avalanche of agricultural commodities was expected), the rice production restrictions continued in a new guise to keep part-time farmers afloat, and the land regime hindering the emergence of commercial agriculture stayed in place. The agricultural iron triangle weakened, but it survived to see another day.

THE SOCIAL FACE OF ABENOMICS

The original three arrows of the Abenomics program were initially successful in shaking the economy out of its stupor and signaling a more comprehensive effort at structural reform than in years past. But they missed their target of avoiding an unequal recovery. This motivated a correction course in fall 2015 with the launch of "Abenomics 2.0." The new arrows in its quiver were a "strong economy" reaching a GDP of 600 trillion yen ($5 trillion) in the next five years; support to families with children to increase the fertility rate from 1.4 percent to 1.8 percent and sustain at least a 100 million population over the next half century; and increased social security with an emphasis on eldercare.[43]

"Workstyle reform" was a centerpiece of the new Abenomics. Japan's employment system—with strong job security and seniority pay for core workers—had been a pillar of the postwar economy and society. With the onset of slow growth in the post-bubble era (1992 onward), labor reforms focused on pairing sustained job protection for regular employees with increased flexibility to hire contract workers without such guarantees. The guiding spirit of employment reform in the second Abe term was very different, however. The crushing labor shortage, depressed wages from the influx of non-regular employees, and the punishing working hours of corporate Japan stood in the way of raising economic activity and labor productivity, boosting consumer demand, and expanding the ranks of the workforce. These were powerful motivations for a conservative prime minister to embark on reforms to promote worker welfare, as Steven Vogel astutely observes.[44]

The main lines of effort concentrated on reducing overtime, achieving equal pay for equal work, and introducing greater diversity in compensation and workstyles. For the first time, a legal cap on overtime was adopted (100 hours per month for a maximum of 720 hours per year), but with an exemption for high-level employees whose compensation was to be based on performance, not on work hours. Firms were also required to ensure employees received at least 5 days of annual leave. In order to address the inequities within firms between permanent and fixed-term workers, the Workstyle Reform Bill enacted in 2019 pushed for greater transparency and equality in compensation and benefits. At the same time, "worker constraint" (i.e., the obligations of core workers to shift positions or transfer to subsidiaries), as well as skills and tenure remained legitimate grounds for compensation differentials. The bill also encouraged a diversity of workstyles through telework or dual jobs for regular employees.[45]

Abenomics 2.0 did not hit its lofty targets in nominal GDP, fertility rate, or wage growth. But its social turn did mark an attempt to correct some of the inequalities of the dual employment system out of a recognition of its high costs for Japan's society and economy. This is, however, unfinished work. Not long after the enactment of the workstyle reforms, the COVID-19 pandemic both accelerated changes in work practices (as telework became a reality at a speed none had imagined), and exposed yet again employment inequities (as non-regular workers suffered the brunt of job losses).

On the bright side, women led the way in filling additional regular jobs during 2020 at 330,000 out of 360,000.[46] During the pandemic, there was a sharp uptick in telework, from 11 percent in 2019 to 67 percent in 2020, a drop in overtime hours, and greater use of paid holiday leave. Over half of Japan's large firms reported implementation of steps toward workstyle reform.[47] But there were also worrisome employment trends in pandemic Japan. Increases in the labor force due to higher labor market participation of females and seniors through the Abenomics years came to a halt, with a labor force contraction of 180,000 due primarily to seniors leaving the labor market. And non-regular workers and female employees suffered the brunt of job losses: of the 750,000 decline in non-regular workers in 2020, two-thirds were female employees.[48]

Securing the future of Japan's middle class remains a pressing task, especially as the country undergoes profound demographic change that will impinge on its ability to improve productivity and sustain the safety net. Much is at stake in current efforts to lay the foundations for sustainable growth and continued societal well-being through climate, digital, and human capital transformations.

NOTES

1. Tobias Harris, *The Iconoclast: Shinzo Abe and the New Japan* (London: Hurst Publishing, 2020).

2. See Haruhiko Kuroda, "Overcoming Deflation–Theory and Practice," (speech, Keio University, Tokyo, June 20, 2016), www.bis.org/review/r160623a .pdf.

3. Gene Park, "The Bank of Japan: Central Bank Independence and the Politicization of Monetary Policy," in *The Oxford Handbook of Japanese Politics*, ed. Robert J. Pekkanen and Saadia M. Pekkanen (New York: Oxford University Press, 2020), 433–50.

4. Takatoshi Ito, "Assessment of Abenomics: Origin, Evolution, and Achievement," working paper, *Asian Economic Policy Review (AEPR) Series*, no. 2020-2-1, Japan Center for Economic Research, Tokyo, October 2020, www .jcer.or.jp/jcer_download_log.php?f=eyJwb3N0X2lkIjo3MDczMywiZmlsZV9 wb3N0X2lkIjoiNzA4MDUifQ==&post_id=70733&file_post_id=70805.

5. Gene Park, "Japan's Deflation, Monetary Policy and Issues Ahead" *East Asian Policy* 11, no. 3 (2019): 68–81.

6. Ito, "Assessment of Abenomics."

7. See OECD, "General Government Debt," 2022, https://data.oecd.org/gga /general-government-debt.htm.

8. Edward J. Lincoln, "A Retrospective on Abenomics," Working Paper no. 378, Center on Japanese Economy and Business, Columbia University Business School, New York, December 2020.

9. Harris, *The Iconoclast*, 211.

10. Takeo Hoshi and Phillip Y. Lipscy, "The Political Economy of the Abe Government," in *The Political Economy of the Abe Government and Abenomics Reforms*, ed. Takeo Hoshi and Phillip Lipscy (Cambridge, UK: Cambridge University Press, 2021), 3–39; and Ko Mishima, "The Presidentialization of Japan's LDP Politics: Analyzing Its Causes, Limits, and Perils," *World Affairs* 182, no. 2 (February 2019): 97–123.

11. See "Japan's Q4 GDP Downgraded to Annualized 7.1% contraction," *Nikkei Asia*, March 9, 2020, https://asia.nikkei.com/Economy/Japan-s-Q4 -GDP-downgraded-to-annualized-7.1-contraction.

12. See "Japan Enacts 19 Tril. Yen Extra Budget to Fight Virus amid Criticism," *Kyodo News*, January 28, 2021, https://english.kyodonews.net/news /2021/01/c5e63041eae7-breaking-news-japan-enacts-1918-tril-yen-extra -budget-to-manage-pandemic.html.

13. See OECD, "General Government Debt."

14. Ito, "Assessment of Abenomics."

15. Mark T. Greenan and David E. Weinstein, "The Crisis That Wasn't: How Japan Has Avoided a Bond Market Panic," Working Paper no. 361, Center on Japanese Economy and Business, Columbia University Business School, New York, November 2017.

16. See Shinzo Abe, "Economic Policy," speech, London, June 19, 2013, https://japan.kantei.go.jp/96_abe/statement/201306/19guildhall_e.html.

17. OECD, "Japan: Productivity," OECD Insights on Productivity and Business Dynamics, Paris, March 2020), www.oecd.org/sti/ind/oecd-productivity -insights-japan.pdf.

18. David Piling, *Bending Adversity: Japan and the Art of Survival* (New York: Penguin Press, 2014).

19. Hoshi and Lipscy, "The Political Economy of the Abe Government."

20. Sebastien Lechevalier and Brieuc Monfort, "Abenomics: Has It Worked? Will It Ultimately Fail?" *Japan Forum* 30, no. 2 (2018): 277–302.

21. Ken Hokugo and Alicia Ogawa, "Corporate Governance and Steward-ship Program," Working Paper no. 1, Center on Japanese Economy and Business, Columbia University Business School, New York, 2017.

22. Franz Waldenberger, "'Growth Oriented' Corporate Governance Reform—Can It Solve Japan's Performance Puzzle?" *Japan Forum* 29, no. 3 (2017): 354–74.

23. See The Council of Experts on the Stewardship Code (FY2019), "Principles for Responsible Institutional Investors «Japan's Stewardship Code»," Tokyo, Financial Services Agency, March 24, 2020, www.fsa.go.jp/en/refer/councils/stewardship/20200324/01.pdf.

24. OECD, "OECD Economic Surveys, Japan 2019," (Paris: OECD Publishing, April 2019), 46.

25. Steven Vogel, "Japan's Ambivalent Pursuit of Shareholder Capitalism," *Politics and Society* 47, no. 1 (2019): 117–44.

26. Curtis J. Milhaupt, "Evaluating Abe's Third Arrow: How Significant Are Japan's Recent Corporate Governance Reforms?" Revised draft paper presented at the Symposium Celebrating the 25th Anniversary of the Chair in Japanese Law, University College London, 2017.

27. Japan has the highest ratio of cash holdings to GDP at 60 percent, compared to 30 percent in the Eurozone and 10 percent in the United States. See Mike Bird, "Stock Market Investors Must Keep an Eye on the Corporate Cash Mountain," *The Wall Street Journal*, April 23, 2021, www.wsj.com/articles/stock-market-investors-must-keep-an-eye-on-the-corporate-cash-mountain-11619171580.

28. Kathy Matsui, Hiromi Suzuki, and Kazunori Tatebe, "Womenomics 5.0," Goldman Sachs, New York, April 2019, www.goldmansachs.com/insights/pages/womenomics-5.0/.

29. Linda Hasunuma, "Political Targets: Womenomics as an Economic and Foreign Relations Strategy," *Asie Visions*, no. 92, Institut français des relations internationales (Ifri), [French Institute for International Relations], April 2017, www.ifri.org/en/publications/notes-de-lifri/asie-visions/political-targets-womenomics-economic-and-foreign-relations.

30. Hiroko Goto, "Will Prime Minister Abe's 'Womenomics' Break Glass Ceilings in Japan?" *Hastings International and Comparative Law Review* 44 (2016): 441–57; and Matsui et al., "Womenomics 5.0."

31. Matsui et al., "Womenomics 5.0," 14.

32. Nobuko Nagase, "Has Abe's Womenomics Worked?" *Asian Economic Policy Review* 13, no. 1 (January 2018): 68–101.

33. Yukiko Amano, Kyo Kitazume, and Eriko Sunayama, "Gender Gap Persists in Japan as Women earn 74% as Much as Men," *Nikkei Asia*, March 8,

2022, https://asia.nikkei.com/Spotlight/Society/Gender-gap-persists-in-Japan-as-women-earn-74-as-much-as-men.

34. Bill Emmott, *Japan's Far More Female Future: Increasing Gender Equality and Reducing Workplace Insecurity will make Japan Stronger*, (Oxford, UK: Oxford University Press, 2020).

35. Masayoshi Honma and Aurelia George Mulgan, "Political Economy of Agricultural Reform in Japan under Abe's Administration," *Asian Economic Policy Review* 13, no. 1 (January 2018): 128–46.

36. Patricia L. Machlachlan and Kay Shimizu, "Japanese Farmers in Flux: The Domestic Sources of Agricultural Reform," *Asian Survey* 56, no. 3 (2016): 442–65.

37. Mireya Solís, *Dilemmas of a Trading Nation: Japan and the United States in the Evolving Asia-Pacific Order* (Washington, DC: Brookings Institution Press, 2017).

38. Ibid., 186.

39. Ibid.

40. See Aurelia George Mulgan, "Can Abe's Third Arrow Pierce Japan's Agricultural Armour?" East Asia Forum, April 6, 2014, www.eastasiaforum.org/2014/04/06/can-abes-third-arrow-pierce-japans-agricultural-armour/.

41. Hironori Sasada, "The 'Third Arrow' or Friendly Fire? The LDP Government's Reform Plan for the Japan Agricultural Cooperatives," *Japanese Political Economy* 41, no. 1–2 (2015): 14–35.

42. Kazuhiko Yamashita, "A First Step Toward Reform of Japan's Agricultural Cooperatives System," Nippon.com, April 20, 2015, www.nippon.com/en/currents/d00169/; and Machlachlan and Shimizu, "Japanese Farmers in Flux."

43. Hideo Hayakawa, "Reading between the lines of Abenomics 2.0," Nippon.com, December 16, 2015, https://www.nippon.com/en/currents/d00207/.

44. Steven Vogel, "Japan's Labor Regime in Transition: Rethinking Work for a Shrinking Nation," *Journal of Japanese Studies* 44, no. 2 (2018): 257–92.

45. Japan Institute for Labour Policy and Training, "Workstyle Reform Bill Enacted," *Japan Labor Issues* 2, no. 10 (November 2018): 7; and Ulrike Schaede, *The Business Reinvention of Japan: How to Make Sense of the New Japan and Why It Matters* (Stanford: Stanford University Press, 2020).

46. Jun Saito, "Changes in Japanese Employment under COVID-19," Japan Center for Economic Research, April 10 2021, www.jcer.or.jp/english/changes-in-japanese-employment-under-covid-19.

47. See Cabinet Office, "感染症拡大の下で進んだ柔軟な働き方と働き方改革【説明資料】," [Flexible Workstyles and Workstyle Reform Progression under the Spread of Infectious Disease (Explanatory Materials)], 年次経済財政報告, [Annual Economic and Fiscal Report], November 2020, https://www5.cao.go.jp/keizai3/2020/1106wp-keizai/setsumei02.pdf.

48. Saito, "Changes in Japanese Employment under COVID-19."

CHAPTER 5

The Quest for Revitalization

HOW FARES THE MIDDLE-CLASS SOCIETY?

Historically, Japan has maintained a slim welfare state, with the bulk of social spending geared toward the provision of universal healthcare and public pensions. Transfers for working families, social services, and human capital development have been modest compared to those of other industrialized nations, giving rise to what Miura Mari calls "welfare through work"—that is, prioritizing employment protection in lieu of income support.[1] Japan's redistribution efforts did help sustain a middle class when both the economy and population were growing through support for the elderly and transfers to rural areas and sunset industries.[2] Tighter public finances, the shrinking working-age population, and the rise of precarious employment, however, have strained the nation's ability to provide social security. And yet, deepening socioeconomic cleavages have not led to political polarization. While this is a testament to the resilience of the safety net, the future of Japan's middle class is being decided today in the ongoing attempts to seize the opportunities of green, digital, and technological innovations. Ultimately, it will be Japan's investments in human capital that will yield the most needed transformation.

DEMOGRAPHIC DECLINE AND INEQUALITY, BUT NOT POLARIZATION

There have been and will continue to be dramatic demographic changes in Japan in this century (see Figure 5.1). From the postwar period on,

Japan's population increased, peaking in 2010 at 128 million people. But the population has since entered an era of contraction. By 2019, Japan's population had decreased to 126.2 million, and it is expected to shrink well beyond the 100-million level in the course of the next four decades. Equally significant is the change in the composition of the population due to the combined effect of low fertility rates (1.3 births per woman) and high life expectancy (82 years for men and 88 years for women) as measured in 2020.[3] Seniors are projected to represent 38 percent of the population in the next fifty years, while the share of the working-age population (15–64 years of age) is expected to decrease markedly (see Figure 5.2).

The ways in which an ageing and contracting population undercut Japan's growth potential and the viability of its safety net are well understood. Labor shortages hamper economic activity, and the ageing of the workforce lowers productivity and innovation.[4] Moreover, these demographic changes put a heavier burden on younger generations to sustain higher social security expenditures given the growing demand for healthcare, pensions, and eldercare. Dire demographic trends, therefore,

Figure 5.1. Actual and projected total population of Japan: Low-, medium-, and high-fertility (medium-mortality) projections

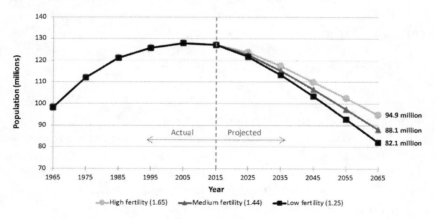

Sources: Actual population from National Institute of Population and Social Security Research, "人口統計資料集(2021)" [Population Statistics Collection (2021)], www.ipss.go.jp/syoushika/tohkei/Popular/P_Detail2021.asp?fname=T01-01.htm; projected population stats from National Institute of Population and Social Security Research, "Population Projections for Japan (2017): 2016 to 2065," http://www.ipss.go.jp/pp-zenkoku/e/zenkoku_e2017/pp29_summary.pdf.

Figure 5.2. Japan's population share of the major three age groups

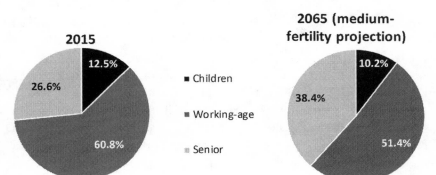

Sources: 2015 population data from Japan Statistics Bureau of the Ministry of Internal Affairs and Communications, "Population and Households of Japan (Final Report of the 2015 Population Census)," www.stat.go.jp/english/data/koku-sei/2015/final_en/final_en.html; 2065 projected population data from National Institute of Population and Social Security Research, "Population Projections for Japan (2017): 2016 to 2065," www.ipss.go.jp/pp-zenkoku/e/zenkoku_e2017/pp29_summary.pdf.

have been at the center of prognostications of Japan's inevitable decline. Yet, the storyline of Japan as the outlier among industrialized nations due to its unique demographic burden has not stood well against the test of time. Rather, Japan now appears to be an early case of a shared and challenging future for a large set of countries that must also navigate an era of a graying and shrinking population.

Across the world, with the exception of Africa, populations are ageing: the fastest-growing cohort are people above 65 years of age. The share of seniors in the world population is expected to double to 16.4 percent by 2050.[5] Scores of countries are reporting fertility rates of 1.5 or less (much lower than the 2.1 replacement ratio), with South Korea at the bottom with a fertility rate below 1.[6] Hence, the United Nations estimates that between 2019 and 2050, fifty-five countries will experience some population contraction, of which twenty-seven will see drops of 10 percent or more. Countries with high levels of projected depopulation include many European nations (Bulgaria, Lithuania, Italy, Germany, and Spain), Russia, and several Asian countries (Japan, South Korea, Thailand, and China).[7] China's depopulation challenges will be much more severe in the second half of the twenty-first century, with the UN projecting a drop of 24 percent in population levels between 2050 and

2100.[8] But the burden of adverse demographic change, with a marked drop in the working-age population, will be felt much sooner in many large economies (see Figure 5.3). Transitioning to an economy defined by chronic labor shortages and avoiding a fiscal cliff that could reduce the safety net is no longer Japan's imperative alone.

Convergence is afoot in other areas. Japan has not escaped the deepening social inequality that has afflicted the rest of the industrialized world. Quite the opposite, in a span of twenty-five years Japan's Gini coefficient (which measures income inequality) grew by fifteen points, converging with the G7 average in 2010. In 2019, Japan had the third-largest Gini coefficient among G7 nations after the United States and United Kingdom, and the second-largest poverty rate after the United States.[9] But the drivers of inequality are markedly different in the United States and Japan. In the former, the concentration of wealth in the top 1 percent of the population is much steeper (the top 1 percent hold 43 percent of household net wealth), while in Japan the top 1 percent hold 11 percent.[10]

The rise of inequality in Japan has been fueled in no small measure by the increase in precarious employment. In lean economic times, Japanese companies have resorted to hiring non-regular workers in order to retain flexibility in their payrolls, and in 2021 non-regular workers represent 36.7 percent of the workforce.[11] Because non-regular workers do not enjoy the same level of pay and benefits, do not partake to the

Figure 5.3. Working-age population (15–64 years old) as percent of total population (1965–2030)

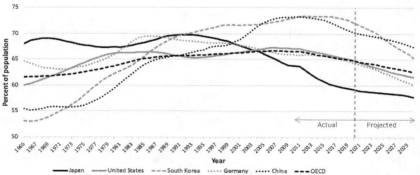

Source: OECD, "Working Age Population (indicator)," https://data.oecd.org/pop/working-age-population.htm.

same extent in on-the-job training opportunities, and do not have secure career paths, their growing ranks have depressed wages and contributed to social inequality. Women have suffered disproportionately from the increase in atypical employment. More than half of all female employees are in non-regular positions. One group of women in particular—single mothers—is most vulnerable, as many of them live below the poverty line.

A long-standing socioeconomic cleavage has also intensified in the era of slow growth and depopulation: urban-rural disparities. Japan's postwar economic takeoff accelerated the forces of urbanization and industrialization, leaving behind the countryside as populations migrated to the cities and economic opportunities diminished in rural areas. Redistribution to rural areas was central to Japan's model of shared growth and to the electoral clout of the Liberal Democratic Party (LDP) in the countryside.[12] However, dwindling fiscal resources undercut regional transfers and the forces of depopulation were felt much more acutely in rural areas. A vicious cycle of population decline, economic stagnation, and unsustainable service infrastructure contributed to a drop by almost half in the overall number of Japanese municipalities during the 2000s.[13]

With the intensification of socioeconomic cleavages, public confidence in sustaining a middle-class society has eroded. Two-thirds of Japanese respondents to the International Social Survey Programme (ISSP) believe that the income gap has grown too large, and this concern was especially high in the aftermath of the Global Financial Crisis (see Figure 5.4). Consistently, the Japanese public has identified the ideal social structure as one in which the vast majority of the population occupies the middle-income brackets (a diamond-shaped income distribution); but over time, survey respondents have felt that the country is moving further away from that mass middle-class ideal (Figure 5.5).

Japan has grown more unequal, but not more polarized. ISSP surveys over the span of two decades show that across potential divides (labor vs. management, rich vs. poor, and young vs. old), public opinion does not see society as torn apart by social conflict (see Figure 5.6). In fact, the share of respondents who believe Japanese society values social cohesion (ties among individuals) grew from 33 percent in 1999 to 42 percent in 2019.[14] And even though public awareness of socioeconomic inequality is high in Japan, most people still self-identify as middle class (89.1 percent in latest Cabinet Office survey of 2021).[15]

Figure 5.4. Is the income gap too large?

Note: "Other" includes answers indicating neither too large/too small, not knowing, and no reply. Total may be more than 100% due to rounding.

Source: Toshiyuki Kobayashi, "減少する中流意識と変わる日本人の社会観" [Decreasing Identification with Middle Class and Changing Societal Views of Japanese People], 放送研究と調査 [Broadcast Research and Survey], NHK Broadcasting Culture Research Institute, May 2020, www.nhk.or.jp/bunken/research/yoron/20200501_7.html.

Employment dualism has not generated polarized labor politics;[16] nor has regional decline turned into rural support for anti-establishment movements.[17] A number of factors have played a role in mitigating social divisiveness despite growing income inequality. Some core pillars of the extended social protection system have endured. The moderate attrition

Figure 5.5. Mass middle-class society: Ideal and actual social structure

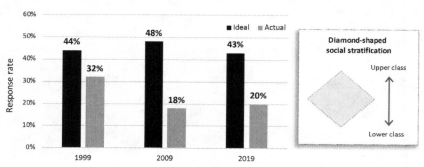

Source: Toshiyuki Kobayashi, "減少する中流意識と変わる日本人の社会観" [Decreasing Identification with Middle Class and Changing Societal Views of Japanese People], 放送研究と調査 [Broadcast Research and Survey], NHK Broadcasting Culture Research Institute, May 2020, www.nhk.or.jp/bunken/research/yoron/20200501_7.html.

Figure 5.6. Conflict between social groups

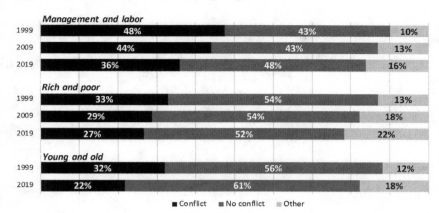

Note: "Other" includes answers indicating not knowing and no reply. Total may be more than 100% due to rounding.

Source: Toshiyuki Kobayashi, "減少する中流意識と変わる日本人の社会観" [Decreasing Identification with Middle Class and Changing Societal Views of Japanese People], 放送研究と調査 [Broadcast Research and Survey], NHK Broadcasting Culture Research Institute, May 2020, www.nhk.or.jp/bunken/research/yoron/20200501_7.html.

of regular workers who enjoy strong employment protection (in absolute numbers, a decrease from 38 million in 1992 to 34 million in 2017)[18] and continued government largesse toward politically overrepresented rural areas[19] have eased the sharper edges of social conflict. Japan's social spending has increased to represent 22.3 percent of GDP, ahead of 20.6 percent for the United Kingdom and 18.7 percent for the United States in 2019.[20] The egalitarian bent of Japanese welfare through universal access to healthcare and old-age pensions has curbed backlash against economic injustice, notes Shiozaki Akihisa.[21] Japan's high living standards—which include efficient transportation and infrastructure, quality public education, and a strong record of public safety help—sustain social cohesion. In a broad measure of well-being, the Human Life Indicator, which tracks not just life expectancy at birth but also the equality of life spans within the population, shows that Japan ranks near the top.[22]

There is no room for complacency, however. The demographic trends highlighted above will dramatically increase the social security burden, with public welfare spending estimated to increase 57 percent by 2040;[23]

and the task to redirect social spending toward working families and social services has just begun (these two programs currently receive less than a quarter of social expenditures). Stagnant household incomes have frayed expectations of upward social mobility. For instance, in a 2021 Pew Research Center survey, only 16 percent of respondents expected their children to be better off financially than their parents.[24]

UNFINISHED TRANSFORMATIONS: GREEN, DIGITAL, AND HUMAN CAPITAL IMPERATIVES

The future of Japan's middle-class society will depend in no small measure on how it traverses the ongoing revolutions in climate change, digitalization, and human-centered technological innovation.

Decarbonizing Japan

An ambitious climate change agenda opened a new chapter for Japan after Prime Minister Abe Shinzo stepped down in 2020. The toll inflicted by extreme weather had already manifested through deadly heat waves and devastating typhoons, while rising sea levels continue to pose danger to some of the country's urban centers. And yet, Japan lagged behind other countries in making meaningful contributions to achieving the Paris Climate Accord objective of capping world temperature rises to below 2 degrees Celsius. Japan's 2015 pledge to reduce greenhouse gas (GHG) emissions by 26 percent from 2013 levels (a base year of high emissions) by 2030 were deemed utterly insufficient and a demerit in the country's otherwise strong track record of international cooperation.[25]

In striking a balance between the goals of energy security, economic competitiveness, and climate change mitigation, Japanese policymakers have favored the former two. The 2011 nuclear accident at the Fukushima Daiichi power plant indelibly altered Japan's energy outlook and environmental goals. But the weakening of Japan's climate ambitions predates the disasters in Fukushima. In 2010, the administration of Prime Minister Kan Naoto from the Democratic Party of Japan (DPJ) dealt a severe blow to the Kyoto Protocol (which had mandated that thirty-seven industrialized countries cut GHG emissions by 5.2 percent from 1990 levels) when it announced its opposition to a second commitment period.[26]

However, the Fukushima Daiichi incident did have a profound effect, with the loss of public confidence in the safety of nuclear power and the onset of coal addiction. Lax regulatory oversight and human error brought the horror of a nuclear power plant accident to Japan and forced an immediate shutdown of all reactors across the country. With the abrupt loss of one-third of the power supply, Japanese policymakers turned to fossil fuels—natural gas and coal in particular—and Japan's emissions went up. Tighter safety protocols have been put in place, but the public remained skeptical that the benefits of nuclear power outweigh the risks, so nuclear restarts moved very slowly with only four reactors (out of the original fifty-four) in operation a decade after the 2011 accident.[27]

The nuclear accident did not spur a revolution in renewables. The DPJ government created a feed-in tariff system whereby consumers pay a premium on their electricity bills to support green energy investments. After a few years, however, the Abe administration scaled it down through more exacting participation requirements and reduced subsidies for participants. This put a damper on the development of renewables and reflected, as pointed out by Incerti and Lipscy, the higher priority the government attached to economic growth.[28] As the fifth-largest emitter of greenhouse gases and an active funder of coal power plants at home and abroad, Japan's modest climate mitigation ambitions complicated the chances for international cooperation. A bigger blow to the Paris Climate Accord was meted out by U.S. President Donald Trump's decision in 2017 to withdraw the United States from the pact.

A few years later, political change in both Japan and the United States brought on an about-face in climate policy and greater prospects for a shared green agenda between the allies. Upon assuming office in fall 2020, Prime Minister Suga Yoshihide put climate change at the top of his agenda as an essential pillar of Japan's future economic competitiveness. Suga significantly scaled up Japan's climate objectives, calling for achieving a carbon-free society by 2050 and reducing emissions by 46 percent from 2013 levels by 2030, with best endeavors to reach a 50-percent target.[29]

This required new thinking about the future of the country's energy mix, which was presented in the Sixth Strategic Energy Plan of August 2021.[30] By 2030, government officials foresaw a doubling in the share of renewables (mostly hydropower) from 18 percent in 2019 to 36–38 percent, a major increase in nuclear power's share from 6 percent to

20–22 percent, and the development of hydrogen/ammonia power projects to supply 1 percent of energy needs. The policy document envisioned winding down the role of oil from 7 percent to 2 percent, nearly halving the supply of natural gas from 37 percent to 20 percent, and reducing dependence on coal from 32 percent to 19 percent by the end of the decade. In a significant move, the government joined a G7 pledge to cease financing new overseas coal power plants by the end of 2021.[31]

The energy strategy was overambitious and underwhelming at the same time. The major leap in renewables and nuclear power appeared unrealistic given Japan's weak track record in shifting to new energy sources and the long road ahead for nuclear restarts. The Japanese government's goal to tap into cutting-edge fuel cell technology in the pursuit of a hydrogen-powered industrial base faces challenges, since the technology is not yet commercially viable and questions remain about the ability to switch hydrogen's supply base from fossil fuels to renewables.[32] But Japan's energy plan disappointed many with its projected continued reliance on coal, preventing Tokyo from playing a proactive role in coal phase-out discussions at the 2021 UN Climate Change Conference.

The 2022 Russian invasion of Ukraine once again raised energy security to the top of the national agenda. The negative effects of soaring oil prices and possible electricity blackouts have taken a toll on consumers and dampened economic recovery prospects. While Japan only imports 4 percent of its oil and 9 percent of its gas from Russia, the worldwide hike in energy prices and the loss of supply sources that had underpinned its diversification strategy put Japan in a more precarious position (hence the government's insistence that Japanese companies continue their Sakhalin liquefied natural gas projects).[33] The administration of Prime Minister Kishida Fumio provided temporary relief through gasoline subsidies but made a big gamble on a nuclear energy comeback with plans to restart five more nuclear reactors in 2022. This is a gamble as well on shifting public views on the merits of nuclear energy at a time when oil prices are driving an unusual phenomenon in the country: inflation.[34]

Digital Transformation and Human Capital

The rapid pace of technological change with the arrival of artificial intelligence (AI), big data, the Internet of Things, cloud computing, edge computing, and 5G telecommunication networks is reconfiguring societies and economies. Digitalization affords significant opportunities to capitalize on new sources of economic competitiveness, increase efficiency and productivity, and raise living standards. Its realization, however, requires hefty investments in critical infrastructure, human capital development, and new governance and management systems. Success in the digital transition will also hinge on the ability of countries to ensure social inclusion, privacy protection, and adequate cybersecurity to ameliorate the downsides and risks of an increasingly wired future.

Japan is keenly aware of how much hangs in the balance in its digital shift. Strategy documents abound on the fourth industrial revolution (with robotization and complex virtual shop management systems) and the emergence of "Society 5.0" (with smart cities connecting hardware and software) that will supply a wide array of digital services.[35] The business world is abuzz with discussions of the competitive plays required for Japanese companies to rise in the ranks of the global digital economy. And both former Prime Minister Suga and current Prime Minister Kishida have made digitalization a signature policy of their administrations.

This active national conversation on Japan's digital transformation (or "DX," to use the abbreviation of choice in Japan) fixes its gaze on three key factors: the assets that a technologically advanced nation can harness to propel its digitalization, the special promise of digital technologies for a nation facing demographic decline and chronic labor shortages, and the many areas where Japan is currently underperforming in its digitalization drive but seeks to improve by closing the digital talent gap.

While newspaper stories about the persistent use of fax machines and *hanko* (a seal used to stamp official documents) are popular, the reality is more complex. In terms of overall digital competitiveness, Japan sits in the middle of the pack, ranking twenty-eighth out of sixty-three in the 2021 Digital Competitiveness Index. It is far behind the United States (first place) and several of its East Asian peers: Singapore (fifth), Taiwan (eighth), South Korea (twelfth), and China (fifteenth).[36] But it is important to look beyond the aggregate ranking since it masks areas where Japan is a leader and where it lags behind. Japan has an excellent telecommunications infrastructure, placing number two in wireless broadband.[37] Corporate Japan is an international leader in automation and was the second-largest adopter of robots in 2017.[38] In contrast, the penetration of digital technologies has been sluggish in the sectors of telemedicine (5 percent), mobile banking (7 percent), government e-services (7.5 percent), and e-commerce (9 percent).[39]

These digitalization deficits proved costly to Japan's COVID-19 pandemic response. They hobbled the ability of the government to transmit medical information across the hospital network, disburse cash handouts to the population, and roll out vaccination appointments.[40] A new Digital Agency tasked with promoting digital government services and streamlining technology policy was introduced in September 2021. It has a full docket that includes boosting IT capabilities in the civil service, adopting interoperable data management systems across ministries and local governments, and making e-services more easily available using My Number Cards (a personal ID system), which currently cover a little over a third of potential users.[41]

Digitalization is unlikely to spread evenly across corporate Japan. Leading Japanese firms are finding their own paths to the forefront of the digital economy, as Ulrike Schaede points out, by tapping into their deep manufacturing expertise in creating a virtual shopfloor and positioning themselves as "data drillers" generating industrial global supply chains.[42] But many other Japanese companies remain wedded to the analog era. A 2020 survey of nine hundred firms found that less than 40 percent are pursuing digital transformation.[43] There is a marked digital divide between large and small firms: digital adoption among firms with more than five hundred employees is 70 percent but only 10 percent in small enterprises.[44]

A major bottleneck to Japan's DX, irrespective of sector or firm size, is the current scarcity of qualified IT professionals.[45] In achieving its national AI strategy goals, Japan has strong technology assets (computing power, AI funding, patent submissions, and AI startups) but is weaker in human capital resources (number of STEM graduates, hiring specialists in AI, and technology skill penetration), according to a cross-national study of forty-four countries.[46] And yet, this picture is bound to change. Another important finding of this multicountry study is that Japan's current AI job market is weak, but the country is better prepared for the future with a robust cohort of STEM students joining the professional ranks. In contrast, the insufficient number of STEM students in the United States is a serious liability for the country.[47] Education and reskilling efforts are underway in Japan, with the introduction of IT curricula in high schools and colleges, as well as digital training in large firms.[48] Japan's DX ambitions will also hinge on its ability to attract digital talent from abroad. Reopening the border is critical to Japan's post-pandemic economic competitiveness.[49]

INVESTING IN HUMAN CAPITAL: WILL KISHIDA'S "NEW CAPITALISM" DELIVER?

Upon becoming prime minister in October 2021, Kishida Fumio rolled out his economic strategy of "New Capitalism," which placed front and center investments in human capital to achieve a complementary relationship between growth and distribution. The economic program is focused on three areas: human capital, technology and innovation, and economic security[50] (this last component is discussed at length in Chapter 10). Noting stagnating wages in Japan and meager corporate spending on human resources by international standards, Kishida has promised that the government will help one million Japanese workers (including non-regular employees) to acquire new skills, find jobs, and move into new occupations. The prime minister has also asked corporate Japan for a fundamental rethinking of their human resource strategies, moving away from viewing wages as merely a cost to seeing them as investments in human capital that add value to the corporation.[51]

Spurring technology and innovation through public-private partnerships is also a priority. Japan's gross domestic R&D investment has remained flat over the last decade and is way behind the investments of the United States and China.[52] Startups in Japan have grown quickly in the past five years, but still remain a fraction of what the United States boasts.[53] The Kishida administration called for greater high-tech investment of 120 trillion yen between 2022 and 2027, of which the government plans to invest 30 trillion in new technology fields (AI, quantum computing, semiconductors, and biotechnology) and in supporting both green and digital transformations.[54] Realizing that the rate at which Japanese companies introduce new products and services lags behind some of their G7 peers, the Kishida administration has made a push for a tenfold increase in the number of startups to help cultivate the next generation of new companies. To this growth element, Kishida has appended a redistribution agenda, planning for regional revitalization by seeding digital garden cities and offering financial support to families with children and seniors.

In some ways, there is little that is new about Kishida's vision of a capitalism with a human face. Achieving a society that leaves no one behind in a low-growth environment has been central to the national conversation for decades. And Kishida's economic agenda shares key objectives pursued by his predecessors: increasing real wages and house-hold consumption; addressing the inequities of the dual employment system; and pushing green, digital, and technological transformations in Japanese society and the economy.

Nonetheless, New Capitalism is not a simple recitation of prior eco-nomic blueprints. Political signaling and the economic environment matter. There is no clarity yet on whether the government can effec-tively encourage corporate Japan to raise wages and adopt the human capital paradigm—an early idea to raise the capital gains tax was nixed and subsidies for companies that raise wages may be insufficient. But Kishida has gone further than his predecessors in making the human capital imperative the yardstick by which his economic strategy will be evaluated. He has accepted a political cost for failure to deliver on this effort. This is new.

Moreover, the international environment has changed in a direction that will force more poignant choices from the Japanese government. During Abenomics, Japan was a trendsetter with monetary easing, but today it is an outlier. With rampant inflation, the United States Federal Reserve and the European Central Bank have raised interest rates, but the Bank of Japan has stayed the course, fearing a global economic con-traction. A sharp depreciation of the yen (25 percent in the course of 2022) has exerted a toll on consumers and producers and pushed up the energy import bill, with consumer inflation now running at 4 percent.[55] It will be up to Kuroda's successor as BOJ governor, Ueda Kazuo (an unconventional pick from academia), to fight inflation and correct the course of monetary policy. Raising interest rates carries its own risks given the high levels of government debt and the demand for larger bud-gets to address pandemic recovery and long-term transformation. To alleviate the rising cost of living and facilitate wage increases, the Diet approved a $267 billion second supplementary budget toward the end of 2022.[56] Investments in the triple transformation (digital, green, and human capital) and the projected increase in defense expenditures raise questions about the ability to sustain deficit financing for an unprec-edented level of fiscal spending.

In promoting a gentler form of capitalism, the Kishida administration has downplayed the structural reform agenda. But deregulation in some sectors and reregulation in others will be required to achieve the desired transformations. In fact, Kishida may oversee growth in the regulation of business activity for national security purposes as part of his economic security program. The battles over spending tradeoffs and the winners and losers from the economic reform agenda will spill into the political arena and dim the idyllic image of win-win capitalism.

NOTES

1. Mari Miura, *Welfare through Work: Conservative Ideas, Partisan Dynamics, and Social Protection in Japan* (Ithaca, NY: Cornell University Press, 2012).

2. Margarita Estévez-Abe, *Welfare and Capitalism in Postwar Japan* (Cambridge, UK: Cambridge University Press, 2008).

3. See The World Bank, "Fertility Rate, Total (Births Per Woman)—Japan," https://data.worldbank.org/indicator/SP.DYN.TFRT.IN?locations=JP; and The World Bank, "Life Expectancy at Birth, Female (Years)—Japan," https://data .worldbank.org/indicator/SP.DYN.LE00.FE.IN?locations=JP.

4. Yihan Liu and Niklas J. Westelius, "The Impact of Demographics on Productivity and Inflation in Japan," IMF Working Paper, WP/26/237, 2016, www .imf.org/en/Publications/WP/Issues/2016/12/31/The-Impact-of-Demographics -on-Productivity-and-Inflation-in-Japan-44449.

5. United Nations, "World Population Prospects 2022: Summary of Results," UN DESA/POP/2022/NO.3, Population Division, Department of Economic and Social Affairs, New York, 2022, www.un.org/development/desa/pd /sites/www.un.org.development.desa.pd/files/wpp2022_summary_of_results .pdf.

6. Kazuo Yanase et al., "The New Population Bomb," *Nikkei Asia*, September 22, 2021, https://asia.nikkei.com/Spotlight/The-Big-Story/The-new -population-bomb.

7. Marcin Pawel Jarzebski et al., "Ageing and Population Shrinking: Implications for Sustainability in the Urban Century," *npj Urban Sustainability* 1, no. 17 (2021): 11, https://doi.org/10.1038/s42949-021-00023-z.

8. See United Nations, "World Population Prospects 2019: Volume I, Comprehensive Tables," ST/ESA/SER.A/426, Population Division, Department of Economic and Social Affairs, New York, 2019, 27, www.un.org/development/ desa/pd/sites/www.un.org.development.desa.pd/files/files/documents/2020/Jan /un_2019_wpp_vol1_comprehensive-tables.pdf.

9. See OECD, "Income Inequality," https://data.oecd.org/inequality/income -inequality.htm; and OECD, "Poverty Rate," https://data.oecd.org/inequality/ poverty-rate.htm#indicator-chart.

10. See OECD, "Wealth," OECD.Stat, https://stats.oecd.org/Index.aspx ?DataSetCode=WEALTH#.

11. Ministry of Health, Labour and Welfare, "非正規雇用（有期・パート・派遣労働）" [Non-Regular Employment (Fixed-Term, Part-Time, Temporary

Work)], https://www.mhlw.go.jp/stf/seisakunitsuite/bunya/koyou_roudou/part
_haken/index.html.

12. David Chiavacci, "Social Inequality in Japan," in *The Oxford Hand-book of Japanese Politics*, ed. Robert J. Pekkanen and Saadia M. Pekkanen (New York: Oxford University Press, 2021), 450–70.

13. Peter Matanle, "Understanding the Dynamics of Regional Growth and Shrinkage," in *Social Inequality in Post-Growth Japan*, ed. David Chiavacci and Carola Hommerich (New York: Routledge, 2017), 213–30.

14. Toshiyuki Kobayashi, "減少する中流意識と変わる日本人の社会観" [Reduced Middle-Class Awareness and Changing Japanese Social Perspective], *ISSP Survey on Social Inequality*, ＮＨＫ放送文化研究所 [NHK Broadcasting Culture Research Institute], May 2020, 9, https://www.nhk.or.jp/bunken/research/yoron/pdf/20200501_7.pdf.

15. Japan Cabinet Office, "世論調査報告書令和3年9月調査" [Public Opinion Survey Report: September 2021 Survey], 国民生活に関する世論調査 [Public Opinion Survey on the Life of the People], January 2022, https://survey.gov-online.go.jp/r03/r03-life/index.html.

16. Steffen Heinrich, "Does Employment Dualization Lead to Political Polarization? Assessing the Impact of Labour Market Inequalities on Political Discourse in Japan," in *Social Inequality in Post-Growth Japan*, ed. David Chiavacci and Carola Hommerich (New York: Routledge, 2017), 73–87.

17. Chiavacci, "Social Inequality in Japan."

18. Andrew Gordon, "Making Sense of the Lost Decades: Workplaces and Schools, Men and Women, Young and Old, Rich and Poor," in *Examining Japan's Lost Decades*, ed. Yoichi Funabashi and Barak Kushner (New York: Routledge, 2015), 77–100. However, non-regular employment has remained high; see "Level of Non-Regular Employment Remains High in Japan at 37.3%," Nippon.com, https://www.nippon.com/en/features/h00175/.

19. For a discussion of how these dynamics played out in the last general election of fall 2021, see Motoko Rich, Makiko Inoue, and Hikari Hida, "In Japan, Rural Voters Count More than Those in Big Cities. It Shows." *The New York Times*, October 28, 2021, www.nytimes.com/2021/10/28/world/asia/japan-election-rural-urban.html.

20. See OECD, "Social Expenditure Database (SOCX)," www.oecd.org/social/expenditure.htm.

21. Akihisa Shiozaki, "Japan's Homogeneous Welfare State: Development and Future Challenges," in *The Crisis of Liberal Internationalism: Japan and the World Order*, ed. Yoichi Funabashi and John Ikenberry (Washington, DC: Brookings Institution Press, 2020), 203–36.

22. See International Institute for Applied Systems Analysis, "The Human Life Indicator," February 19, 2019, https://iiasa.ac.at/web/home/research/researchPrograms/WorldPopulation/Reaging/HLI.html.

23. Shiozaki, "Japan's Homogeneous Welfare State," 216.

24. Shannon Schumacher and J. J. Moncus, "Economic Attitudes Improve in Many Nations Even as Pandemic Endures," Pew Research Center, July 21,

2021, www.pewresearch.org/global/2021/07/21/economic-attitudes-improve -in-many-nations-even-as-pandemic-endures/.

25. "Japan Outlines 2030 Carbon Target Ahead of Paris Climate Summit," *The Guardian*, April 30, 2015, https://www.theguardian.com/environment /2015/apr/30/japan-outlines-2030-carbon-target-ahead-of-paris-climate -summit.

26. See Stacy Feldman, "Japan's Motion to Kill Kyoto Protocol a 'Slap in the Face,' Advocates Say," *Reuters*, December 2, 2010, www.reuters.com/article/ idUS2196082629202010202.

27. Gavin Blair, "Why Japan Still Plugs In to Nuclear," *Christian Science Monitor*, February 26, 2021, https://www.csmonitor.com/World/Asia-Pacific /2021/0226/Why-Japan-still-plugs-into-nuclear.

28. Trevor Incerti and Phillip Y. Lipscy, "The Politics of Energy and Climate Change in Japan under Abe," *Asian Survey* 58, no. 4 (2018): 610, 617.

29. Satoshi Kurokawa, "Can the US-Japan Climate Partnership Lead Decarbonization in Asia?" *East Asia Forum*, June 2, 2021, https://www .eastasiaforum.org/2021/06/02/can-the-us-japan-climate-partnership-lead -decarbonisation-in-asia/.

30. See Agency for Natural Resources and Energy, "Outline of Strategic Energy Plan," Ministry of Trade, Economy and Industry, October 2021, www .enecho.meti.go.jp/en/category/others/basic_plan/pdf/6th_outline.pdf.

31. See Shuang Liu, Ye Wang, and Yan Wang, "South Korea and Japan Will End Overseas Coal Financing. Will China Catch Up?" World Resources Institute, June 14, 2021, www.wri.org/insights/south-korea-and-japan-will-end -overseas-coal-financing-will-china-catch.

32. Jane Nakano, "Japan's Hydrogen Industrial Policy," Center for Strategic and International Studies, October 21, 2021, www.csis.org/analysis/japans -hydrogen-industrial-strategy.

33. Diana Schnelle, "Japan's Energy Mix after the Ukraine Crisis," East Asia Forum, www.eastasiaforum.org/2022/05/10/japans-energy-mix-after-the -ukraine-crisis/.

34. Soon after the Russian invasion of Ukraine and the energy price hikes, public opinion in Japan shifted, showing for the first time a slim majority supporting a faster pace for restarting nuclear power reactors. See "Majority in Japan Backs Nuclear Power for the First Time since Fukushima," *The Japan Times*, March 28, 2022, www.japantimes.co.jp/news/2022/03/28/national/ nuke-power-poll/.

35. Mayumi Fukuyama, "Society 5.0: Aiming for a New Human-Centered Society," *Japan Spotlight*, Special Article 2 (July/August 2018): 47–50, https:// www.jef.or.jp/journal/pdf/220th_Special_Article_02.pdf.

36. IMD World Competitiveness Center, "World Digital Competitiveness Ranking," 2021, www.imd.org/centers/world-competitiveness-center/rankings /world-digital-competitiveness/.

37. Ibid.

38. Hiroshi Fujiwara, "Why Japan Leads Industrial Robot Production," International Federation of Robotics, December 17, 2018, https://ifr.org/post/why -japan-leads-industrial-robot-production.

39. McKinsey & Company and the American Chamber of Commerce in Japan, "Japan Digital Agenda 2030," February 2021, www.accj.or.jp/japan -digital-agenda-2030.

40. See Jun Mukoyama, "COVID-19 and Japan's Long-Awaited Digital Transformation," East Asia Forum, September 25, 2021, www.eastasiaforum .org/2021/09/25/covid-19-and-japans-long-awaited-digital-transformation/.

41. Marie Yanaka, "Will New Agency Save Japan from 'Digital Defeat'?" *NHK World*, September 2, 2021, www3.nhk.or.jp/nhkworld/en/news/ backstories/1747/.

42. Ulrike Schaede, *The Business Reinvention of Japan: How to Make Sense of the New Japan and Why It Matters* (Stanford: Stanford University Press, 2020).

43. Naoki Togawa, "日本のDXは本当に遅れているのか？「DXサーベイ」から見る900社の実態" [Is Japan's DX Truly Behind? The Situation of 900 Companies Seen From the DX-Survey, *Fujitsu Journal*, April 17, 2020, www.fujitsu .com/downloads/JP/microsite/fujitsutransformationnews/journal-archives/pdf /2020-04-17-01.pdf.

44. Japan Cabinet Office, "年次経済財政報告" [Annual Report of the Japanese Economy and Public Finance], September 2021, https://www5.cao.go .jp/j-j/wp/wp-je21/index_pdf.html.

45. Koichi Iwamoto, "日本企業のDX導入が遅れている背景" [Background on the Delayed Introduction of DX of Japanese Firms], Research Institute of Economy, Trade, and Industry (RIETI), July 20, 2021, www.rieti.go.jp/users/ iwamoto-koichi/serial/130.html.

46. Samar Fatima et al., "Winners and Losers in the Fulfillment of National Artificial Intelligence Aspirations," Brookings Institution, October 21, 2021, www.brookings.edu/blog/techtank/2021/10/21/winners-and-losers-in-the -fulfilment-of-national-artificial-intelligence-aspirations/.

47. Samar Fatima et al., "The People Dilemma: How Human Capital Is Driving or Constraining the Achievement of National AI Strategies," Brookings Institution, November 10, 2021, www.brookings.edu/blog/techtank/2021 /11/10/the-people-dilemma-how-human-capital-is-driving-or-constraining-the -achievement-of-national-ai-strategies/.

48. Ulrike Schaede and Kay Shimizu, *The Digital Transformation and Japan's Political Economy* (Cambridge, UK: Cambridge University Press, 2022).

49. See Mireya Solís, "In Vying for Economic Preeminence in Asia, Openness Is Essential," Brookings Institution, January 14, 2022, www.brookings .edu/blog/order-from-chaos/2022/01/14/in-vying-for-economic-preeminence -in-asia-openness-is-essential/.

50. Harukata Takenaka, "Demystifying Kishida's New Capitalism: Deputy Chief Cabinet Secretary Kihara Seiji Talks Policy (Part 1)," Nippon.com, July 13, 2022, www.nippon.com/en/in-depth/a07705/demystifying-kishida%E2

%80%99s-new-capitalism-deputy-chief-cabinet-secretary-kihara-seiji-talks
-.html.

51. Fumio Kishida, "新しい資本主義" [New Capitalism], Bungei Shunju,
January 7, 2022, https://bungeishunju.com/n/nf0aaa6d2c57c.

52. The United States' gross domestic R&D expenditures (in 2015 constant
prices) grew from $361.6 billion in 2000 to $664.1 billion in 2020. China's
increased from $39.8 billion to $563.3 billion, and Japan showed a small increase from $133.3 billion to $167.1 billion in that period. See OECD, "Gross
Domestic Spending on R&D," 2022, https://data.oecd.org/rd/gross-domestic
-spending-on-r-d.htm. For a good discussion of Japan's technology policy, see
L. James Schoff, "U.S.-Japan Technology Policy Coordination: Balancing Tech-
nonationalism with a Globalized World," Carnegie Endowment for International Peace, 2020, https://carnegieendowment.org/files/Schoff_US-Japan.pdf.

53. Startup investments in Japan grew from $1.4 billion in 2014 to $3.8 billion in 2018 (compared to $118.9 billion in the United States in 2018). See Gen
Isayama, "Innovation, Entrepreneurship and Change Management in Japan,"
Japan Forum Webinar Series, UC San Diego, July 28, 2021, www.youtube.com/
watch?v=2HB0wKhfDC4. Kenji Kushida provides a good overview of the regulatory shifts and changes in the business environment that have supported the
development of Japanese startups, including the growth of venture capital, the
ability of universities to develop ties with industry, and Japanese firms' partnerships with startups for collaborative innovation. See Kushida, "Is the Lack of
'Unicorns' in Japan Good News or Bad News?" Nippon Institute for Research
Advancement (NIRA) Opinion Paper, no. 39, November 2018, https://english
.nira.or.jp/papers/opinion_paper/2018/11/is-the-lack-of-unicorns-in-japan
-good-news-or-bad-news--injecting-a-historical-institutional-perspec.html.

54. See Takenaka, "Demystifying Kishida's New Capitalism."

55. Takatoshi Ito, "Down Goes the Yen," Project Syndicate, October
20, 2022, www.project-syndicate.org/commentary/japan-yen-depreciation
-intervention-foreign-exchange-market-by-takatoshi-ito-2022-10;   Yuri
Kageyama, "Japan Parliament Ok's Ueda as BOJ Chief to Fight Inflation," *AP
News*, March 11, 2023, https://apnews.com/article/boj-ueda-inflation-japan
-economy-2e2ac3e81e9dc42519078b15924901a8.

56. "Cabinet Approves 29-Trillion-Yen Extra Budget, Inflation Package,"
Asahi Shimbun, October 28, 2022, www.asahi.com/ajw/articles/14754498.

SECTION 3

Politics

CHAPTER 6

Change and Continuity
in Japanese Politics[1]

It is common to assert that during Japan's "lost" decades the country was gripped by immobilism on all fronts. In fact, Japanese politics have been anything but stagnant in the past three decades. During this period, Japan adopted a different set of electoral rules, which profoundly changed the nature of political competition. The country experienced the onset of a two-party system, only to see the rising opposition party falter during its stint in power and the opposition camp dwindle due to the fragmentation and low survival rates of fledging political parties. Japanese politics shifted from a period of fast turnover of prime ministers and sharp swings in voter support for rival parties during the second half of the 2000s, to the return of a dominant Liberal Democratic Party (LDP)–Komeito ticket in six national elections and Abe Shinzo becoming the longest-serving prime minister in Japan's history.

The nature of executive leadership experienced profound change in this era as well. Electoral and administrative reforms gave the prime minister the power to initiate policy proposals, create advisory councils to advance landmark policies, and overcome bureaucratic sectionalism. The office of the prime minister acquired greater clout over factions, policy tribes in the LDP, and civil servants. The combination of political stability and augmented policymaking authorities created two distinct periods of top-down leadership under Koizumi and Abe. Abe went further in making the *Kantei* (Prime Minister's Office) a control tower in policymaking and established whole-of-government structures to tackle national security and foreign economic policy.

Nevertheless, COVID-19 changed the direction of Japanese politics, hastening the end of Abe's long tenure and sealing the fate of Prime Minister Suga's brief stint in power. The tragic assassination of former Prime Minister Abe on July 8, 2022, cut short the life of the country's most influential politician who, up until his death, was still shaping the public debate on domestic economic management and foreign policy from his perch as the leader of the LDP's largest faction. In winning two national elections within his first year in office, Prime Minister Kishida cleared essential hurdles to a more stable and long-lasting administration. Yet, his political challenges have compounded—internal LDP coordination will be harder as the Abe faction is in transition, and his support levels took a hit as the public demanded greater transparency and accountability after several politicians were linked to a problematic religious group.

THE OLD REGIME

During the Cold War era, unbroken rule by the LDP since its creation in 1955 earned Japan the designation of an "uncommon democracy." The moniker underscored a political system with free elections and media as well as civil and political rights where, nevertheless, one party stays in power for decades.[2] Japanese politics operated under a "one-and-a-half party system," with the Socialist Party and LDP squaring off mostly on foreign policy issues (e.g., the Peace Constitution and the U.S.-Japan alliance). The LDP was a party of factions, so the primordial concern to retain its hold on power was to avoid defection from disgruntled party members. It relied on the organizational vote (from agricultural cooperatives and postmasters) and mustered fundraising prowess among big business with its embrace of pro-growth policies. A party with roots in agricultural conservatism, the LDP was able to weather Japan's profound economic transformation and urbanization through its deliberate effort to become a catch-all party and its cunning political instinct, co-opting popular policies from the opposition (e.g., pollution control, support for small businesses).[3]

At the onset of the 1990s, however, the stress in the political system was beginning to show. The LDP was no longer a nimble machine capable of reinvention to meet new political tests. The last and uncrossed Rubicon was political reform to improve the quality of Japanese democracy—a strong expectation from the growing ranks of urban voters.

Japan's electoral system (multimember districts with a single nontransferable vote) pitted members of the same party against each other to compete in the same electoral district. This weakened the appeal of party labels and electoral campaigns were candidate-centered affairs. Factions inside the LDP managed these competitive dynamics as they vied for electoral nominations, government appointments, and funds for their faction members. Because electoral rules framed politics as a clientelist transaction of voter/interest group support for a specific candidate in exchange for a stream of constituent services, pork-barrel projects, and/or favorable legislation, money politics thrived.

The 1955 system had profound implications for policymaking dynamics during the decades of the uninterrupted LDP government. In his role as party president, the prime minister acted largely as broker to manage factional competition and avoid costly defections. Internal unity in a party of competitive factions was a constant concern. The prime minister had little sway over backbenchers, who could always threaten defection or run as independents, since the LDP would take them back if they proved successful.[4] To keep the faction leaders at peace, frequent Cabinet turnovers were used to reward veteran politicians with senior appointments. The prime minister's capacity to direct the bureaucracy or advance legislation was very limited. The Cabinet could only propose legislation with the sign-off of the bureaucracy (the meeting of senior vice ministers) and the party (its policymaking body the Policy Affairs Research Council).[5] Iron triangles—of bureaucrats, interest groups, and LDP policy tribes—flourished.

ELECTORAL, POLITICAL, AND ADMINISTRATIVE REFORMS

The LDP's inability to deliver political reform was a more glaring deficiency amid a number of high-profile scandals in the 1990s that revealed corrupt ties between corporations and senior politicians. Eventually, the party's worst fear materialized when a group of LDP members defected in 1993 in support of a no-confidence motion that brought the LDP administration down. Opposition parties formed a short-lived coalition government that had one major achievement: new electoral and political fundraising rules. A hybrid electoral system for Lower House elections, in effect since 1994, gives Japanese voters two votes: one for a candidate in single-member districts, and another for a party in regional blocs that are allocated proportional representation seats.

Political funding rules were tightened in 1994 and 2000, with stiffer penalties for electoral campaign violations, increased transparency through a system of public subsidies for parties, and eventually a ban on corporate contributions to individual politicians.[6] Redistricting efforts have continued to address the overrepresentation of the rural vote. The malapportionment problem led the Japanese Supreme Court to rule that the Lower House elections of 2009, 2012, and 2014 were in an "unconstitutional state" (although it did not void the electoral results). The 2017 redistricting effort eliminated ten seats from the Lower House, yielding 289 single-member districts and 176 proportional representation seats, for a total of 465 seats. The latest redistricting effort, approved by the Diet in November 2022, shifted more seats from low-density to high-density electoral districts in order to balance apportionments to a level deemed constitutional for the next general election.[7]

These institutional reforms aimed to "modernize" Japanese politics by encouraging a shift toward electoral competition based on policy platforms, the emergence of a competitive party system, and the attenuation of the strong redistributive character of Japanese politics. Progress was made on some fronts but not others. With the shift to single-member districts, party labels and programmatic proposals became more important in election campaigning.[8] Moreover, the prime minister has a much better chance of reining in backbenchers, who depend on the party for nomination and whose own political fortunes are now more influenced by the overall popularity of the party leader. The influence of the factional bosses has diminished, but the factions have survived and are still central to the competition for the party leadership.[9] The political funding reforms managed to excise the flow of funds from corporations to individual politicians, and political corruption diminished with greater transparency in fundraising practices.[10]

By undercutting the role of factions, the electoral reform helped strengthen the hand of the prime minister within the party. The prime minister's policymaking clout grew as well with administrative reforms that took effect in 2001. The reform of the Cabinet Law for the first time gave the prime minister the power of initiative to send proposals to the Cabinet. It expanded the role of the Cabinet Secretariat to include policy planning. A newly established Cabinet Office gave the prime minister the authority to coordinate bureaucracies, establish advisory councils to promote signature policies, and be at the center of policy formulation.[11] In 2014, the centralization of decision-making in the Cabinet Office advanced through control over the appointments of senior bureaucrats through the establishment of the Cabinet Bureau of Personnel Affairs.

Altogether, these were profound changes to the rules of political competition and the balance of power in decision-making. They brought new fluidity to Japanese political dynamics that could allow for two important potential outcomes: transition to a competitive two-party system and the emergence of a strong executive, with the prime minister setting the strategic direction of domestic and foreign policy.

POLITICAL DYNAMICS IN THE POST-REFORM ERA

Japanese politics were in flux during the 1990s and 2000s, but three main trends were discernable: the flurry of parties created and disbanded, the onset of coalition governments (some ephemeral, some durable), and the emergence of viable opposition parties that appeared to be finally capable of offering an alternative to the LDP. In many of these developments, Ozawa Ichiro, an LDP political operative and maker and breaker of political parties, played an outsized role. Ozawa and his supporters endorsed the opposition parties' no-confidence motion that produced the ouster of the LDP in 1993. After the seven-party coalition fragmented a few months later, Ozawa led the splinter parties into the creation of the New Frontier Party in December 1994 that, until its demise in early 1997, appeared poised to become the main challenger of the LDP.

The post-reform era by and large put an end to exclusively LDP governments. The liberal democrats returned to high office after just a few months in the opposition but had to establish alliances with other parties to assure their hold on power. The political alliances have brought together parties of dissimilar ideological inclinations for the sake of political expediency. The first tie-up in 1994 with its postwar archrival, the Japan Socialist Party, was brief. The 1999 coalition with the Komeito—the political offshoot of the lay Buddhist sect Soka Gakkai—was started as a collaboration to gain ground in the Upper House, and it continues today. There was plenty of animosity between the parties before the coalition experiment, with Komeito participating in the rival coalition government of 1993 and later joining the New Frontier Party, and LDP politicians decrying Komeito as breaching the separation of religion and politics.[12] Yet, the LDP-Komeito collaboration developed into a symbiotic electoral alliance (with an agreement to maximize the seats each party can capture in single-member districts and proportional representation seats) and policy accommodations to heed Komeito's top priorities (e.g., the LDP watering down security reforms and constitutional revision proposals).[13]

With the creation of the Democratic Party of Japan (DPJ) in 1996, it appeared Japan was on its way toward a two-party system. Founded by former LDP politicians Hatoyama Yukio and Kan Naoto from the Socialist Democratic Federation through the fusion of several parties, the DPJ grew in strength as it yet again absorbed several smaller parties in 1998 and Ozawa's Liberal Party in 2003.[14] Throughout the 2000s, the LDP and DPJ competed intensely to gain ground against each other in both rural and urban settings. This entailed courting a rural vote that swung widely depending on which party appeared willing to extend largesse to the countryside, as well as mobilizing urban and independent voters with promises of genuine reform by doing away with traditional LDP politics.

In 2001, it was the unconventional LDP Prime Minister Koizumi Junichiro who captured the zeitgeist of reform. Throughout his tenure, which ended in 2006, public support remained strong for his promise to confront the "forces of resistance" within his own party, his disavowal of traditional factional politics, and his pledge to pursue reform with "no sacred cows."[15] The Japanese public rewarded him with a landslide victory when he called for a snap election in 2005 to define the future of his signature initiative, postal reform. But voters were soon disenchanted when subsequent short-lived LDP administrations walked back reform efforts and struggled to demonstrate competent governance.

When Koizumi left at the height of his popularity, he was succeeded by his protégé Abe Shinzo. Reflecting his political lineage as former Prime Minister Kishi Nobosuke's grandson, Abe's political project had long been animated by a desire to restore Japan to major power status by breaking away from what he viewed as the shackles of the postwar settlement: the pacifist constitution, passive dependence on the United States, and a historical narrative that undercut national pride. Abe figured prominently in the LDP's historical revisionist wing, but as his biographer Tobias Harris notes, his was a nationalism deployed for the sake of statism.[16] In other words, the paramount objective was to strengthen national capabilities, especially in the security realm. His first term delivered anything but. Abe formed a kitchen cabinet of individuals who shared his world outlook but were less adept at governing, and he pushed for unpopular security measures, downplaying the public's desire to focus on wallet issues. Abe's few months in office were consumed by gaffes from Cabinet ministers and a raging scandal over missing public pension records that cost the LDP the loss of the Upper House election in July 2007. Afflicted by a chronic, debilitating disease, Abe abruptly resigned soon thereafter.

Two more short-lived LDP premierships followed under Fukuda Yasuo and Aso Taro. Their political strategies floundered. Fukuda's attempts at a grand coalition with the DPJ came to naught, and Aso was unable to call for a general election to bolster his position during the Global Financial Crisis. Both LDP leaders struggled to advance a legislative agenda without control of the Upper House. Because a two-thirds majority in the Lower House is required to overturn an Upper House veto or inaction on a bill, a "twisted Diet" (opposing parties controlling different houses) created legislative gridlock and contributed to the demise of these LDP administrations.[17]

Koizumi's attacks on the privileges of the postmasters and cutbacks on public works in the countryside weakened the LDP's organized vote in rural Japan. A swelling of support across the country delivered a novel electoral outcome: an opposition party winning a landslide victory in the 2009 general election. The DPJ promised more than just an alternation of power. It advertised a restructuring of the fundamentals of policymaking. Seeking a more responsive body politic, the DPJ vowed to make bureaucrats compliant with politicians' directives, promised to inject new life into politics by banning hereditary Diet seats, and pledged to reduce wasteful spending and deliver income subsidies to the average Japanese with generous child allowances.

But the DPJ-led government soon ran aground. The campaign to slash government expenditures devolved into the *shiwake* process, which amounted to a public-shaming campaign of bureaucrats for wasteful spending but did not do much to cut expenditures. The party's attempt to usher in a better, more responsive government did not yield its promised results. The breakdown in communication with the bureaucracy produced policy paralysis.[18] The DPJ lost the 2010 Upper House election and struggled to advance its legislative program, as it now operated within the constraints of the twisted Diet. There was significant political instability at the top, with three DPJ prime ministers in three years. Prime Minister Hatoyama's botched policy on the relocation of the Futenma Air Base in Okinawa, Prime Minister Kan's ineffectual response to the

3/11 triple disaster, and Prime Minister Noda Yoshihiko's need to coordinate with opposition parties to advance his position due to internal DPJ divisions doomed each prime minister's administration. The final blow to the party was Ozawa and his supporters' defection in the summer of 2012.[19] There were policy disagreements, such as on the consumption tax, but the split was fundamentally a struggle over control of the party. In the December 2012 Lower House election, the Japanese public showed buyers' remorse and abandoned the DPJ.

A major reversal of fortune was evident in the election outcomes. The DPJ was reduced to 57 seats while the LDP secured 294 seats and Komeito held 31. The vote was a rejection of the DPJ but not a warm embrace of the LDP. Twenty million fewer people voted in 2012 than 3 years prior, and the lower turnout favored the LDP.[20] A new political dynamic set in with the return of the LDP-Komeito coalition and the remarkable comeback of Abe Shinzo. The sharp swings in electoral outcomes during the heyday of LDP-DPJ competition came to an end. The Lower House elections of 2012, 2014, and 2017 showed remarkably consistent results: a dominant ruling party in coalition with Komeito and low rates of voter turnout. The emergence of a two-party system was trounced (see Figure 6.1 in the next section).

ABE'S LONG TENURE: POLITICAL MANAGEMENT AND POLICYMAKING DYNAMICS

Abe orchestrated not only a remarkable comeback to the highest office in 2012, but also managed to consolidate his grip on national politics, cinching the record of longest-serving prime minister in Japan's history. The stability of the second Abe administration derives in no small part from the marked improvement in the areas of political management and policy implementation. Learning from past mistakes, in his second administration Abe looked beyond his inner circle to appoint a more balanced and competent Cabinet and dealt more expeditiously with corruption scandals afflicting Cabinet members.[21] The prime minister displayed improved political instincts by choosing to emphasize his economic agenda to appeal to voters (given the unpopularity of constitutional revision, nuclear power plant restarts after the incident in Fukushima, and consumption-tax hikes).

The first major electoral test was the Upper House poll in the summer of 2013. This was a key election if Abe was to avoid the trap of a twisted

Diet, especially considering that a few months earlier he had tested the will of the agricultural lobby by making the decision for Japan to join the Trans-Pacific Partnership (TPP). The LDP and its partner Komeito secured a handsome win, thereby cementing the ability of the Abe administration to push its legislative agenda. The electoral dominance of the LDP (with the decimation of the DPJ in the last general election) left the agricultural lobby bereft of a large national party to champion its anti-TPP crusade. Politics shifted toward greater pragmatism in securing *through* the LDP its core interests in future trade negotiations.[22]

The LDP under Abe demonstrated political acumen in other ways. The prime minister utilized his power to call for a snap election to win policy battles, prevent coordination among opposition parties, and steal the momentum from new party tickets. Robert Pekkanen and his co-authors deem the decision to call for a snap election in December 2014 an instance of Abe's "proactive governance," for it secured him a mandate to postpone the second consumption-tax hike and quelled opposition from LDP tax hawks and Ministry of Finance officials.[23] The October 2017 snap election sought to forestall the rise of potential challengers and left the largest opposition party in further disarray. Koike Yuriko, formerly of the LDP, had continued to amass political momentum. After running as an independent and winning the Tokyo governor's race, she struck a collaboration between her local party "Tokyoites First" and Komeito, which resulted in a landslide victory in the summer 2017 Tokyo Metropolitan Assembly election. When Abe announced the snap election in the fall, Koike quickly created the Party of Hope to contend in the general election. The Democratic Party (DP, a product of the 2016 merger of the DPJ with a faction of the Nippon Ishin no Kai [Japan Innovation Party, marked *Ishin* in Figure 6.1 below]) took the monumental decision to run under the banner of the newly minted Party of Hope.

Hope, however, fizzled quickly. Koike's decision to remain as Tokyo governor deflated voter enthusiasm because the face of the party was not in the running to become prime minister. Koike's refusal to accept all DP members into her party and make support for constitutional revision a prerequisite for admission botched the merger. The Democratic Party splintered, with some members running as independents, others joining the Hope ticket, and the liberal wing forming another party on the eve of the election: the Constitutional Democratic Party of Japan (CDP).[24] Opposition fragmentation yet again played in favor of the LDP.

Figure 6.1. General election results: Share of Lower House seats by leading parties and voter turnout

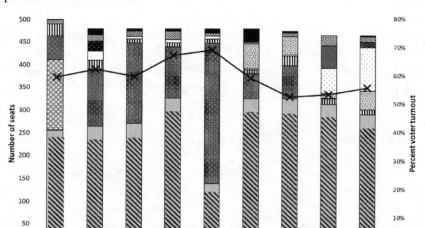

Note: In 1996, the LDP coalition partners were the Social Democratic Party (SDP) and the New Party Sakigake. From 2000 to present, the LDP coalition partner has been Komeito.

Source: Ministry of Internal Affairs and Communications, "衆議院議員総選挙・最高裁判所裁判官国民審査結果" [House of Representatives General Elections and Supreme Court Justice Appointment Results], www.soumu.go.jp/senkyo/senkyo_s/data/shugiin/ichiran.html.

The electoral prowess of the ruling coalition during the second Abe administration (2012–2020) is impressive: it achieved three wins in the Lower House and three wins in the Upper House. The LDP and Komeito ticket secured a two-thirds majority in the general elections of 2012, 2014, and 2017, creating traction for its legislative agenda. The ability of Abe to deliver a long winning streak for the LDP increased his hold over the party. As his second term as party president came to a close, the LDP reformed its rules so Abe could run for a third term. He won the LDP presidency for a third time in September 2018.

Political longevity enabled the Abe administration to utilize—and expand—the augmented powers of the Prime Minister's Office in policymaking. Not only did Abe revive the Koizumi-era policy advisory councils to advance economic reforms, he also went further. The creation of a TPP headquarters and especially the establishment of a National Security Council in 2013 enabled whole-of—government decision-making in foreign and trade policy. The Cabinet Secretariat's policymaking capabilities expanded considerably, comprising forty different policy units in 2017, and the number of civil servants on appointment doubled from the Koizumi era to nearly three thousand during Abe's second term.[25] The Prime Minister's Office instituted itself as a "control tower" capable of reining in bureaucratic sectionalism, in no small measure due to its greater sway over civil servant appointments. With Suga Yoshihide as chief cabinet secretary, the Abe administration became the embodiment of the dictum that "personnel is power."

The pitfalls of overly responsive bureaucrats as a result of the expansion of prime ministerial powers were revealed in scandals that haunted the Abe administration. In 2017, two prominent scandals erupted around the question of whether undue political influence facilitated the sale of government land with a steep discount to a controversial private school (Moritomo Gakuen) and led to the approval of a new veterinary school for a friend of the prime minister (Kake Gakuen). Although no direct intervention from the prime minister and his wife could be proved, a year later the Moritomo Gakuen scandal resurfaced upon news that Ministry of Finance officials had doctored documents related to the sale. A novel aspect of these scandals is the phenomenon of *sontaku*: government officials awarding policy favors to individuals who they believe enjoy the prime minister's support. In the aftermath of the scandals, the government adopted new measures to extend the period for the preservation of public documents and increased penalties for tampering with the official record.[26]

Public support for Abe dipped in the wake of these scandals, but eventually it bounced back. During the seven-plus years of his second administration, Abe was able to sustain robust levels of public support, for the most part above 40 percent and with brief interludes when the withholding of support surpassed sentiments of support (see Figure 6.2). The ability of the prime minister to portray himself as a steady hand in the pursuit of domestic economic revitalization and managing a more challenging external environment—an assertive China, a threatening North Korea, and an unpredictable America—played a role in his staying power.

A different sort of crisis changed this perception. The onset of the COVID-19 pandemic had profound consequences for Japan's economy,

Figure 6.2. Public support for the second Abe administration

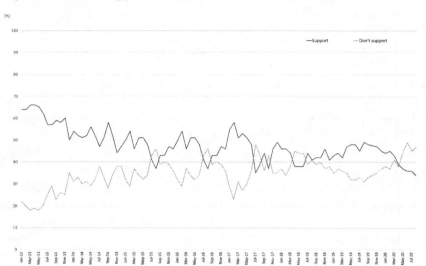

Note: No data for October 2019.

Source: NHK, "内閣支持率" [Cabinet Approval Rating], 2013–2020, https://www.nhk.or.jp/senkyo/shijiritsu/archive/2020_07.html.

which at the time was still reeling from the second increase of the consumption tax and shook public confidence in the government's competence in handling the health crisis. The Abe administration appeared neither decisive nor effective, delaying the call for a national health emergency and botching the disbursement of cash payments. A public opinion poll in April 2020 showed that 53 percent of respondents did not approve of the government's response.[27] Public support for the Abe Cabinet dropped by almost 10 percent between February and August of 2020. That year was supposed to be a landmark one for the legacy of Prime Minister Abe with the celebration of the Tokyo Olympics. Instead, the games were postponed and on August 28, Abe once again abruptly resigned from office due to a resurgence of his chronic disease. The pandemic had opened a new chapter in Japanese politics.

JAPANESE POLITICS AFTER ABE

Abe's sudden departure reopened the question of whether a return to the politics of indecision and frequent turnover in the premiership would occur. The LDP quickly rallied around Abe's right-hand man Suga Yoshihide, his chief cabinet secretary of almost eight years who had no factional affiliation, as the candidate of continuity. The Japanese public seemed to concur and upon his appointment in September 2020, Prime Minister Suga enjoyed record levels of public approval at 74 percent.[28] Suga promptly laid out ambitious plans for Japan's long-term transformation in two areas where Abenomics had underdelivered or was missing in action: digital transformation and climate change. But the mandate from the party and the public was for Suga to provide a steady hand in the most uncertain of times, and it was in the immediate task of pandemic response that he floundered.

The fate of Suga as a caretaker prime minister was decided early on. Because of the social distance protocols required for COVID-19 mitigation, he gave up on calling a snap election at the height of his popularity. That meant he had one year to prove his mettle on the pandemic response and structural change before facing an LDP presidential election in September 2021 and a general election later that fall. Suga's decision to go forward with the postponed Tokyo Olympics while Japan's vaccination campaign had a very slow start cost him the public's confidence. Public support for the Suga Cabinet dropped to 42 percent in December 2020 and continued to hemorrhage in the run up to the Olympics, which eventually took place the following July and August. His approval rate plummeted below 30 percent by August of 2021.[29] Suga decided to bow out of his reelection bid to party president.

Kishida Fumio won the contest. This was not his first attempt to win the party presidency, nor had he received the endorsement of former Prime Minister Abe despite having served in his administration as foreign minister for close to five years. Hailing from a more liberal LDP faction and seen as a more understated personality, Kishida displayed sharper elbows and rebranded himself as more of a hawk in security policy as he sparred with the other contenders in televised debates. Upon his appointment as party president and prime minister, Kishida led the LDP to a solid win with coalition partner Komeito in the Lower House election later that fall. Still facing an Upper House contest the following summer, the Kishida administration focused on its economic revitalization program, reimposed strict border controls with the arrival of the Omicron variant SARS-CoV-2, and made plans for a major update to Japan's national security strategy for the winter of 2022. Within the LDP, Kishida's goal was to strike a balance between securing buy-in from the party's largest faction led by former Prime Minister Abe and staking his own distinctive course with plans for a "new capitalism" and "new realism" in foreign policy.

The tragic assassination of former Prime Minister Abe during a campaign stop in Nara on July 8, 2022, shook Japan and the world. For a country with almost no gun violence thanks to strict firearm controls and where there is no recent memory of political assassination, there was bewilderment at the news of a befallen Abe. Additional shock came from reports that the assassin was motivated by a grudge against the Unification Church, which he blamed for the financial ruin of his family, and had decided to target Abe to underscore what he suspected were the politician's ties to the religious cult. In the Upper House election a fortnight later, the ruling coalition once again retained majority control while the opposition remained fragmented. But the mood was somber.

The reverberations of Abe's assassination in Japanese politics are still unfolding. Managing the fallout will be an acute test for Prime Minister Kishida. The public has bristled at the revelations of the connections of the Unification Church to Japanese politicians from across the political spectrum, but predominantly the LDP. The Unification Church scandal and Kishida's decision to hold an uncommon and controversial state funeral for Abe, plus rising COVID-19 cases and increases in the cost of living have reduced public support for the Kishida Cabinet. Following the resignation of three Cabinet ministers in one month, support for the Kishida administration dipped to 33.1 percent in November 2022 polls.[30] Having scored wins in the Lower and Upper House elections in the first months of its tenure, the Kishida administration does not face a required national election for the next three years. Yet, critical to Kishida's ability to restore public trust is his administration's follow through on pledges to thoroughly examine party member's ties to the Unification Church and to provide relief to those who have fallen into the church's grift.[31] One first step was the Diet's approval in late 2022 of a bill supported by all major parties which aims to crack down on exploitative solicitations from organizations (both secular and religious).[32]

Responsiveness to public demands will matter greatly to the future of Japanese politics. In addition to an effective pandemic response, voters in Japan are mostly concerned with the pocketbook issues of today (wages and the cost of living) and of tomorrow (social security in an ageing society).[33] They do not feel that politicians have prioritized the concerns of ordinary citizens, instead pursuing issues like constitutional reform, and many are disincentivized from political participation by the lack of meaningful party alternatives. Responsive politicians and engaged citizens are critical ingredients to ensuring Japan's democratic dynamism, as discussed in the next chapter.

NOTES

1. Some portions of this chapter appeared in the policy brief "Japan's Consolidated Democracy in an Era of Populist Turbulence," Democracy and Disorder, Brookings Institution, February 2019, www.brookings.edu/research/japans-consolidated-democracy-in-an-era-of-populist-turbulence/.

2. T. J. Pempel, ed., *Uncommon Democracies: The One-Party Dominant Regimes* (Ithaca, NY: Cornell University Press, 1990).

3. Gerald Curtis, *The Japanese Way of Politics* (New York: Columbia University Press, 1988); and Kent Calder, *Crisis and Compensation: Public Policy and Political Stability in Japan* (Princeton, NJ: Princeton University Press, 1988).

4. Steven Reed, "Japanese Electoral Systems since 1947," in *The Oxford Handbook of Japanese Politics*, ed. Robert J. Pekkanen and Saadia M. Pekkanen (Oxford, UK: Oxford University Press, 2021): 41–55.

5. Aurelia George Mulgan, "Japan's 'Un-Westminster' System: Impediments to Reform in a Crisis Economy," *Government and Opposition* 38, no. 1 (Winter 2003): 73–91.

6. Alisa Gaunder, "The Institutional Landscape of Japanese Politics," in *The Routledge Handbook of Japanese Politics*, ed. Alisa Gaunder (New York: Routledge, 2011); and Matthew M. Carlson and Steven R. Reed, *Political Corruption and Scandals in Japan* (Ithaca, NY: Cornell University Press, 2018).

7. "Japan Enacts Law to Rebalance Lower House Electoral Districts," *Kyodo News*, November 18, 2022, https://english.kyodonews.net/news/2022/11/5bd15951a42a-japan-enacts-law-to-rebalance-lower-house-electoral-districts.html.

8. Amy Catalinac, *Electoral Reform and National Security in Japan: From Pork to Foreign Policy* (New York: Cambridge University Press, 2016).

9. Ellis S. Krauss and Robert K. J. Pekkanen, *The Rise and Fall of Japan's LDP: Political Party Organizations as Historical Institutions* (Ithaca, NY: Cornell University Press, 2010).

10. Matthew M. Carlson and Steven R. Reed, *Political Corruption and Scandals in Japan* (Ithaca, NY: Cornell University Press, 2018).

11. Harukata Takenaka, "Expansion of the Prime Minister's Power in the Japanese Parliamentary System," *Asian Survey* 59, no. 5 (2019): 844–69.

12. Axel Klein and Levi McLaughlin, "Komeito: The Party and Its Place in Japanese Politics," in *The Oxford Handbook of Japanese Politics*, ed. Robert

J. Pekkanen and Saadia M. Pekkanen (Oxford, UK: Oxford University Press, 2021): 201–22.

13. Adam Liff and Ko Maeda, "Electoral Incentives, Policy Compromise, and Coalition Durability: Japan's LDP-Komeito Government in a Mixed Electoral System," *Japanese Journal of Political Science* 20, no. 1 (2019): 53–73.

14. Kenji E. Kushida and Phillip Lipscy, "The Rise and Fall of the Democratic Party of Japan," in *Japan under the DPJ: The Politics of Transition and Governance*, ed. Kenji E. Kushida and Phillip Lipscy (Stanford: Walter H. Shorenstein Asia-Pacific Research Center, Stanford University, 2013): 3–42.

15. Ikuo Kabashima and Gill Steel, "The Koizumi Revolution," *PS: Political Science and Politics* 40, no. 1 (2007): 81.

16. Tobias Harris, *The Iconoclast: Shinzo Abe and the New Japan* (London: Hurst Publishers, 2020).

17. Harukata Takenaka, "Evolution of Japanese Security Policy and the House of Councilors," *Japanese Journal of Political Science* 22, no. 2 (June 2021): 96–115.

18. Ko Mishima, "Unattainable Mission? The Democratic Party of Japan's Unsuccessful Policy-Making System Reform," *Asian Politics and Policy* 7, no. 3 (2015): 433–54.

19. Ethan Scheiner and Michael F. Thies, "The Political Opposition in Japan," in *The Oxford Handbook of Japanese Politics*, ed. Robert J. Pekkanen and Saadia M. Pekkanen, (Oxford, UK: Oxford University Press, 2021): 223–42.

20. Aurelia George Mulgan, "How Significant Was the LDP's Victory in Japan's Recent General Election?" East Asia Forum, December 31, 2012, www .eastasiaforum.org/2012/12/31/how-significant-was-the-ldps-victory-in-japans -recent-general-election/.

21. Masahisa Endo and Robert J. Pekkanen, "The LDP: Return to Dominance? Or a Golden Age Built on Sand?" in *Japan Decides 2014: The Japanese General Election*, ed. Robert J. Pekkanen, Steven R. Reed, and Ethan Scheiner (New York: Palgrave Macmillan, 2016): 41–54.

22. Mireya Solís, *Dilemmas of a Trading Nation: Japan and the United States in the Evolving Asia-Pacific Order* (Washington, DC: Brookings Institution Press, 2017).

23. Robert J. Pekkanen, Steven R. Reed, and Daniel M. Smith, "Japanese Politics between the 2012 and 2014 Elections," in *Japan Decides 2014: The Japanese General Election*, ed. Robert Pekkanen, Steven R. Reed, and Ethan Scheiner (London: Palgrave Macmillan, 2016): 20.

24. Alisa Gaunder, "Resolved: Japan Needs a Two-Party System," Debating Japan, Center for Strategic and International Studies, July 29, 2019, www.csis .org/analysis/resolved-japan-needs-two-party-system.

25. Takenaka, "Evolution of Japanese Security Policy."

26. See Matthew M. Carlson, "*Sontaku* and Political Scandals in Japan," *Public Administration and Policy* 23, no. 1 (2020): 33–45, www.emerald.com/ insight/content/doi/10.1108/PAP-11-2019-0033/full/html.

27. See "Majority in Japan Don't Approve Abe Govt's Coronavirus Response: Mainichi Poll," *The Mainichi*, April 20, 2020, https://mainichi.jp/english/articles/20200420/p2a/00m/0na/016000c.

28. Yukio Tajima and Yuki Fujita, "Honeymoon over as Suga Faces Make-or-Break Moment on Virus," *Nikkei Asia*, December 29, 2020, https://asia.nikkei.com/Spotlight/Coronavirus/Honeymoon-over-as-Suga-faces-make-or-break-moment-on-virus.

29. Takahiro Hirata, "内閣支持率 26% 菅政権に「明かり」は見えず," [Cabinet Approval at 26%, Public Says to Suga Administration It Doesn't See "the Light"], *Mainichi Shimbun*, August 31, 2021, https://mainichi.jp/premier/politics/articles/20210829/pol/00m/010/003000c.

30. "Kishida Cabinet Support Rate Plunges to Lowest Level since Launch," *The Japan Times*, November 27, 2022, https://www.japantimes.co.jp/news/2022/11/27/national/politics-diplomacy/kishida-support-rate-lowest-poll/.

31. "LDP Execs and Ministers Must Sever Church Ties, Kishida Says," *The Japan Times*, August 22, 2022, www.japantimes.co.jp/news/2022/08/22/national/politics-diplomacy/ldp-code-of-conduct-unification-church/.

32. "Japan Enacts Law to Prohibit Malicious Solicitation for Donations," *Nikkei Asia*, December 10, 2022, https://asia.nikkei.com/Politics/Unification-Church-and-politics/Japan-enacts-law-to-prohibit-malicious-solicitation-for-donations.

33. Cabinet Office, "Overview of the Public Opinion Survey on the Life of the People," Public Relations Office, Government of Japan, January 2022, 51, https://survey.gov-online.go.jp/r03/r03-life/gairyaku.pdf.

CHAPTER 7

Japan's Democracy in the Populist Era

While the rise of populism has upended politics in the West, it has yet to disrupt the national politics of one major industrial democracy: Japan. Economic stagnation and greater social disparities should make Japan a likely candidate for the politics of grievance that in other places has paved the way for populist forces. Yet, Japan has not experienced the toxic polarization that has given rise to exclusionary politics elsewhere. The vast majority of the Japanese public does not show an appetite for populism, nor have anti-establishment political figures in Japan peddled anti-pluralism. Japan has been spared the populist trap of hyperpartisanship, all-out attacks on the institutions of representative democracy, and weakened electoral integrity.

In an era of democratic backsliding, Japan plays an important global role as a consolidated democracy that has adjusted to economic globalization and avoided populist disruption. Its democracy, however, is not immune to challenges. There are troubling signs of declining democratic dynamism: a deflated opposition camp, disengaged voters, and weakened channels of accountability. Robust interparty competition with alternation in office was tried once, but now appears a remote possibility. Reconstructing a viable opposition that can offer credible alternatives to the electorate will be essential to adding greater vitality to Japanese democracy.

ESCAPING (SO FAR) THE POPULIST TRAP

Populism is far from a new political phenomenon, but it has lately risen to new prominence in Western democracies with the electoral inroads of far-right parties in Continental Europe, the success of the Brexit campaign, and the 2017 arrival of populist candidate Donald Trump to the American presidency. The political turmoil in many consolidated democracies and a marked inward turn, with growing anti-immigration and protectionist sentiments, show that the consequences of populism for liberal democracies and an open international order are profound.

The Perils of Populism

Rather than a specific policy orientation or leadership style, populism is best understood as an ideology that interprets politics as a fundamental clash between two homogenous groups, the people (pure and virtuous) and the elite (corrupt and exploitative), and which mandates that the unmediated general will must dictate political decisions in any society. A Manichean worldview and the moralization of politics are essential traits of populism.[1] At the core of populist movements are two fundamental elements: anti-elitism and anti-pluralism. The denunciation of elites and the status quo is a necessary condition of populism, but not a sufficient one. Populism is ultimately about the rejection of pluralism. The essential claim of populist leaders is that they alone represent the will of the people, therefore calling into question the legitimacy of opposition forces and institutions that protect minority rights.[2] The pluralist view that society is composed of multiple groups, whose interests should not be subsumed under majoritarian preferences, and that politics is the art of compromise among diverse constituencies is at odds with the populist understanding that only the "proper" people are sovereign and pure majoritarian rule is legitimate.

Populism emerges in societies that feel existential insecurity and where the political elite remains unresponsive. As Hawkins explains, populism thrives where there is political institutional failure (with endemic corruption, weak rule of law, and/or structural inequities fueling a legitimacy crisis) and where society's woes go beyond policy failure.[3] The electoral success of a populist movement requires a leader who can mobilize these frustrations. The appeal to a "new politics" can come from outsiders, political novices erupting into electoral politics, or maverick old-timers renouncing the existing elite and aiming to reshape their own party.[4]

The most critical distinction is between anti-establishment politicians, who decry the status quo, attack existing elites, and target policy reform, and populist leaders, who challenge the regime of liberal democracy itself (with its constitutional protections for minority rights and institutional checks and balances) by claiming that they alone represent the will of the people.

The consequences of populism for liberal democracies and the international order are steep. As Müller warns, the casualty is not just liberalism but democracy itself, because at the core of anti-pluralism lies a denial that all citizens are free and equal.[5] The electoral triumph of a populist project in a country will likely impact the conduct of its foreign policy. An inward turn follows from populism's emphasis on national sovereignty over international cooperation and the attribution of a country's ills to outside forces.[6]

Anti-Establishment Politics in Japan

The pull of the establishment in Japan is strong. The same party, the Liberal Democratic Party (LDP), has ruled the country since 1955, with the notable exception of two instances of a non-LDP government (1993–1994 and 2009–2012). The LDP's exclusivity to rule has also changed over the years, specifically with the onset of LDP coalition governments most of the time since a change in electoral rules in the 1990s. The postwar-era pantheon of Japanese leaders does not feature populist figures in the image of Hungary's Viktor Orbán, America's Donald Trump, or France's Marine Le Pen; nor have mass populist parties akin to France's Front National (National Front), Germany's AfD (Alternative for Germany), and Italy's Movimento 5 Stelle (Five-Star Movement) emerged. In contrast, continuity is conspicuous in Japan with the prevalence of second- and third-generation politicians. In a carefully documented study of dynastic politics, Daniel Smith shows that at their peak in 1993, legacy parliamentarians represented 33 percent of all members of the Lower House. With the new electoral rules deemphasizing candidate-centered campaigns, there has been some attrition of legacy Diet members, but lineage candidates still predominate in LDP Cabinets (on average representing 60 percent of all appointments).[7] Politics is largely an inherited business in Japan.

Periodic calls in Japan to deliver "new politics" have come less often from outsiders making a debut in electoral contests than from already established career politicians promising to remove the establishment from which they themselves emerged. Many political figures in Japan labeled as "populist" are not outsiders but creatures of the establishment—following their family elders into politics and with tenures in the ruling party. Such is the case of former Prime Ministers Koizumi Junichiro and Hatoyama Yukio, who captured the national spotlight in their reinvention as mavericks. Both decried the hold of political elites on policymaking, but neither mounted a populist assault to weaken the legitimacy of the institutions of representative democracy; nor did they attempt to rule through majoritarian plebiscites or the vilification of a perceived external enemy to justify domestic changes. Telegenic or subdued, competent or ineffective, these Japanese leaders offered an anti-establishment, but not an anti-pluralist, alternative to politics as usual.

The pinnacle of Koizumi's premiership was his call for a snap election in 2005 to challenge his own party's rejection of the postal privatization bill. Koizumi expelled the postal rebels from the party and challenged these incumbents by hiring "assassin" candidates (novices to politics) to run in their districts. The public rewarded Koizumi's campaign by showing up in force at the polls and electing eighty-three new candidates, baptized by the media as "Koizumi's children." Koizumi was implacable vis-à-vis the vested interests he set out to overhaul in a number of policy bailiwicks (including postal services and highway construction), and he was more than willing to trample on the privileges of incumbents by diminishing factional influence and bringing new blood into politics. A master communicator, he engaged in theatrical politics in his quest against the "forces of resistance."[8] But Koizumi did not seek to undermine the institutions of representative democracy, nor did he bypass legislative procedures or attack the free press.[9] As soon as he left office, his mentee and successor—Abe Shinzo—invited the rebels back into the LDP. The establishment had quickly roared back.

Populist politicians have not taken by storm Japanese national politics, but some regional governors have been labeled as populist. Hashimoto Toru transfixed Osaka politics with his election as governor in 2008. A lawyer by training, Hashimoto had acquired notoriety as an outspoken TV celebrity. He thrived on oppositional politics, targeting public servants and teachers' unions and pushing for cutbacks in social spending.

His signature policy was the creation of an Osaka Metropolis, fusing the prefectural and city administrations. To further his political ambitions, Hashimoto created in 2010 a new local party called Osaka Ishin, and then set his eyes on national politics with the launch of Nippon Ishin no Kai (The Japan Innovation Party) in 2012.[10]

Hashimoto thrived on controversy, aware that his command of the political cycle was a key asset. His penchant for top-down decision-making (he once praised dictatorship as more effective than slow, deliberative democratic institutions) and his denials of the "comfort women" issue captured headlines, but cost him votes.[11] Yet, Hashimoto was not made in the mold of a xenophobic demagogue. He supported the Korean community in Osaka, embraced international economic engagement, and did not contest adverse electoral results.[12] Hashimoto lost the Osaka Metropolis referendum of 2015 and resigned from Nippon Ishin after the party's poor results in the 2017 election.[13]

Koike Yuriko started her professional career as a TV anchor, but by the time she set her sights on the Tokyo governorship she was a decade-and-a-half veteran in the LDP with two Cabinet postings under her belt. Her reinvention as maverick entailed a direct challenge to the local LDP establishment (which refused to endorse her and supported another candidate) built on the promise to bring greater transparency in decision-making and do away with the opaque old-boy network. She hit a nerve with Tokyo residents who had seen the last two governors resign amid money scandals, but her appeal did not rest on populist ideology. In fact, as a conservative politician, many of her policy positions were close to that of the Abe wing of the LDP establishment that had housed her for so long. Surveys looking at the 2017 Tokyo Metropolitan Assembly and Lower House elections in that same year found weak support among voters for key planks of populist ideology: a Manichean world view, popular sovereignty, and anti-elitism.[14] Neither the supply nor the demand for populism was strong in those elections.

More recently, other anti-establishment parties have entered the fray. The Party to Protect the People from NHK established by Tachibana Takeshi does not have a coherent platform other than its opposition to mandatory fees for Japan's public broadcasting network NHK. But it deploys populist rhetoric, calling for a peasant rebellion against the elites and opposing foreign aid.[15] Another example is the Reiwa Shinsengumi. Created by retired actor Yamamoto Taro, it offers an anti-establishment critique of the ruling elite for its failures to address the concerns of average citizens, opposes nuclear energy, and positions itself as a genuine grassroots party. Yamamoto's messaging is not populist, though. A careful analysis of the party's platform and Yamamoto's speeches by Axel Klein finds no evidence of an ideology that views people as a homogenous group whose will is above representative institutions.[16] On the contrary, one of Yamamoto's trademarks is the protection of minority rights, in particular those of people with disabilities. Yet another party is Sanseito, a far-right party established in 2020 with strong populist leanings. It decries globalism, calls for restrictions on foreign workers, and rejects COVID-19 vaccines and masking requirements.[17]

These newer parties are small, rely on social media to reach voters, and have secured seats through the proportional representation (PR) vote. In the Upper House election of 2019, the Party to Protect the People from NHK won just one seat and Reiwa Shinsengumi two seats. Reiwa Shinsengumi won three PR seats in the Lower House election of 2021. In the Upper House poll of 2022, the Party to Protect the People from NHK won one more seat, Reiwa Shinsengumi claimed three more seats, and in its electoral debut Sanseito captured one seat. These disparate parties do not represent a consolidated populist movement in Japanese politics. Not all of them espouse a populist ideology and they lack the organizational clout or general voter appeal to alter the balance of power in the all-important Lower House. Rather, their emergence underscores that growing segments of the Japanese population, especially younger voters, do not believe extant national parties can address their concerns.

Avoiding Political Polarization

All over the world, toxic polarization has contributed to steep democratic backsliding. Hyper-partisanship devolves political life into a zero-sum competition with greater tolerance for extra-constitutional measures to score wins. It promotes rigid divides in a country with groups increasingly at odds with each other. The space for deliberation, tolerance of different viewpoints, compromise solutions, and respect for due process diminishes.[18] Polarization creates the conditions for the election of populist leaders using Manichean rhetoric to mobilize voters. The arrival of populist leaders in turn feeds exclusionary politics and can wound democracy when a political party and its supporters refuse to abide by a sacrosanct principle: accepting the will of the voters in an election.[19]

The United States and Japan are headed in very different directions regarding political and social polarization. According to a 2021 Pew Research Center survey, 90 percent of American respondents say there are strong conflicts among political parties, compared to 39 percent in Japan.[20] Political conflict has divided American society. Another Pew poll shows that since 2016, in the United States there has been a sharp increase in the negative views Democrats and Republicans hold of each other, believing the opposite side to be narrow-minded, dishonest, and immoral.[21] Expert ratings in the Varieties of Democracy project place the United States and Japan at markedly different places on the continuum of political polarization (hostile party competition ranked from 0 to 4) at 3.6 and 1.2, respectively.[22] Protracted hyper-partisanship does not bode well for the future of American democracy given that the historical track record points to democratic degradation in political systems afflicted by long-term polarization.[23] The spread of the "Big Lie" (the spurious claim that the 2020 U.S. presidential election was rigged) has undermined confidence in electoral integrity and triggered organized violence to prevent the peaceful transfer of power on January 6, 2021.

Japan's democracy is not in the throes of toxic polarization, nor have demagogue leaders damaged the fabric of society by sowing ideological divisions. Rather, the challenges that Japan's democracy faces are of a different nature: apathy and disengagement.

THE DOWNSIDES OF POLITICS WITHOUT ALTERNATIVES

There are troubling signs of waning democratic dynamism in Japan such as tepid interparty competition, voter apathy, and the weakening of accountability channels. The less than successful experience with a Democratic Party of Japan (DPJ) government dashed the hope among the electorate that party turnover could bring genuine political and economic reform. Ever since, opposition parties have failed to become a viable alternative capable of eliciting a wave of support from voters. The irrelevance of opposition parties derives from many factors; one of them, as pointed out by Scheiner and Thies, is their inability to generate credible plans to tackle the nation's economic problems or foreign policy management.[24]

With party breakups, new mergers, and short-lived parties, it has been difficult to generate public confidence that the opposition in government is a viable option. The fragmentation of the opposition camp has played into the hands of the LDP at election time. By splitting the non-LDP vote in single-member districts, opposition parties lose the opportunity to capture seats. Electoral coordination is necessary, but pitfalls abound. By teaming up with disparate parties, there is a risk of confusing voters and diluting the party's image. In particular, an electoral alliance with the Japanese Communist Party (JCP) has been a source of internal friction for center-left parties. The Constitutional Democratic Party of Japan's (CDP) bet on electoral cooperation with the JCP in the fall 2021 general election did not deliver good results. The party lost seats—from 110 on the eve of the election to 96 in its aftermath—and its strongest support group, the Japan Trade Union Confederation (commonly known as Rengo), given their historical animosity toward the JCP, rebuked the CDP's decision to team up with the JCP.[25]

Becoming the perennial opposition in the Diet generates other dilemmas. For some, the only way to influence policy is to cooperate with the government, even if that diminishes the party's appeal as an alternative to the current administration or forecloses future cooperation with other opposition forces.[26] Another center-left party, the Democratic Party for the People (DPP, established in 2018 through the merger of the DPJ and the Party of Hope) voted in favor of the LDP's draft budget in February 2022 after obtaining a concession on a trigger mechanism to lower gas prices. Other opposition parties decried the move and cited it as a barrier to future cooperation with the DPP.[27]

Public support for the opposition parties is in the low single digits: voters support the Nippon Ishin at 5.1 percent, CDP at 4.8 percent, JCP at 2.5 percent, DPP at 2.1 percent, Sanseito at 1.6 percent, Reiwa Shinsengumi at 1.5 percent, Social Democratic Party at 0.4 percent, and the Party to Protect the People from NHK at 0.4 percent. Support for the LDP is far more robust at 36.2 percent, and its coalition partner Komeito boasts a loyal followership and public support at 2.9 percent. Perhaps the most remarkable statistic is that 34.9 percent of respondents claim they do not support any party.[28] The lack of a competitive party system has had two major consequences for voting behavior in Japan: dealignment with the rise of floating voters, and low political participation both on election day and in other political activities. Independent voters can sway elections in bursts of mobilization by a party promising to deliver change (they came in force to support Koizumi and the DPJ in consecutive general elections), or they may choose to stay home, disillusioned by broken reform vows or unenthused by the lack of meaningful political alternatives to LDP rule.

Since the return to power of the LDP-Komeito coalition in 2012, voter apathy has been the norm. The general election of 2014 registered the lowest turnout rate in the postwar era, and it remained stubbornly low in 2017 at 53.7 percent, to recover slightly at 55.9 percent in 2021. Without an upswell of support, opposition parties cannot close the gap with the LDP-Komeito ticket, which relies more heavily on the organized vote. There is frustration with the less-than-desired level of responsiveness of political parties. According to a 2018 Pew Research Center poll, 62 percent of respondents believe that no matter who wins, things will not change much.[29] The incentive for ordinary citizens to become involved in other types of political activities is therefore low: 70 percent of respondents to a 2014 NHK survey had no intention to partake in political assemblies, demonstrations, or letter writing to parliamentarians or media outlets.[30]

The weakening of meaningful political competition in Japan does not only encourages citizen passivity toward the political process. It also dulls legislative deliberations and, without the prospect of alternation in office between competing political tickets, weakens transparency and accountability. Robust electoral competition incentivizes governments to remain attuned to public demands. The LDP, and Prime Minister Abe in particular, mounted a comeback in 2012 showing such responsiveness, running on a platform of economic revitalization and an unconventional reflationist strategy.[31] But along the way, the Abe administration lost some of its luster, with Cabinet appointments that led to scandals (e.g., Defense Minister Inada Tomomi's resignation over "lost" daily activity records of the Self-Defense Force's peacekeeping mission in Sudan),[32] testy relations with some media outlets,[33] and the over-deference from public officials that was at the heart of the school scandals.

The far-reaching reforms to the rules of the political game and decision-making of the 1990s and 2000s aspired to create a more competitive party system and bolster the prime minister's leadership power. While the first goal stalled, the reality of strong executive power materialized, especially when the prime minister's office under Abe asserted greater influence over the LDP and bureaucracy.[34] Strong executive leadership has served Japan well in tackling the deflationary economy and orchestrating a more proactive foreign policy. But the lack of a viable center-left party has weakened checks and balances against a dominant

LDP.[35] This situation is well captured in how the LDP itself runs electoral campaigns under slogans such as the somewhat ominous-sounding "There Is No Alternative," and celebrates itself as the party of "Decision and Execution."

Japan and the United States belong to a shrinking group of liberal democracies. However, the challenges that each society and political system face in preserving and renewing their democratic governance are of a different nature (see Table 7.1). The overall ranking of each country in the Liberal Democracy Index is very close, but the areas where Japan and the United States excel and struggle are markedly different. Japan ranks very high in the egalitarian component, which measures equal access of groups to political participation (including resource equity in welfare, education, and health), but the United States trails far behind in this measure. Japan is a few places behind the United States in the liberal component, which measures horizontal checks and balances such as the ability of the legislative branch to hold the executive to account.

Table 7.1. Comparison of Japan and U.S. on measures of liberal democracy

	Liberal Democracy Index (LDI)		Electoral Democracy Index (EDI)		Liberal Component Index (LCI)		Egalitarian Component Index (ECI)		Participatory Component Index (PCI)		Deliberative Component Index (DCI)	
	Rank	Score	Rank	Score	Rank	Score	Rank	Score	Rank	Score	Rank	Score
Japan	28	0.74	24	0.83	31	0.88	8	0.92	73	0.56	20	0.92
United States	29	0.74	29	0.82	26	0.90	76	0.65	26	0.66	61	0.78

Source: Vanessa A. Boese, Nazifa Alizada, Martin Lundstedt, Kelly Morrison, Natalia Natsika, Yuko Sato, Hugo Tai, and Staffan I. Lindberg, "Autocratization Changing Nature?" *Democracy Report 2022* (Gothenburg: Varieties of Democracy Institute, March 2022), www.v-dem.net/publications/democracy-reports.

On the other hand, Japan is ahead of the United States in the electoral component, which includes a clean election index and a freedom of expression index. On the latter, Japan has had a lackluster performance in press freedom rankings due to close-knit ties between journalists and public officials through the *kisha kurabu* (reporters' club) system. Since some media outlets receive exclusive access to public figures, this hinders the participation of outside media and more robust investigative journalism. Hayashi Kaori's study of Japan's media landscape shows that self-censorship and media indifference are the biggest issues, not direct censorship or a lack of trust from the Japanese public of news sources.[36]

The apathy-populist upheaval dichotomy that separates Japan and the United States also comes through in areas where each country has a low score. Japan places at a low seventy-third in the participatory component, which measures civil society's involvement in politics. The United States ranks sixty-first on the deliberative component, which measures the extent to which the common good motivates reasoned political decisions.

Bolstering democratic dynamism for Japan and strengthening democratic resilience for the United States are urgent tasks in an era when the competence of democracies in addressing their citizens needs is crucial to the redefinition of the global order.

NOTES

1. Cas Mudde and Cristóbal Rovira Kaltwasser, *Populism: A Very Short Introduction* (New York: Oxford University Press, 2017).

2. Jan-Werner Müller, *What Is Populism?* (Philadelphia: University of Pennsylvania Press, 2016).

3. Kirk A. Hawkins, *Venezuela's Chavismo and Populism in Comparative Perspective* (New York: Cambridge University Press, 2010).

4. Robert R. Barr, "Populists, Outsiders, and Anti-Establishment Politics," *Party Politics* 15, no. 1 (2009): 29–48.

5. Müller, *What Is Populism?* 106.

6. Cristóbal Rovira Kaltwasser, "Explaining the Emergence of Populism in Europe and the Americas," in *The Promise and Perils of Populism*, ed. Carlos de la Torre (Lexington: The University Press of Kentucky, 2015), 189–226.

7. Daniel M. Smith, *Dynasties and Democracy: The Inherited Incumbency Advantage in Japan* (Stanford: Stanford University Press, 2018), 23, 44.

8. Hideo Otake, "Neoliberal Populism in Japanese Politics: A Study of Prime Minister Koizumi in Comparison with President Reagan," in *Populism in Asia*, ed. Pasuk Phongpaichit and Kosuke Mizuno (Singapore and Japan: National University of Singapore Press and Kyoto University Press, 2009).

9. Olli Hellman, "Populism in East Asia," in *The Oxford Handbook of Populism*, ed. Cristóbal Rovira Kaltwasser et al. (Oxford, UK: Oxford University Press, 2017), 161–78; and Yu Uchiyama, *Koizumi and Japanese Politics: Reform Strategies and Leadership Style* (New York: Routledge, 2010).

10. Charles Weathers, "Reformer or Destroyer? Hashimoto Toru and Populist Neoliberal Politics in Japan," *Social Science Japan Journal* 17, no. 1 (2014): 77–96.

11. Ibid.

12. Ken Victor Leonard Hijino, "Winds, Fevers, and Floating Voters," in *The Crisis of Liberal Internationalism: Japan and the World Order*, ed. Yoichi Funabashi and G. John Ikenberry (Washington, DC: Brookings Institution Press, 2020): 247–48.

13. See Eric Johnston, "Hashimoto Cuts Ties with Nippon Ishin after Party's Poor Election Showing," *The Japan Times*, October 27, 2017, www.japantimes.co.jp/news/2017/10/27/national/politics-diplomacy/hashimoto-cuts-ties-nippon-ishin-partys-poor-election-showing/.

14. Takashi Hieda, Masahiro Zenkyo, and Masaru Nishikawa, "Do Populists Support Populism? An Examination through an Online Survey Following the 2017 Tokyo Metropolitan Assembly Election," *Party Politics* 27, no. 2 (2019): 1–12; and Robert A. Fahey, Airo Hino, and Sebastian Jungkunz, "Populist Attitudes and Party Preferences in Japan," North-Eastern Workshop on Japanese Politics, 2019, https://cpb-us-e1.wpmucdn.com/sites.dartmouth.edu/dist/d/274/files/2019/09/Fahey-NEWJP-Paper-Draft.pdf

15. Robert A. Fahey, Airo Hino, and Robert J. Pekkanen, "Populism in Japan," in *The Oxford Handbook of Japanese Politics*, ed. Robert J. Pekkanen and Saadia M. Pekkanen (Oxford, UK: Oxford University Press, 2021), 317–51.

16. Axel Klein, "Is There Left Populism in Japan? The Case of Reiwa Shinsengumi," *The Asia-Pacific Journal* 18, no. 10 (2020): 1–19.

17. "Political Newcomer Sanseito Making Waves in Okinawa Elections," *The Japan Times*, August 8, 2022, https://www.japantimes.co.jp/news/2022/08/08/national/politics-diplomacy/okinawa-sanseito-popularity/.

18. William Galston, "The Populist Challenge to Liberal Democracy," *Journal of Democracy* 29, no. 2 (2019): 5–19.

19. For an excellent discussion of the perils of toxic polarization for democracy that forty countries today are experiencing, see V-Dem Institute, "Democracy Report 2022: Autocratization Changing Nature?" University of Gothenberg, Gothenburg, Sweden, 2022, https://v-dem.net/media/publications/dr_2022.pdf.

20. Laura Silver, Janell Fetterolf, and Aidan Connaughton, "Diversity and Division in Advanced Economies," Pew Research Center, October 13, 2021, www.pewresearch.org/global/2021/10/13/diversity-and-division-in-advanced-economies/.

21. Pew Research Center, "As Partisan Hostility Grows, Signs of Frustration with the Two-Party System," August 9, 2022, www.pewresearch.org/topic/politics-policy/political-parties-polarization/political-polarization/.

22. V-Dem Institute, "Democracy Report 2022."

23. Jennifer McCoy and Benjamin Press, "What Happens When Democracies Become Perniciously Polarized?" Carnegie Endowment for International Peace, January 18, 2022, https://carnegieendowment.org/2022/01/18/what-happens-when-democracies-become-perniciously-polarized-pub-86190.

24. Ethan Scheiner and Michael F. Thies, "The Political Opposition in Japan," in *The Oxford Handbook of Japanese Politics*, ed. Robert J. Pekkanen and Saadia M. Pekkanen, (Oxford, UK: Oxford University Press, 2021), 223–42.

25. Ko Maeda, "The Continuing Predicament of Japan's Opposition," Sasakawa Peace Foundation USA, January 13, 2022, https://spfusa.org/publications/the-continuing-predicament-of-japans-opposition/.

26. Steven Reed, "Japanese Electoral Systems since 1947," in *The Oxford Handbook of Japanese Politics*, ed. Robert J. Pekkanen and Saadia M. Pekkanen (Oxford, UK: Oxford University Press, 2021), 41–55.

27. "Japan Ruling Party Welcomes Opposition Votes for Draft Budget," *The Japan Times*, February 25, 2022, www.japantimes.co.jp/news/2022/02/25/national/politics-diplomacy/dpp-votes-for-budget/.

28. All figures are for September 2022. See "各党の支持率は NHK世論調査," [Political Support for Each Party, NHK Public Opinion Poll], NHK, September 2022.

29. Bruce Stokes and Kat Devlin, "Despite Rising Economic Confidence, Japanese See Best Days behind Them and Say Children Face a Bleak Future," Pew Research Center, November 12, 2018, www.pewresearch.org/global/wp-content/uploads/sites/2/2018/11/Pew-Research-Center_Despite-Rising-Economic-Confidence-Japanese-See-Best-Days-Behind-Them-and-Say-Children-Face-Bleak-Future_2018-11-121.pdf.

30. The results of the NHK Broadcasting Cultural Research Institute's survey are reported by Kaori Hayashi, "The Silent Public in a Liberal State: Challenges for Japan's Journalism in the Age of the Internet," in *The Crisis of Liberal Internationalism: Japan and the World Order*, ed. Yoichi Funabashi and G. John Ikenberry (Washington DC, The Brookings Institution Press, 2020), 335.

31. Tobias Harris, *The Iconoclast: Shinzo Abe and the New Japan* (London: Hurst Publishers, August 2020).

32. See Ankit Panda, "Tomomi Inada, Japan's Defense Minister, Resigns Following Weeks of Scandal," *The Diplomat*, July 28, 2017, https://thediplomat.com/2017/07/tomomi-inada-japans-defense-minister-resigns-following-weeks-of-scandal/.

33. See Mizuho Aoki, "Abe Tells Asahi Shimbun to Help in 'Recovering Japan's Honor,'" *The Japan Times*, October 6, 2014, www.japantimes.co.jp/news/2014/10/06/national/politics-diplomacy/abe-tells-asahi-shimbun-to-help-in-recovering-japans-honor/.

34. Aurelia George Mulgan, "The Role of the Prime Minister in Japan," in *The Oxford Handbook of Japanese Politics*, ed. Robert J. Pekkanen and Saadia M. Pekkanen (Oxford, UK: Oxford University Press, 2021), 56–73.

35. Gerald Curtis, "Weak Opposition Is a Cancer in Japan's Political System," East Asia Forum, September 18, 2016, www.eastasiaforum.org/2016/09/18/weak-opposition-is-a-cancer-in-japans-political-system/.

36. Kaori Hayashi, "The Silent Public in a Liberal State."

SECTION 4

Geoeconomics

CHAPTER 8

Japan as Champion of Connectivity in a Rules-Based Order

Japan's determination to advance economic connectivity in large swaths of the world significantly raised the country's stature in world affairs. The push for cross-border economic integration was comprised of efforts to make rules for trade, investment, and data governance; supply private and public capital to promote development; and cultivate a newfound political will to open protected markets enough to strike bigger bargains at the negotiation table. In this manner, Japan shed the image of a passive actor in the international trading system (at best) and a mercantilist free rider benefitting from the openness of others (at worst). With a new level of ambition in its development finance and digital governance, and a track record as broker of mega trade agreements, Japan reinvented itself as champion of the rules-based economic order.

ARCHITECT OF MEGA TRADE DEALS

At the outset of the twenty-first century, Japan was a laggard in international trade diplomacy. While most countries had begun to negotiate preferential trade agreements to bypass the negotiation deadlock at the World Trade Organization (WTO), Japan had yet to ink even one free trade agreement (FTA). Two decades later, Japan boasts twenty-one FTAs (signed or in force) that cover close to 80 percent of its total trade. But not all trade agreements are created equal, and it is the Trans-Pacific Partnership (TPP) project (in its different iterations) that has redefined Japan.

In summer 2013, Japan was the last country to join the TPP negotiations. Given its well-known defensive position in trade negotiations,
there were skeptical voices in the United States who warned that Japan
would water down liberalization targets or preclude a timely conclusion
of the talks.[1] Japan, however, defied these expectations. Tokyo demonstrated a newfound level of ambition and came prepared to negotiate
with a unified voice, thanks in part to the creation of a TPP headquarters housed in the Cabinet Office with seconded elite officials, which
allowed the overcoming of impediments caused by traditional differences among Japanese ministries. In the TPP talks, trade ceased to be
mostly a bilateral irritant in U.S.-Japan relations and heralded the much
greater potential for strategic convergence in drafting an economic rulebook for the region.[2]

Japan and the United States reached compromises on long-divisive
market issues in the agricultural and automobile sectors. Japan kept its
five sacred agricultural commodities off-limits from tariff liberalization,
while the United States punted the elimination of auto and truck tariffs
to 25–30 years down the road. Notwithstanding these domestic political sensitivities, the overall TPP agreement achieved a 99 percent tariff
elimination target, and Japan bested its record with a commitment to
scrap 95 percent of overall tariff lines. Moreover, the United States and
Japan worked together to codify new rules on trade and investment that
would essentially update a toolkit that the WTO had left dormant for 20
years. A comprehensive set of disciplines covering newer areas like the
digital economy, service and investment liberalization, and disciplines
on state-owned enterprises was a remarkable achievement for a trade
grouping comprising both developed and developing nations.

Japan's participation in the TPP was transformative because it marked
the first time that Tokyo clearly articulated a whole set of national interests to advance through trade leadership. In making the case for TPP
entry, Prime Minister Abe Shinzo referred to the trade deal as the "prov-
ident masterstroke" to position Japan at the heart of the Asia-Pacific
century. He noted that the transformation of the Pacific Ocean into a
vast inland sea of commerce would help Japan overcome some of its economic and demographic limitations, but fundamentally would preclude
its turning into an inward-looking nation. Abe saw in TPP a platform to
coordinate with countries that share its values of democracy, rule of law,
and human rights and to work together to enhance peace and stability
in the region.[3]

The TPP promised immediate geopolitical dividends by anchoring the United States to the regional economic architecture at a critical moment of shifting power with the rise of China. A multifaceted U.S. role in the region beyond its traditional role of security guarantor, the ability to shape the rules of the road in the Asia-Pacific, and a reconceptualization of the U.S.-Japan alliance as a force multiplier in the geoeconomic sphere appeared within reach. The United States, however, left these gains on the table when President Donald Trump withdrew from the signed agreement in January 2017.

The TPP looked hopelessly wounded. However, after some initial hesitation, Prime Minister Abe decided to put the full weight of Japan as the largest remaining economy behind the trade pact to rescue it. There were powerful incentives for Japan and other TPP members to ensure that the agreement would live to see another day. For one, the TPP's economic rulebook and the liberalization of trade and investment flows would facilitate the operation of global supply chains, which is essential to the region's economic growth. Tokyo was keen to fill the void created by U.S. retrenchment so as not to cede to China the initiative on the regional integration push. Keeping the TPP project alive left open the possibility of an eventual American return (even though U.S. officials have given no encouraging signs), but it also showcased the willingness and ability of the parties to move forward without the United States.

The pragmatism of the remaining eleven TPP members was critical to the rescue effort. Three decisions in particular paved the road to success. First, there was a clear recognition that renegotiating market access commitments would prove too unwieldy, so the TPP-11 countries agreed to maintain ambitious schedules for tariff liberalization. Second, the vast majority of TPP rules were left intact, with a targeted suspension of twenty-two disciplines (mostly on the intellectual property chapter) and a narrowing down of the operation of the investor-state dispute mechanism. And third, the entry-into-force provisions were relaxed, requiring only ratification by six members. The end result was a renamed Comprehensive and Progressive TPP (CPTPP) agreement that retained the high level of ambition of the original agreement but with a pragmatic nod to the sensitivities of the remaining parties and an easier road for acting on the agreement.

The CPTPP was the prelude to a burst of middle-power diplomacy seeking to shore up rules-based trade and provide insurance against growing protectionism from the great powers. Such was the spirit that brought to fruition Japan's second mega trade agreement, cinched with the European Union at the end of 2017. Japanese and European leaders highlighted the broader strategic meaning of the trade pact and their desire to operate as standard-bearers for free trade in an increasingly challenging international environment. A subsequent agreement on data flows introduced the adequacy rule facilitating the free movement of data among the parties, and Japan and the EU further cemented their relationship with a strategic partnership agreement.[4]

A few years later in November 2020, in the aftermath of the U.S.-China trade war and in the throes of the COVID-19 pandemic, fifteen nations signed the largest preferential trade agreement in the world. The Regional Comprehensive Economic Partnership (RCEP) includes all ten Association of Southeast Asian Nations (ASEAN) countries, China, Japan, South Korea, Australia, and New Zealand to comprise 30 percent of global GDP and trade flows, and it entered into force in January 2022. India's decision to withdraw in the last stages of negotiations was a blow to RCEP members, but the shock was felt most acutely by Japan. Tokyo had long championed the inclusion of democracies like India to serve as a counterweight to China's influence, and as part of the effort to build a deeper Japan-India strategic partnership.

RCEP is an important pillar of the emerging regional economic architecture. While it is not as comprehensive as CPTPP, the liberalization outcomes are significant: a 91 percent tariff elimination to be achieved in the next 20 years and commitments on investment, services, and digital trade. A key trait of RCEP is the flexible rules of origin, mandating, for example, only 40 percent of regional content to qualify for the duty preferences. With RCEP, member economies are doubling down on regional production networks at a time when pressure for the onshoring of manufacturing is growing.

A hallmark of negotiation success is when all parties can claim significant gains from the bargain struck. RCEP passes muster here. For Southeast Asia, there is much to like in RCEP: its endorsement of ASEAN centrality, the flexibilities in implementation to reflect gaps in development, and the creation of a secretariat to advance liberalization efforts in the future. For the three Northeast Asian economies, RCEP introduces, for the first time, preferential trading among them. Peter Petri and Michael Plummer estimate that the largest gains from trade in RCEP will accrue to these three nations, with annual income gains in 2030 of $85 billion for China, $48 billion for Japan, and $23 billion for

South Korea.[5] Though China did not lead the RCEP talks, it was still able to derive some handsome benefits. Its membership in the largest global trade deal to date makes the narrative of decoupling appear less credible. Moreover, China did not have to sacrifice any of the levers of its industrial policy since RCEP does not contain disciplines on subsidies and state-owned enterprises. Even China's much-vaunted acceptance of commitments on free data flows in RCEP can be easily subverted given that there is a broad self-judging national security exemption attached.

CPTPP and RCEP are important drivers of regional connectivity. Despite their differences, the two mega trade agreements share a commitment to grow their membership and to update their rulebooks.[6] Another commonality is the absence of the United States from both deals. The risk of American marginalization from the regional economic architecture is high, since both Republican (Trump) and Democratic (Biden) administrations have refused to use trade liberalization as a driver of economic engagement with Asia.[7] Ruling out a return to CPTPP, President Joe Biden launched during his visit to Tokyo in May 2022 the Indo-Pacific Economic Framework (IPEF). The IPEF is not a traditional trade agreement since it will not award market access preferences through tariff cuts, nor will it be subjected to ratification by the U.S. Congress. Instead, the framework is composed of four pillars: 1) resilient trade (labor, environment, and digital economy standards), 2) green infrastructure, 3) supply chain resilience, and 4) tax administration and anti-corruption initiatives. Thirteen countries agreed to join the U.S.-led framework, and all but India agreed to participate in all four pillars. Whether this negotiation can yield substantial outcomes in the absence of market access benefits and enforceable provisions is still unclear. Negotiated by the Biden administration as an executive agreement, the IPEF's ability to survive the vagaries of American domestic politics is also a concern. Prime Minister Kishida Fumio welcomed IPEF as an important sign of U.S. engagement with the region, but continued to urge an eventual American return to the CPTPP, the most robust economic grouping.[8]

China agrees on the value of the CPTPP. In fall 2021, Beijing formally requested accession. Taiwan emulated this move a week later with its own bid. The politics of CPTPP enlargement have become very complex in light of these developments. While the Japanese government welcomed Taiwan's application, it struck a more cautious tone with China out of a concern that Beijing may seek to water down the disciplines of the agreement. Regardless, neither application is bound to advance quickly. Generating support for Taiwan's accession among current CPTPP members will be difficult—not because of Taiwan's ability to meet the trade agreement standards, but due to concern over damaging relations with China. Some CPTPP members like Malaysia and Singapore have been enthusiastic about China's application, but others, including Japan, Australia, and Mexico, have been more subdued, emphasizing that prospective applicants must abide by the high-level CPTPP standards and respect rules-based trade.[9] In the meantime, the United Kingdom is poised to become the next CPTPP member as it continues to make progress in its accession negotiations.

DOUBLING DOWN ON INFRASTRUCTURE INVESTMENT

Supplying capital to close the infrastructure finance gap in Asia and other parts of the developing world is an essential pillar of economic connectivity. The Asian Development Bank (ADB) has estimated the region's infrastructure investment deficit to be as high as $459 billion per year.[10] The Asian powers, China and Japan, have stepped up to cover part of this gap, aiming to further unlock the region's economic potential and to advance their foreign policy interests along the way. China's forays into development finance have been conditioned by its own experience as a recipient of economic aid, much of which originated from Japan. Hence, as Katada and Liao point out, some key planks of Chinese economic assistance mirror long-standing Japanese practices: a focus on infrastructure projects (over social programs), a preference for loans (over grants), and a request-based system where recipient governments put forward project proposals (frequently at the recommendation of contractors from the donor nation).[11]

A key commonality is that both China and Japan have made economic connectivity central to their bid for regional and global leadership and have invested heavily based on their respective visions for Asia. Nevertheless, there are also significant differences in the blueprint of economic integration each Asian power is advancing, the transparency of their economic assistance programs, and the terms attached to their infrastructure finance. Importantly, infrastructure finance in Asia remains a two-horse race, as Western powers have raised concerns about China dominating the field but have not supplied enough funding to become a major player.

The crown jewel of China's economic engagement diplomacy is the Belt and Road Initiative (BRI). The concept was first floated by President Xi Jinping in two speeches in 2013 and was later incorporated into the Constitution of the Communist Party of China. A vastly ambitious undertaking promising to mobilize $1 trillion to build the hard and soft infrastructure of vast inland and maritime corridors across Eurasia and Africa, BRI seeks to promote Chinese national interests in a variety of ways, from helping China secure supplies of strategic commodities, gain access to foreign markets, and expand its economic and political influence among recipient countries, to stimulating domestic economic growth and the development of hinterland Chinese provinces. China's leaders have conceptualized BRI as both a driver and testament of the country's ascent.[12]

China has pursued development finance on a variety of tracks. Multilaterally, China launched in 2013 the Asian Infrastructure Investment Bank (AIIB), the newest addition to the constellation of multilateral development banks. The AIIB offered to address a major bottleneck to regional growth by closing the financing gap in infrastructure, and it was predicated on a different governance model to cut red tape and facilitate faster decision-making. Currently capitalized at $100 billion with 105 members, the AIIB has proceeded cautiously, with a large share of its financing done in tandem with other multilateral development banks such as the World Bank and the ADB. As of December 2021, 54 percent of AIIB projects were co-financed.[13]

It is the bilateral track of Chinese policy banks financing with little transparency huge infrastructure projects at near commercial rates that has generated the most concern about the motives and geopolitical consequences of the BRI. As a bilateral donor, China can more easily channel development finance to advance narrow foreign policy interests, acquire stakes in critical infrastructure (e.g., Hambantota International Port in Sri Lanka), and/or increase its leverage by making recipients of Chinese capital dependent. While the concerns over "debt-trap diplomacy" seem overblown, Chinese lending practices are a matter of concern. Looking at the share of debt commitments over national income among Southeast Asian recipients of BRI financing before the COVID-19 pandemic erupted in early 2020, David Dollar concluded that only Laos was at risk of default.[14] A broader look at countries borrowing from China shows they have diversified their sources of finance.[15] Still, some unique traits in Chinese lending continue to create concerns. A study of one hundred contracts by Chinese state-owned enterprises with developing countries underscored three problematic areas: stiff confidentiality clauses, commitments to keep debt out of collective restructuring efforts, and undue policy influence by including clauses for immediate repayment in case of significant legal or policy changes.[16]

China has not joined multilateral forums such as the Development Assistance Committee (DAC) or the Paris Club of creditor nations. Hence, there is little transparency regarding its practices and weak peer pressure to improve the quality of its aid or to partake in collective debt relief efforts. These concerns became more acute as the COVID-19 crisis put pressure on developing countries to service their extant debts. China joined the debt service moratorium for poor countries initiative of 2020, but its willingness to participate in broader debt relief efforts is being tested. Beijing was reluctant to roll over BRI loans prior to the Sri Lankan default in May 2022;[17] but this position may begin to change as the debt problem grows. A positive sign was China's agreement to participate in a debt relief package for Zambia just a few months later.[18]

Japan is *the* peer competitor to China in the field of infrastructure finance. Japan's lead among Western nations in infrastructure finance was not blunted by the slashing of official development assistance (ODA) budgets in lean times or by Tokyo's attempts during the 1990s to converge with mainstream donor philosophy by deemphasizing investments in physical infrastructure in favor of social programs and poverty reduction efforts. Figure 8.1 shows that the lion's share of DAC nation's economic assistance provided for infrastructure in the past forty years originated from one source. Japan's share of total DAC commitments, at 42.7 percent, is larger than the combined share of the next four top donors: Germany, the United States, France, and the United Kingdom. In fact, the desire to revive the domestic economy and the keen awareness of growing competition from China motivated the then newly installed Abe administration to embrace infrastructure exports as a key tenet of its economic revitalization programs.[19] In March 2013, the Abe government established the Ministerial Meeting on Strategy relating Infrastructure Export and Economic Cooperation, which set a target for Japanese companies to triple their infrastructure exports to 30 trillion yen by 2020.[20]

This move represented, as Sasada Hironori puts it, the comeback of the "Japan model," defined by the return to a focus on infrastructure finance predicated on close business-government coordination.[21] But

Figure 8.1. Japan leads the West in infrastructure finance

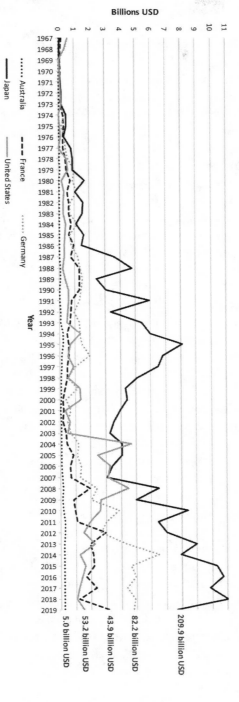

Note: Amounts to the right of the graph represent the cumulative total of ODA commitments in economic infrastructure per donor country for 1967–2019.

Source: OECD, Query Wizard for International Development Statistics (QWIDS), https://stats.oecd.org/qwids.

Japan was not returning to its mercantilist past by enlisting state support for narrow commercial gain, as Katada Saori has persuasively argued.[22] Rather, the infrastructure push was an important manifestation of the advent of a more strategically oriented Japan during the Abe era. In providing the hard infrastructure for the region's development, Japan was pursuing larger national interests: preventing China from dominating the regional order and directing it instead toward Japan's own vision of a Free and Open Indo-Pacific. The strategic articulation of development assistance was evident in the 2015 revision of the ODA Charter, which more explicitly connected aid to Japan's national interests. China's diplomatic coup with the launch of the AIIB and BRI and Japan's loss of a high-speed rail bid in Indonesia to China (deemed a harbinger of things to come) spurred Japanese policymakers to further action.

For the first time, the Japanese government launched its own brand of development finance, the Partnership for Quality Infrastructure, destined to be a crucial component of its broader Indo-Pacific strategy. In 2015, Prime Minister Abe announced the launch of a $110 billion fund, later increased to $200 billion. The Abe administration also enunciated the set of quality standards that would guide Japanese infrastructure finance, drawing an implicit but obvious contrast to China: transparency of procurement, debt sustainability, complementarity with development strategy, and efficiency throughout the project's life cycle. Having found its voice in rulemaking, Tokyo launched a campaign to disseminate the quality infrastructure standards across major international forums such as the G7, G20, Asia-Pacific Economic Cooperation (APEC), and the Organization for Economic Cooperation and Development (OECD). In this manner, quality infrastructure became Japan's calling card and an accepted international norm.

Southeast Asia has been regarded as the epicenter of U.S.-China strategic competition, but the infrastructure investment contest in this region is truly between China and Japan. In the estimates of Roland Rajah, Chinese commitments to the region's infrastructure between 2008 and 2016 amounted to $42.3 billion, while Japan's funding was close to $37 billion. Far behind were Australia ($1.8 billion) and the United States ($1.1 billion).[23] When it comes to private investment flows, Japan has a hefty lead over China in Southeast Asia. ASEAN statistics show that annual investment flows from Japan in the 2010–2018 period averaged $138 billion compared to China's $71.7 billion.[24]

There are several corollaries to the growing importance of infrastructure finance as an engine of growth and arena for competitive statecraft. First, the ability of the United States and like-minded partners to make an effective and coordinated push on infrastructure finance has been limited. In 2018, the United States, Japan, and Australia launched a trilateral infrastructure partnership, but to date they have only financed one project, an undersea cable in Palau. Their Blue Dot Network initiative to promote private sector participation in high-quality infrastructure financing through project certification has struggled to gain traction. To better respond to BRI, the United States established a $60 billion Development Finance Corporation in 2019, although in its first years of operation the brunt of financing has been allocated to finance and insurance, not infrastructure.[25] The G7 global infrastructure initiative seeking to raise $600 billion in five years faces the two main challenges of effective coordination among disparate development finance institutions and the mobilization of the private sector.[26] Neither problem has proven easy to tackle in the past.

Second, neither Japan nor China have been interested in defining their regional integration policies as zero-sum competition. In fact, infrastructure finance diplomacy was part of an attempt to stabilize Sino-Japanese relations after a period of major strain. When Prime Minister Abe visited China in 2018, fifty memoranda of understanding were signed as part of an initiative to promote business cooperation on infrastructure projects in third countries. The projects remained mostly on paper, but the larger message this sends to the region—that no binary choices are presented to the recipients of economic assistance—increases the attractiveness of their development finance programs.

Third, the ascent of Japan and China as top infrastructure financiers has not been linear: they both have had to contend with important challenges and setbacks. Onerous lending terms in Chinese BRI projects and distrust over China's underlying intentions has generated pushback and on occasion renegotiation of terms (e.g., for Malaysia's East Coast Railway Link).[27] With the COVID-19 crisis, China faces a major test in stepping up as a responsible creditor and effectively coordinating an international response to an intensifying debt crisis. Japan has finite budgetary resources and has had to innovate by reforming its credit disbursing agencies to tolerate greater risk in its financing to keep up with China and avoid becoming a legacy power. Its new push on infrastructure exports was predicated on greater coordination with the private sector (through public-private partnerships), but it has been slow to materialize.[28]

THE NEW FRONTIER: DATA GOVERNANCE

Digitization has emerged as a central driver of economic competitiveness, transforming sources of innovation and productivity, reshaping social interactions, and flattening borders with greater ease of communication. The growth of the digital economy and digital trade enabled by new technologies such as artificial intelligence (AI), the Internet of Things (IOT), and cloud computing has been staggering. According to the United States International Trade Commission (USITC), with half the world online, global e-commerce grew to $27.7 trillion in 2016, with China and the United States as the largest e-commerce markets.[29] At the center of the digital economy is the generation of data at unprecedented levels and unfathomable speeds. For instance, it is expected that the amount of data produced globally will grow from 12 zettabytes[30] in 2015 to 160 zettabytes in 2025.[31] Reconciling the efficient use of data, including its overseas transfer, with privacy protections and national security controls has emerged as a central concern for policymakers.

While digitization has advanced in great and uneven strides across the world, international digital governance has lagged behind. The establishment of the WTO preceded the internet era and comprehensive rules on digital trade at the multilateral level have yet to be adopted. Until recently, the most notable efforts of the WTO on digital trade revolved around a recurrent moratorium on customs duties on online transmissions. International digital rulemaking faces the daunting challenge of seeking common ground among disparate domestic data governance regimes that reflect profound philosophical differences and regulatory traditions. While the United States does not have federal privacy laws and advocates freedom of cross-border data flows with precautionary safeguards proportionate to risk, the European Union has enshrined the protection of personal information as a fundamental human right. With the 2018 adoption of the General Data Protection Regulation (GDPR), the EU now restricts the transfer abroad of personal data only to locations that award similar levels of protection. Japan's Act on the Protection of Personal Information establishes obligations for firms to disclose to consumers their methods of data collection and to ensure that personal information is protected from theft or unauthorized disclosure.[32] China, on the other hand, embodies a security-first approach to data governance, giving the state broad discretion in accessing personal information from telecommunications firms and internet providers for the sake of internal political stability and cybersecurity.[33]

There is growing concern about the balkanization of the international digital regime due to its disparate rules and standards and the spread of digital protectionism with restrictive measures on data transfers. While WTO-wide digital rules are absent, there has been a marked proliferation of free trade agreements containing e-commerce disciplines. According to some estimates, of the 348 FTAs negotiated between 2000 and 2020, more than half had some sort of e-commerce provisions. And yet, only a fraction (twelve agreements) included binding provisions on data governance and freedom of information flows.[34] Two related risks follow: The first is that divergent disciplines and lack of interoperability among digital regimes may become sizable barriers to the further development of the digital economy. And second, while deep commitments on digital governance are still rare, digital restrictive measures are expanding rapidly. The USITC notes that worldwide data localization requirements doubled between 2010 and 2016.[35] The European Centre for International Political Economy (ECIPE) created a digital restrictiveness index that shows that while China practices digital protectionism the most, it is not alone. Russia, India, Indonesia, and Vietnam also significantly restrict digital trade.[36]

China's digital protectionism is far-reaching and includes a variety of measures such as walling off internet access, pervasive data localization requirements, obligations for foreign companies to surrender source code and encryption keys as a condition for market entry, investment and licensing restrictions, and the use of subsidies and tax benefits to nurture its own technology firms. As Ferracane and Lee-Makiyama point out, China's decision to shield its technological ecosystem is motivated by a complex mix of objectives, including commercial gain, domestic political stability, and the protection of core national interests by creating a "secure and controllable" digital ecosystem. Hence, market access negotiations stand to make limited progress in convincing Chinese leadership to dismantle digital restrictions geared to serve its core political and strategic goals.[37]

China's digital prowess has raised concerns not only because of the inaccessibility of its domestic market and its growing authoritarian tilt at home, but also because China is using digital connectivity to expand its international influence in ways that create concerns about an illiberal digital regime taking hold in Asia and elsewhere.[38] The export of surveillance technology to authoritarian governments is one area of concern, but it is only one part of a broader push centered around the Digital Silk Road, which launched in 2015 and now covers memoranda of understanding with sixteen countries. China is financing the physical infrastructure of digital connectivity (such as undersea fiber-optic cables that channel most of the world's internet traffic), promoting ICT networks powered by its 5G technology to connect smart cities, shaping international technology standards, and helping generate and capture vast amounts of data through the large presence of Chinese firms in online marketing, apps, and cashless payment systems.[39]

The United States and Japan have adopted a more market-oriented approach to the digital economy, seeking to maximize the efficiency gains of free data flows across national borders, tempered by precautionary standards to protect consumers and sensitive personal data as well as manage cyber risks. Washington has long sought to add e-commerce provisions to its trade agreements, but it gave up on the one regional trade agreement (TPP) with far-reaching disciplines on digital connectivity trade.[40] While the United States has adopted—and strengthened—the digital governance disciplines of the original TPP into subsequent trade negotiations, these efforts engage a limited number of partners—including Canada and Mexico in the United States-Mexico-Canada Agreement and Japan with a bilateral executive agreement—stalling the wider dissemination of U.S.-preferred digital standards.

Japan's digital diplomacy has included the negotiation of binding trade agreements, promotion of interoperability of data governance regimes, and a push for the WTO to adopt more comprehensive digital trade rules. The CPTPP is a landmark agreement for digital rulemaking. It bans the localization of data (with exceptions for financial data) and embraces the principle of free data flows with limited exemptions to achieve legitimate public policy objectives. The agreement disallows the transfer of source code as a condition for market entry, customs duties on electronic transmissions, and discrimination against digital products.[41] Japan has advocated for interoperable data governance regimes built on trust. Prime Minister Abe launched the "Data Free Flow with Trust" (DFFT) initiative at the 2019 World Economic Forum meeting in Davos, and Tokyo has pushed for its adoption in forums like the OECD, G7, and G20. Twenty-four countries signed on to the Osaka Declaration on Digital Economy, ushering in the Osaka Track on data governance under the WTO umbrella. Japan is also a co-convener of the WTO's e-commerce plurilateral negotiations, which launched in 2019 with seventy-six nations.

Nevertheless, Japan's "trust" brand for data governance faces significant challenges. Four nations (Egypt, India, Indonesia, and South Africa) refrained from supporting the Osaka Track to digital governance.[42] And finding common ground in the WTO's e-commerce negotiations is no easy task. China's position in the plurilateral talks does not anticipate commitments on data localization and cross-border data flows. And while the European Union has been prepared to adopt clauses on freedom of data flows and a ban on forced transfer of source code, it insists on adequacy principles for data protection.[43] In the Asia-Pacific, the United States and Japan have yet to regain lost ground in working together on a regional digital agreement. While China has requested accession to the Digital Economic Partnership Agreement (launched by New Zealand, Singapore, and Chile in 2020), the United States and Japan have not. Instead, the United States has offered IPEF to realize this ambition, but it is unclear that far-ranging digital commitments from developing country participants will be forthcoming in the absence of market access preferences.

Japan's connectivity agenda is at a crossroads. Trust is becoming an increasingly scarce commodity in a world of deepening geopolitical divides, where actors increasingly hedge against the risks of economic interdependence.

NOTES

1. Howard Schneider, "Japan's Possible Entry to Trade Talks Sparks Opposition in Congress," *The Washington Post*, March 15, 2013, www.washingtonpost .com/business/economy/japans-possible-entry-to-trade-talks-sparks-opposition -in-congress/2013/03/14/831582bc-8ce4-11e2-b63f-f53fb9f2fcb4_story.html.

2. Mireya Solís, *Dilemmas of a Trading Nation: Japan and the United States in the Evolving Asia-Pacific Order* (Washington, DC: Brookings Institution Press, 2017).

3. Cabinet Public Affairs Office, "Press Conference by Prime Minister Abe," March 15, 2013, https://japan.kantei.go.jp/96_abe/statement/201303/15kaiken _e.html.

4. Andrei Lungu, "Japan and Europe's Triple Partnership: Parsing the new EU-Japan Strategic, Economic and Digital Agreements," *The Diplomat*, Feb-

ruary 14, 2019, https://thediplomat.com/2019/02/japan-and-europes-triple -partnership/; and Mireya Solís and Shujiro Urata, "Abenomics and Japan's Trade Policy in a New Era," *Asian Economic Policy Review* 13, no. 1 (January 4, 2018): 117.

5. Peter Petri and Michael Plummer, "East Asia Decouples From the United States: Trade War, COVID-19, and East Asia's New Trade Blocs," Peterson Institute of International Economics, Washington, DC, June 2020, www.piie .com/system/files/documents/wp20-9.pdf.

6. On RCEP's potential for future rulemaking, see Deborah Elms, "Getting RCEP across the Line," *World Trade Review* 20, no. 3 (July 2021): 1–8.

7. Mireya Solís, "Heyday of Asian Regionalism? Implications of the Regional Economic Comprehensive Economic Partnership for the United States," ERIA Discussion Paper, no. 435, Economic Research Institute for ASEAN and East Asia, August 2022, www.eria.org/publications/heyday-of-asian-regionalism -the-implications-of-the-regional-comprehensive-economic-partnership-for-the -united-states/.

8. Ibid.

9. Masaya Kato and Kosuke Takeuchi, "With an Eye on China, Japan Refuses to Ease TPP Rules for New Members," *Nikkei Asia*, December 18, 2020, https://asia.nikkei.com/Economy/Trade/With-eye-on-China-Japan-refuses-to -ease-TPP-rules-for-new-members.

10. Asian Development Bank (ADB), "Meeting Asia's Infrastructure Investment Needs," Mandaluyong City, Philippines, 2017, www.adb.org/sites/default /files/publication/227496/special-report-infrastructure.pdf.

11. Saori Katada and Jessica Liao, "China and Japan in Pursuit of Infrastructure Investment Leadership in Asia: Competition or Convergence?" *Global Governance* 26 (2020): 449–72.

12. Nadège Rolland, "A Concise Guide to the Belt and Road Initiative," National Bureau of Asian Research, April 11, 2019, www.nbr.org/publication/a -guide-to-the-belt-and-road-initiative/.

13. See Martin A. Weiss, "Asian Infrastructure Investment Bank," Congressional Research Service (CRS), March 17, 2022, https://crsreports.congress.gov /product/pdf/IF/IF10154.

14. David Dollar, "Seven Years into China's Belt and Road," Order from Chaos, The Brookings Institution, Washington, DC, October 1, 2020, www .brookings.edu/blog/order-from-chaos/2020/10/01/seven-years-into-chinas -belt-and-road/.

15. David Dollar, "China and the West Competing over Infrastructure in Southeast Asia," The Brookings Institution, Washington, DC, April 2020, www .brookings.edu/research/china-and-the-west-competing-over-infrastructure-in -southeast-asia/.

16. Anna Gelper et al., "How China Lends: A Rare Look at 100 Contracts with Foreign Governments," Policy report, Peterson Institute for International Economics; Kiel Institute for the World Economy, Center for Global Devel-

opment; and AidData at William & Mary, March 2021, www.aiddata.org/publications/how-china-lends.

17. See Mohamed Zeeshan, "Sri Lanka's Meltdown Puts China's Strategic Influence in Jeopardy," *The Diplomat*, May 18, 2022, https://thediplomat.com/2022/05/sri-lankas-meltdown-puts-chinas-strategic-influence-in-jeopardy/.

18. See Editorial Board, "China's Shift on Debt Relief," *The Christian Science Monitor*, August 1, 2022, www.csmonitor.com/Commentary/the-monitors-view/2022/0801/China-s-shift-on-debt-relief.

19. Saori Katada, *Japan's New Regional Reality: Geoeconomic Strategy in the Asia-Pacific* (New York: Columbia University Press, 2020),182.

20. Shiro Armstrong, "Economic Diplomacy and Economic Security under Abe," *Asian Economic Policy Review* 16, no. 2 (July 2021): 283–99.

21. Hironori Sasada, "Resurgence of the 'Japan Model'? Japan's Aid Policy Reform and Infrastructure Development Assistance," *Asian Survey* 59, no. 6, (2019): 1044–69.

22. Saori Katada, *Japan's New Regional Reality*.

23. Roland Rajah, "Mobilizing the Indo-Pacific Infrastructure Response to China's Belt and Road Initiative in Southeast Asia," The Brookings Institution, Washington, DC, 2020, www.brookings.edu/research/mobilizing-the-indo-pacific-infrastructure-response-to-chinas-belt-and-road-initiative-in-southeast-asia/.

24. See ASEAN Stats Data Portal, www.aseanstats.org/.

25. See Shayerah I. Akhtar and Nick M. Brown, "U.S. International Development Finance Corporation: Overview and Issues," Report no. R47006, Congressional Research Service, Washington, DC, January 10, 2022, https://crsreports.congress.gov/product/pdf/R/R47006.

26. See "The G7 at Last Presents an Alternative to China's Belt and Road Initiative," *The Economist*, July 7, 2022, www.economist.com/china/2022/07/07/the-g7-at-last-presents-an-alternative-to-chinas-belt-and-road-initiative.

27. See Alifah Zainuddem, "What Happened to China's BRI Projects in Malaysia?" *The Diplomat*, October 5, 2021, https://thediplomat.com/2021/10/what-happened-to-chinas-bri-projects-in-malaysia/.

28. Saori Katada, *Japan's New Regional Reality: Geoeconomic Strategy in the Asia-Pacific* (New York: Columbia University Press, 2020), 173.

29. U.S. International Trade Commission (USITC), "Global Digital Trade 1: Market Opportunities and Key Foreign Trade Restrictions," Publication no. 4716, Investigation no. 332-561, August 2017, www.usitc.gov/publications/332/pub4716.pdf.

30. For the sake of comparison, one zettabyte is equal to one trillion gigabytes.

31. Figures cited in Joshua P. Meltzer, "Governing Digital Trade," World Trade Review 18, Special Issue S1: Digital Trade (2019): 23–54.

32. Simon Abendin and Pingfang Duan, "Global E-Commerce Talks at the WTO: Positions on Selected Issues of the United States, European Union, China, and Japan," *World Trade Review* 20, no. 5 (December 2021): 707–24.

33. Rachel F. Fefer, "Data Flows, Online Privacy, and Trade Policy," Report no. R45584, Congressional Research Service, Washington, DC, March 26, 2020, https://fas.org/sgp/crs/misc/R45584.pdf.

34. Mira Burri, "Towards a New Treaty on Digital Trade," *Journal of World Trade* 55, no. 1 (2021): 77–100.

35. USITC, "Global Digital Trade 1."

36. The index ranks 64 countries across 100 policy measures on market access, investment requirements, data policies, and trading restrictions. China ranked first with a score of 0.70, the United States twenty-second at 0.26, and Japan fiftieth at 0.18. See Martina F. Ferracane, Hosuk Lee-Makiyama, and Erik van der Marel, "Digital Trade Restrictiveness Index," European Center for International Political Economy, Brussels, https://ecipe.org/wp-content/uploads/2018/05/DTRI_FINAL.pdf.

37. Martina F. Ferracane and Hosuk Lee-Makiyama, "China's Technology Protectionism and Its Non-Negotiable Rationales," European Centre for International Political Economy, Brussels, June 26, 2017, 12, 15, https://ecipe.org/publications/chinas-technology-protectionism/.

38. Lisa Curtis, Joshua Fitt, and Jacob Stokes, "Advancing a Liberal Digital Order in the Indo-Pacific," Center for New American Security, Washington, DC, May 2021, www.cnas.org/publications/reports/advancing-a-liberal-digital-order-in-the-indo-pacific.

39. Dai Mochinaga, "The Expansion of China's Digital Silk Road and Japan's Response," Asia Policy 15, no. 1 (2020): 41–60.

40. Robert Holleyman, "Data Governance and Trade: The Asia-Pacific Leads the Way," The National Bureau of Asian Research (NBR), January 9, 2021, www.nbr.org/publication/data-governance-and-trade-the-asia-pacific-leads-the-way/.

41. The U.S.-Japan Digital Trade Agreement strengthened these provisions by laying out conditions for the transfer of financial data, banning not only the forced transfer of source code but also of algorithms and encryption keys, limiting the liability for third-party content on internet platforms, and adding commitments on open access to non-sensitive e-government data. See Ibid.

42. Graham Greenleaf, "G20 Makes Declaration of "'Data Free Flow with Trust': Support and Dissent," *Privacy Laws & Business International Report*, 2019, 18–19.

43. Burri, "Towards a New Treaty on Digital Trade."

CHAPTER 9

The Sharp Edge of Japan's Economic Statecraft

A major recalibration of Japanese economic statecraft is underway. The deterioration of Sino-American relations, the growing weaponization of economic interdependence, and production dislocations amid the pandemic have given rise to a new track of economic security. The strategy is both defensive, as an effort to hedge against supply chain risks and diminish economic coercion vulnerabilities, and offensive, with a return of industrial policy to excel in advanced manufacturing and propel high-tech research as avenues for economic prosperity and international influence.

As Japan builds its economic security strategy, it confronts a delicate balancing act. It must create a more resilient technological ecosystem and supply chain network and coordinate with allies and partners to align best practices on economic security measures. But Tokyo should be mindful not to overcorrect its course in ways that compromise openness and innovation, robust international exchange, trade and investment flows, and the efficiency of supply chains central to its own economic competitiveness. As foreign economic transactions are increasingly distilled through the lenses of national security, the contours of deep Japan-China economic ties are being redrawn.

A HARSHER WORLD ECONOMIC ORDER

In fits and starts, economic interdependence among sovereign states operating in an anarchical world deepened over the past few decades.

Anchored in the multilateral trading system built upon the General Agreement on Tariffs and Trade (GATT) and later the World Trade Organization (WTO), obstacles to international trade in the form of tariffs and non-tariff barriers diminished. Governments increasingly entertained "behind the border" obligations in trade and investment agreements and acquiesced to greater levels of legalization—defined by obligation, precision, and delegation.[1] The WTO operated with a significantly strengthened dispute settlement mechanism, setting the international trading system apart from other international regimes for its third-party adjudication of disputes. Economic interdependence also morphed with increasingly complex networks of production and information delivered by global supply chains and the information and communication technology (ICT) revolutions. The favorable outcomes of this growing economic interdependence were tangible as more countries sought integration into the international trading system and the global middle class experienced pronounced growth.

Globalization has been tested before, but a new challenge is upon us: the securitization of international economic relations. Two main forces, state rivalry and technological change, are testing the parameters of economic interdependence. Great power competition between the United States and China has led to a change in priorities—focused less on mutual benefits and more on the implications of relative gains and the minimization of vulnerabilities. The fourth industrial revolution (which includes AI, 5G, cloud and quantum computing, etc.) has raised the competitive stakes because new platform technologies are ever more central to national sources of economic competitiveness and military readiness. Interstate rivalry amid dense global networks has created new tools of state coercion. In addition to the exploitation of bilateral asymmetries, control over economic or information hubs provides new sources of leverage.[2]

Self-reliance has grown in appeal, but it should not be understood as a simple penchant for autarky, which after all diminishes national power. Rather, some of the major players in the international system are aiming to strengthen their domestic capabilities and lead in the technological frontier while encouraging economic dependence from others.

The securitization of economic interdependence is fraught with challenges. States are adopting defensive measures to mitigate the risks of economic interdependence, but these measures are prone to self-fulfilling prophecies: a state's invocation of national security to restrict cross-border economic activities can be motivated by protectionist intent, can overshoot and hurt domestic competitiveness and innovation, and can invite foreign retaliation.[3] The rise of economic security will have major consequences for international economic governance. States have long asserted their right to invoke national security exemptions to trade and investment commitments. That is the essence of Article XXI of the WTO, which reads: "nothing in the treaty shall be construed to prevent a state from taking any action which it considers necessary for the protection of its essential security interests."[4] In the past, governments treaded carefully in invoking a national security exemption, mindful that their actions could open the floodgates to protectionism. That restraint is clearly ebbing as more disputes emerge in the WTO regarding such invocations.

As states carve out more areas of economic activity subject to security controls and/or they weaken the application of judicial review by asserting essential security interests, mercantilism and de-legalization may ensue.[5] A less than judicious management of economic security risks could weaken the rules-based order.

SKEPTICS OF INTERDEPENDENCE: CHINA AND THE UNITED STATES

In both the United States and China, a palpable rethinking of the acceptable parameters of integration into the global economy is underway. Though a single factor is not responsible for this repositioning, the onset of U.S.-China strategic competition over advanced technologies is a main driver. A more skeptical view of globalization from the two largest economies in the world has systemwide implications.

China: Globalization à la Carte

China's integration into the international economic system reshaped the country and transformed the world. China embraced its role as the principal assembly hub in "Factory Asia," receiving large inflows of foreign direct investment (FDI) and developing broad trade links to propel its economic takeoff. This was, however, a carefully managed approach to globalization. The Chinese Communist Party (CCP) kept critical sectors like telecommunications off-limits, mandated joint ventures to secure know-how, practiced industrial policy with generous subsidies, and decoupled digitally from the West under the principle of internet sovereignty. The era of President Xi Jinping witnessed a recommitment to the staunch application of state levers of economic intervention, but with a loftier goal: cultivating domestic prowess in leading technologies. Such was the spirit of the 2013 policy document "Made in China 2025," setting targets for greater self-reliance in the new commanding heights of the economy.

Even before the era of great power competition officially began through the Trump administration's 2017 National Security Strategy, China's views of interdependence had hardened. Julian Gerwitz describes this shift as Xi's embrace of a "big security concept" integrating national security and interdependence.[6] Desirable objectives under this new viewpoint were not just to minimize vulnerabilities from interdependence through indigenization but to continue to cultivate others' economic dependence on China as a tool of influence and potential instrument of state coercion. The sharp deterioration in U.S.-China relations reified this policy orientation.

Trade tensions between the United States and China had long simmered, but they came to a boil in June 2018 when the United States imposed punitive tariffs on $50 billion of Chinese products following a Section 301 investigation on China's unfair intellectual property (IP) and technology practices. A fast-and-furious pace of retaliation and counterretaliation ensued. In a few months, most of bilateral trade was subject to punitive duties. The U.S. tariffs covered $360 billion of Chinese products, and China's tariffs reached $110 billion of American goods. A truce was called in early 2020 with a phase-one trade deal that prevented further escalation but left untouched the sources of grievance. China agreed to purchase $200 billion of American products, but it has not met these targets.[7] The phase-one deal skipped Chinese structural reform with no commitments on subsidies, state-owned enterprises (SOE), or comprehensive IP protection. And the bulk of the tariffs from both sides remain in place. The tariff war was painful, but it has been the exploitation of tech vulnerabilities that has hurt China the most (addressed later in this chapter). Tighter U.S. export controls on China's telecom champion Huawei exposed a major weakness for China: its inability to produce the most advanced semiconductors.

China's 2020 "dual circulation" strategy represents a doubling down on a hard-edged approach to interdependence in the face of a more challenging external environment. It implies both greater emphasis on domestic production, distribution, and consumption and an active diplomatic push to blunt the narrative of decoupling or Chinese isolation. Regarding the latter, China reaped important successes with the conclusion of the largest trade agreement in the world, the Regional Comprehensive Economic Partnership (RCEP), as well as with the Comprehensive Agreement on Investment (CAI) with the EU.[8] Regarding the former, the CCP is dedicating a vast amount of resources to advance its capabilities in the critical field of semiconductors. It boosted spending on its "Big Fund" for developing the domestic integrated circuit (IC) industry and has allocated $1.4 trillion to high-tech development.[9] In response to the American tech curbs, China has produced its own list of unreliable suppliers and adopted an export control law at the end of 2020 that will facilitate retaliatory measures to tech restrictions. China's coercive economic diplomacy—restricting trade as a tool to apply pressure—has also been on full display during the COVID-19 pandemic, with Australia, Lithuania, and Taiwan, among others, as recent targets.

United States: Playing Defense on Globalization

The United States has also experienced a significant recalibration of its approach to economic interdependence. The reorientation has been spurred by growing frustration with the policy of engagement with China and the intensification of the great power rivalry. Concern about overdependence on China for the operation of critical supply chains has intensified greatly as a potential U.S.-China security crisis looms larger on the horizon. The shift, however, is not circumscribed to changing the terms of interaction with China; it is a much broader expansion of national security concerns in the formulation of foreign economic policy.

There is a sharp divide between the central priorities and tactics of Trump's "America First" foreign policy and Biden's pledge that "America Is Back" to multilateralism, democracy support, and alliances. But there is also a crucial area of overlap: the fusion of economics and national security. "Economic security is national security" is a guiding principle of both the Trump administration's 2017 National Security Strategy and the Biden administration's 2021 Interim National Security Strategic Guidance. The concept is certainly flexible and amenable to different interpretations, but in general it attaches greater importance to the protection of the domestic industrial base and the pursuit of technological prowess, pays greater attention to the relative gains from international economic exchange, and uses tariffs and other defensive measures to accomplish these goals.

The China challenge does loom large in the American rethinking of economic interdependence. Skepticism that the WTO system is sufficiently equipped to rein in Chinese state capitalism is running high in Washington. Mark Wu identifies several such limitations: gaps in WTO rules (on subsidies, investment, tech transfer, etc.), the advantages of self-declaration as a developing country, the lax compliance with (subsidy) notification requirements, and the insufficiency of compensation for Chinese transgressions.[10] Both the Trump and Biden administrations have concluded that a WTO-centric approach is ineffective in curbing Chinese mercantilism, but neither has offered a fix to break the stalemate of the WTO's Appellate Body. The hefty tariffs on China that the Biden team inherited from the previous administration have stayed in place, even though they have not achieved any of their stated objectives. The Biden administration is torn between scrapping some of them to fight inflation or keeping them intact to avoid charges of being soft on China in a politically charged environment.[11]

In order to repair relations with allies and partners and facilitate coordination in tackling Chinese state capitalism, the Biden administration finally eliminated the 232 "national security" steel and aluminum tariffs[12] the previous administration had imposed on the EU and Japan, among other nations. However, this was not a return to free trade in metals among trusted parties, since the tariffs were replaced with tariff rate quotas. Still, the Biden administration is engaged on several fronts to coordinate with like-minded countries on economic security measures. This includes the Trans-Atlantic Trade and Technology Council, the emerging technologies working group of the Quad, and, with Japan specifically, the Competitiveness and Resilience (CoRe) Partnership and a new economic 2+2 dialogue.[13]

Tighter U.S. national security controls on international economic policy have manifested in the screening of FDI and export controls and the use of sanctions. The 2018 Foreign Investment Risk Review Modernization Act (FIRRMA) brought important changes to the national security review of foreign acquisitions of American companies. The Committee on Foreign Investment in the United States (CFIUS, in operation since 1975) has expanded its authority to review noncontrolling investments in sectors involving critical technologies, critical infrastructure, and personal data. The new legislation created an incentive for other countries to tighten their national security reviews so that investors from "excepted states" can receive preferred status.[14] The United Kingdom, Canada, and Australia currently qualify for this status. The 2018 Export Control Reform Act foreshadowed a sweeping expansion to cover emerging and foundational technologies in licensing requirements for dual-use products. The business community (both domestic and foreign firms) expressed concern that this overly expansive definition of covered sectors would hamper their research and production activities and hinder their competitiveness. These companies pushed for a more focused approach on military applications of genuinely emerging technologies and for coordinated international standards that would enable efficient cross-border operations.[15]

The weaponization of economic interdependence has been most evident in the exploitation of chokepoints in the semiconductor supply chain.[16] U.S. policymakers have deemed Huawei a national security threat, barring it from participation in American 5G networks and seeking similar actions from allied and partner nations. In 2019, the Trump administration placed Huawei and other Chinese telecom firms on its Entity List, mandating American companies to obtain a license (with the presumption of denial) for the sale of chips and equipment to Huawei. A year later, the U.S. government closed the loopholes that had enabled Huawei to continue to procure the most advanced semiconductors with tighter regulations on U.S. firms and the application of the Entity List strictures to foreign companies if they rely on American technology and equipment.[17]

The Biden administration's redefinition of the nature of technological competition with China and the central role it has awarded export controls to achieve its ramped-up objectives will have profound consequences that go far beyond U.S.-China relations. National Security Advisor Jake Sullivan has provided a clear articulation of the new thinking around "force multiplier" technologies (computing-related technologies, biotech, and green tech), in which the United States can no longer afford to maintain a "sliding scale approach" or relative advantage. China's use of these technologies to develop high-precision weapons makes absolute superiority a requisite in the U.S. government's estimation.[18] Implementation followed quickly. An October 7, 2022, rule relied on unilateral and extraterritorial export controls to prevent sales of advanced chips to China for AI and supercomputing purposes. In a first, the Department of Commerce imposed controls on U.S. persons to restrict activities that would assist with chip manufacture in China. These developments underscore the willingness of the U.S. government to curb technology flows with commercial applications, citing the pervasive Chinese practice of civil-military fusion, but with the far more expansive objective of stalling Chinese technological development by restricting access to advanced chips, production equipment, and highly skilled human capital. Long-term success will largely hinge on the Biden team's bet that it can successfully persuade its allies to implement their own restrictions on technology flows to China.[19]

Vulnerabilities in the supply chain are a top concern for U.S. policymakers. The Biden administration undertook an exhaustive review of supply chains for semiconductors, large-capacity batteries, pharmaceuticals, and critical minerals to identify vulnerabilities and potential countermeasures. The report touted the benefits of coordinating with like-minded countries to boost resilience ("friend-shoring"), but it also included a hefty dose of unilateral measures with "Buy American" commitments, a "strike force" to clamp down on foreign unfair trading practices, and a Section 232 probe into the use of national security tariffs on neodymium magnets that rely heavily on rare earth metals.[20] After extensive partisan wrangling, Congress finally approved the CHIPS and Science Act in the summer of 2022, earmarking $280 billion to a technology competitiveness agenda. This will include $100 billion for the National Science Foundation and the creation of a new Technology Directorate to spur the development of commercial technologies. To boost chip manufacturing in the United States, the bill allocates $39 billion in investment incentives for cutting-edge fabrication plants and $13.2 billion for R&D and workforce development.[21] Firms accepting this funding will not be able to significantly expand their chip manufacturing operations in countries of concern like China,[22] creating further momentum toward fragmentation of the advanced semiconductor supply chain.

JAPAN'S ECONOMIC SECURITY: BALANCING CONNECTIVITY AND RESILIENCE

Japan is no novice to the risks of economic interdependence. After its economic takeoff under the auspices of the Bretton Woods system to become a major exporting nation, the country felt vulnerable to the fissures and readjustments of the postwar regime during the 1970s. The

Nixon shocks (the end of fixed exchange rates, an import surcharge, and the U.S. rapprochement with China with no allied coordination) rocked Japan's officialdom. The intensification of resource nationalism with two oil shocks and food embargoes drove home the stark dependencies of a resource-scarce country. At the initiative of Prime Minister Ohira Masayoshi, Japan rolled out the concept of comprehensive security in 1980 with a major focus on economic vulnerabilities.[23] The state and private sectors sprang into (sometimes coordinated) action to ameliorate these risks. These were the golden days of resource diplomacy—not just to guarantee the stable and cost-effective supply of raw materials and foodstuffs but also to relocate abroad Japan's energy-intensive industries, which had previously been defeated by the law of comparative advantage. The state committed sizable public resources to "national projects" (e.g., aluminum smelting in Brazil), but there was also a cautionary tale to government FDI financing given that shifts in market conditions could compromise the rentability of mammoth projects.[24]

Economic security, therefore, is in the DNA of Japanese statecraft. Yet, the nature of today's challenges and Japan's own capabilities are markedly different. For one, Japan is more deeply integrated into the world economy, as Japanese companies led the way in the development of regional production networks. Whereas in the past Japan was primarily concerned with the procurement of commodities, it is now preoccupied with the opportunities and risks afforded by dense and complex supply chains operating across borders. Moreover, Japan's current attempts to mitigate the risks of interdependence in a more contested geopolitical environment come on the heels of a robust economic connectivity agenda (through trade agreements, digital rules, and infrastructure finance). Nor is the essential geopolitical gambit the same. Today, Japan's largest security challenge is also its main trading partner: China.

This complex array of challenges prompted the Japanese government to once again elevate economic security policy. Prime Minister Shinzo Abe's administration established an economic division in the National Security Secretariat (NSS) in the spring of 2020 composed of twenty elite bureaucrats.[25] With the goal of "strengthening Japan's economy in this new world order," economic security was enshrined in the Basic Policy for Economic and Financial Management Reform published that year by the Cabinet Office.[26] The novel balancing act was evident in the list of core objectives enunciated. On the one hand, Japan was to become an indispensable strategic country for international society by leading the way in the codification of free and fair rules for the international economic system and contributing to international efforts to address transnational challenges like the pandemic and climate change. On the other hand, the country was to develop an economy and society resilient to risks by diversifying supply chains and expanding the focus from "just-in-time" efficiency to "just-in-case" economic security; protecting critical infrastructure, energy sufficiency, and digital and technological developments; and crafting economic security rules for the financing of commodities among countries with shared values.

The Liberal Democratic Party's (LDP) Strategic Headquarters on the Creation of a New International Order released in 2020 recommendations for Japan's economic security strategy anchored in two notable concepts: "strategic autonomy" (eliminating excessive dependencies) and "strategic indispensability" (increasing the number of industrial sectors where the international community finds reliance on Japan essential). It advocated a far-reaching economic security strategy that would include energy security, financial and telecommunications infrastructures, space cybersecurity, technology and data, economic intelligence, infectious diseases, and rulemaking via international organizations, among other areas.

The shift has not just been rhetorical; it has already resulted in tighter screening of FDI, tightened oversight over critical telecommunications infrastructure, supply chain diversification efforts, and a new economic security bill approved by a wide majority in the Diet in May 2022.

Investment Screening

Keenly aware of major economic vulnerabilities at the onset of the postwar era—chronic balance of payments deficits and foreign exchange shortages—the Japanese government asserted complete control over international capital transactions and mandated case-by-case approval of FDI in the 1949 Foreign Exchange and Foreign Trade Act (FEFTA). These sweeping powers brought about the heyday of Japanese industrial policy since the government concentrated and allocated all foreign exchange and largely kept foreign multinationals at bay to nurture infant domestic industries. These broad regulatory powers were surrendered over time. In 1964, as a condition of entry into the OECD, the government abolished the foreign exchange budget and acquired the obligation to liberalize capital flows over time. Two major subsequent reforms of the FEFTA did so: in 1980, making all foreign exchange transactions free in principle, unless explicitly forbidden; and in 1998, relinquishing the prior notification requirement for foreign investments in favor of post-facto reporting, except for some designated sectors.[27]

Japan's shift to a more liberal approach accepting inward investment eliminated a constant source of friction with other advanced market economies, which had long complained about the lack of investment opportunities for their companies. Today, the forces of convergence are still at work, but the direction has shifted to reregulation for national security purposes. In the past few years, several peer countries (Australia, the United States, France, Germany, and the United Kingdom) have all tightened FDI screening to address national security risks. This created a strong incentive for Japan to follow suit to accomplish the "defensive" and "offensive" objectives of avoiding becoming a soft target for the leakage of critical technologies as others tighten their FDI clearance protocols and ensuring that Japanese companies can benefit from expedited procedures in other countries that share strict security controls.

The latest revision of the FEFTA, which went into effect in 2020, entailed three major changes to the FDI screening process. First, it vastly expanded the number of investments subject to government screening by lowering the threshold of share acquisition from 10 percent to 1 percent. Second, it listed a larger number of designated sectors subject to prior notification. Third, it set up exemptions to prior notification requirements depending on the type of investor and the goal of the transaction (passive or active control). Regarding the former, financial institutions and sovereign wealth funds are exempted, but not SOEs. Regarding the latter, regular investors can qualify for an exemption if they do not intend to exert managerial control (appoint a board member, dispose of a business unit, or have access to sensitive nonpublic information). The Japanese government released a list of 518 companies (40 percent of all publicly listed) that are now subject to the national security screening.[28]

The adoption of a new FDI security policy has received mixed reviews. To some, subjecting such a large number of companies and sectors to FDI screening runs counter to the goal of encouraging more investment into Japan, and the government may not be prepared to undertake a massive increase of cases to review.[29] Others worry that if the screening can be used for industrial policy goals, it will undercut corporate governance reforms by disincentivizing the role of activist investors in improving managerial practices.[30] More positive takes emphasize the need for Japan to be aligned with other peer nations and do not anticipate decreased investment activity, since the focus of the screening is to forestall leakage of sensitive technologies to China.[31] With national security embedded in FDI screening, the United States and Japan can share relevant information, but the reform was not enough to secure Japan "excepted foreign state" status under CFIUS, which currently only Five Eyes partner countries enjoy.[32]

Export Controls

Japan has long participated in international export control regimes regulating access to weaponry and dual-use technologies and goods that could potentially be used to develop weapons of mass destruction. During the Cold War, Japan joined the Coordinating Committee for Multilateral Export Controls (COCOM), which was abolished in 1994. Since then, it has been part of other international agreements like the Wassenaar Arrangement. Ensuring compliance to avoid a fissure between it and allies has always been an important objective. Hence, the friction with the United States over the 1987 sale by an affiliate of Toshiba specializing in machine tools that helped Russia improve its submarines has cast a pall over the history of Japanese export controls. And yet, as Marukawa explains, after China's economic opening, the risk perception over technology leakage was low among Japanese corporations eager to expand business opportunities.[33] Only in the 2010s, when Chinese tech capabilities had advanced and bilateral ties soured over territorial disputes, did corporate sentiment shift in favor of stricter protocols.

The U.S.-China tech rivalry has had ripple effects in Japan. The Japanese government shares concerns over China's theft of IP, leaks of critical technologies, and cyber and information security risks posed by Chinese telecommunications giants. In late 2018, the GOJ for the first time introduced public procurement guidelines banning the use of telecommunications equipment it deemed posed a national security risk, thereby shutting out Huawei and other Chinese technology firms without directly naming them.[34] The private sector followed suit soon thereafter. American unilateral export controls against Chinese technology firms through its Entity List, however, have worried the Japanese private sector about losing a significant customer base (annual sales to Huawei of electronic components from Japanese companies were in the neighborhood of $9 billion in 2020)[35] and getting caught between feuding technology restrictions.

China's civil-military fusion and the U.S. decision to impose export controls on emerging and foundational technologies have upped the ante for Japan to develop new export control regimes with like-minded countries (including the United States) given its inability to make progress with the extant multilateral agreements, which operate by consensus and include countries at opposite sides of the geopolitical divide.[36] Russia's invasion of Ukraine and the unprecedented coordination of technology sanctions by the United States and its allies have added impetus to this idea. And yet, the October 7th export control decision—invoking extraterritorial reach to cut off advanced chip supply to Chinese firms and requesting partner nations like Japan and the Netherlands to follow suit with restrictions on exports of advanced semiconductor equipment to China—presented Tokyo with a difficult choice. While a trilateral deal was reportedly reached in early 2023, the exact details have been slow in coming, reflecting allied concerns over Chinese retaliation.[37]

Beyond the export control system, Tokyo is considering tightening visa screenings for foreign students, bolstering protection for cutting-edge technology in universities and research institutions, and tightening the reporting of foreign funding.[38] The GOJ has begun preparations to introduce a comprehensive security clearance system for the public and private sectors. Information security has long been considered a hindrance to intelligence cooperation with international partners and an obstacle to Japanese firms participating in high-tech consortia, but in the past privacy concerns have discouraged the adoption of extensive background checks.[39]

Supply Chain Resilience

Japan is painfully aware of the risks of weaponized interdependence. It was the target of one of China's first acts of economic coercion when in 2010 China enacted an informal embargo of rare earth metal exports following frictions in the East China Sea (see Chapter 10). At that time, the Japanese government and business community organized a multipronged response to address this key vulnerability by recycling and redesigning products to reduce consumption, successfully challenging Chinese practices in the WTO, and executing a sustained diversification campaign through financing mining and processing of rare earths in other locations.[40] Reliance on Chinese sources for rare earths decreased markedly, from 90 percent in 2010 to 58 percent in 2018.[41] The diversification drive continues, with a recent Japan-Australia-United States initiative to reduce dependence on China to below 50 percent by 2025.[42]

Supply chain resilience once again became a top concern due to the COVID-19 pandemic. Early on, the harsh lockdowns in China affected Japanese industries relying on the shipment of components, and some Japanese auto plants had to halt production. Concerns over the scarcity of personal protection equipment and fears of production dislocation prompted the Abe government to announce in the spring of 2020 a new subsidy program to strengthen Japan's supply chains. Seeking to alleviate overdependence on specific locations (all but naming China), the government offered funds both to onshore production and to diversify operations into Southeast Asia. The subsidy program has proven popular, to date awarding $3.1 billion to more than two hundred projects. The sectoral breakdown shows that the government's aim is not only a response to the public health crisis but constitutes a hedge against geopolitical risk. Many of the companies receiving subsidies produce advanced materials (chemicals and rare earths), semiconductors, and electronics.[43] The subsidies are small compared to the stock of Japanese investment in China ($130 billion). They are not meant to bring about decoupling but to ease some of the burden of overdependence on China.

The severe chip crunch during the pandemic spurred broader Japanese efforts to recoup lost ground in this critical sector. The days of Japanese superiority in the semiconductor industry are long gone, and today Japanese firms hold a 10 percent share of the world market. However, there are key nodes in the chip supply chain where Japanese firms are dominant, for example in advanced chemicals, silicon wafers, and some specialized production equipment. The Ministry of Economy, Trade, and Industry's (METI) semiconductor strategy aims to address the supply chain shortages in legacy chips in the short-term, but it has long-term aspirations to advance Japanese competitiveness in more advanced microchips through international alliances with producers from Taiwan, the United States, and other countries.[44] The Japanese government established a $4.42 billion semiconductor fund to help defray the cost of chip manufacturing in Japan (for example, it will pay $3.5 billion or 40 percent of the total cost for TSMC's new fabrication plant in Kumamoto).[45] Other countries have launched even larger semiconductor funds, with the United States allocating $52 billion, the EU $46 billion, India $30 billion, and China over $51 billion.[46]

The comeback of industrial policy in Japan, the United States, and the EU—with plans to promote domestic manufacturing through international alliances—underscores the premiums attached to both location and trust. Fundamental questions loom, however, on how to avoid a subsidy race among like-minded countries, keep in check rent-seeking, and prevent a future glut of semiconductors.[47] The industrial policy turn will also challenge the United States and its partners to reconcile the inherent tension between onshoring and friend-shoring in other advanced industrial sectors. The most poignant example is Biden's landmark climate change bill, the Inflation Reduction Act (IRA) of 2022, which aims to award tax incentives to electric vehicles that are assembled in North America and eventually phase out Chinese content in their batteries.[48] The domestic content measures of the IRA undermine cohesion among like-minded parties and could end up delaying the adoption of clean energy technologies.

Economic Security Promotion Act

Japan's economic security measures have crystallized into a more comprehensive legislative package with four lines of effort: supply chain resilience, protection of critical infrastructure, promotion of research and innovation, and patent protection.[49] With this bill, the government set out to identify critical products (essential to the operation of Japan's economy and society and prone to disruptions of foreign supply) and provide subsidies to companies that submit plans to strengthen their supply chain. For fourteen critical infrastructure sectors (power, transportation, telecommunications, and finance among them), the government will require prior approval for the procurement of hardware and software to eliminate vulnerabilities. To advance public-private cooperation on applied R&D, the government will allocate $3.6 billion to twenty high-tech sectors such as AI, hypersonic transportation, and cybersecurity.[50] And the government has established a system to maintain concealed patents for sensitive technologies that have received government support.

The bill has both a promotion side, with subsidies to strengthen production networks and advance applied technological research, and a regulatory side through greater auditing of acquisitions in infrastructure sectors, monitoring of supply chains, and enforcing research security protocols. The bill paints government intervention in broad strokes, and much remains to be decided regarding the details of implementation and the balance achieved between efficiency and protection. However, as former Economic Security Minister Kobayashi Takayuki stated, the bill does open a new chapter in using economic tools to achieve national interests.[51]

NOTES

1. Kenneth W. Abbot et al., "The Concept of Legalization," *International Organization* 54, no. 3 (2000): 401–19.

2. Anthea Roberts, Henrique Choer Moraes, and Victor Ferguson, "Toward a Geoeconomic Order in International Trade and Investment," *Journal of International Economic Law* 22 (2019): 655–76; James L. Schoff and Satoru Mori, "The U.S.-Japan Alliance in an Age of Resurgent Techno-Nationalism," Asia Strategy Initiative, Policy Memorandum #4, Sasakawa Peace Foundation, Tokyo, March 31, 2020, www.spf.org/jpus-insights/spf-asia-initiative-en/spf-asia-initiative004.html; and Daniel W. Drezner, "Introduction: The Uses and Abuses of Weaponized Interdependence," In *The Uses and Abuses of Weaponized Interdependence*, ed. Daniel W. Drezner, Henry Farrell, and Abraham L. Newman (Washington, DC: Brookings Institution Press, March 2, 2021), 1–16.

3. Mireya Solís, "Comment on 'Economic Diplomacy and Economic Security under Abe,'" *Asian Economic Policy Review* 16 (February 6, 2021): 300–01.

4. Article XXI identifies specific circumstances that apply for the invocation of security interests: fissionable materials, military weaponry, and cases of war or crisis in international relations. A recent WTO panel (Russia-Transit) ruled that the national security exemption is subject to judicial review. See J. Benton Heath, "National Security and Economic Globalization: Toward Collision or Reconciliation?" *Fordham International Law Journal* 42, no. 5 (2019): 1443. And in December 2022, several WTO rulings came down against the U.S. national security tariffs on steel and aluminum imposed by the Trump administration in 2018. The Biden administration strongly rejected the ruling, asserting that the WTO cannot second-guess a member's invocation of security interests. See Doug Palmer, "WTO Says Trump's Steel Tariffs Violated Global Trade Rules," *Politico*, December 9, 2022, https://www.politico.com/news/2022/12/09/wto-ruling-trump-tariffs-violate-rules-00073282. Japan has inserted self-judging national security exemptions in its trade and investment agreements, including the Comprehensive and Progressive Trans-Pacific Partnership (CPTPP). See Tomoko Ishikawa, "Investment Screening on National Security Grounds and International Law: The Case of Japan," *Journal of International and Comparative Law* 7, no. 1 (2020): 71–98.

5. Roberts et al., "Toward a Geoeconomic Order in International Trade and Investment."

6. Julian Gerwitz, "The Chinese Reassessment of Interdependence," *China Leadership Monitor* 64 (June 1, 2020): 4, www.prcleader.org/gewirtz.

7. See Chad P. Bown, "China Bought None of the Extra $200 Billion of US Exports in Trump's Trade Deal," Peterson Institute for International Economics, July 19, 2022, www.piie.com/blogs/realtime-economic-issues-watch/china -bought-none-extra-200-billion-us-exports-trumps-trade.

8. Ryan Hass, "How China Is Responding to Escalating Strategic Competition with the United States," *China Leadership Monitor*, no. 67 (March 1, 2021), www.prcleader.org/hass. The prospects for CAI ratification are low given frostier EU-China relations due to tensions over Chinese economic coercion of Lithuania and its tacit support of Russia's invasion of Ukraine.

9. Douglas B. Fuller, "China's Counter-Strategy to American Export Controls in Integrated Circuits," *China Leadership Monitor*, no. 67 (March 1, 2021), www.prcleader.org/fuller.

10. Mark Wu, "Managing the China Trade Challenge: Confronting the Limits of the WTO," Working Paper for the Penn Project on the Future of U.S.-China Relations, the University of Pennsylvania's Center for the Study of Contemporary China, 2020, https://cpb-us-w2.wpmucdn.com/web.sas.upenn .edu/dist/b/732/files/2020/10/Mark-Wu_Limits-of-WTO_Final.pdf.

11. See Gavin Bade, "Runaway Inflation Brings New Attention to Easing China Tariffs," *Politico*, June 15, 2022, www.politico.com/news/2022/06/15/ inflation-china-tariffs-00039651.

12. The active use of Section 232 of the U.S. Trade Expansion Act (which authorizes tariffs when imports hurt national security) is indicative of this new era. Even though the Department of Defense was clear that extant steel supply was more than sufficient to meet its weapons manufacture needs, the Department of Commerce recommended tariffs based on low steel capacity utilization. Hence, national security tariffs were imposed not for the purpose of military readiness but with an industrial policy objective in mind.

13. See White House, "Fact Sheet: U.S.-EU Trade and Technology Council Establishes Economic and Technology Policies & Initiatives," May 16, 2022, www.whitehouse.gov/briefing-room/statements-releases/2022/05/16/fact-sheet -u-s-eu-trade-and-technology-council-establishes-economic-and-technology -policies-initiatives/; and White House, "Fact Sheet: U.S.-Japan Competitiveness and Resilience (CoRe) Partnership," April 16, 2021, www.whitehouse .gov/briefing-room/statements-releases/2021/04/16/fact-sheet-u-s-japan -competitiveness-and-resilience-core-partnership/.

14. Sarah Bauerle Danzman, "Investment Screening in the Shadow of Weaponized Interdependence," in *The Uses and Abuses of Weaponized Interdependence*, ed. Daniel W. Drezner, Henry Farrell, and Abraham L. Newman (Washington, DC: Brookings Institution Press, 2021), 257–72.

15. James L. Schoff, "U.S.-Japan Technology Policy Coordination: Balancing Techno-Nationalism with a Globalized World," Paper, Carnegie Endowment for International Peace, Washington, DC, June 2020, 19–20,

https://carnegieendowment.org/2020/06/29/u.s.-japan-technology-policy
-coordination-balancing-technonationalism-with-globalized-world-pub-82176.

16. Adam Segal, "Huawei, 5G, and Weaponized Interdependence," in *The Uses and Abuses of Weaponized Interdependence*, ed. Daniel W. Drezner, Henry Farrell, and Abraham L. Newman (Washington DC: Brookings Institution Press, 2021), 149–68.

17. Eurasia Group, "The Geopolitics of Semiconductors," September 2020, 3, www.eurasiagroup.net/live-post/geopolitics-semiconductors.

18. White House, "Remarks by National Security Advisor Jake Sullivan at the Special Competitive Studies Project Global Emerging Technologies Summit," September 16, 2022, www.whitehouse.gov/briefing-room/speeches -remarks/2022/09/16/remarks-by-national-security-advisor-jake-sullivan-at -the-special-competitive-studies-project-global-emerging-technologies-summit /.

19. Martijn Rasser and Kevin Wolf, "The Right Time for U.S. Chip Controls," *Lawfare*, December 13, 2022, www.lawfareblog.com/right-time-chip -export-controls.

20. "White House to Set Up 'Trade Strike Force' Led by USTR, Eyes New 232 Probe," *Inside U.S. Trade*, June 8, 2021, https://insidetrade.com/daily -news/white-house-set-%E2%80%98trade-strike-force%E2%80%99-led-ustr -eyes-section-232-magnet-probe.

21. The White House, "Fact Sheet: CHIPS and Science Act Will Lower Costs, Create Jobs, Strengthen Supply Chains, and Counter China," August 9, 2022, https://www.whitehouse.gov/briefing-room/statements-releases/2022 /08/09/fact-sheet-chips-and-science-act-will-lower-costs-create-jobs-strengthen -supply-chains-and-counter-china/.

22. See Akin Gump Strauss Hauer & Feld LLP, "Senate Passes Chips-Plus Package, House Passage Imminent," July 27, 2022, www.akingump.com/en/ news-insights/senate-passes-chips-plus-package-house-passage-imminent.html.

23. For a detailed discussion of the genesis of the comprehensive security concept and its ultimate fading, see Akihiko Tanaka, "Security: Human, National, and International," *Japan's Diplomacy Series*, Japan Digital Library, The Japan Institute for International Affairs, Tokyo, 2013, https://www2.jiia .or.jp/en/pdf/digital_library/japan_s_diplomacy/160325_Akihiko_Tanaka.pdf.

24. Mireya Solís, *Banking on Multinationals: Public Credit and the Export of Japanese Sunset Industries* (Stanford: Stanford University Press, 2004).

25. "New Government Division Gathers 'Elite Level' Staff to Bridge Gap between Realms of Economy, National Security," *The Japan News*, May 24, 2020.

26. Cabinet Office of Japan, "経済財政運営と改革の基本方針2020 について" [Basic Policy of Economic and Financial Management and Reform 2020], 11th meeting of the Council on Economic and Fiscal Policy and 41st meeting of the Council on Investments for the Future, July 17, 2020, https://www5.cao.go.jp/ keizai-shimon/kaigi/cabinet/2020/2020_basicpolicies_ja.pdf.

27. Solís, *Banking on Multinationals*.

28. Tetsushi Kajimoto and Daniel Kaussink, "Japan Tightens Rules on Foreign Stakes in 518 Firms, Citing National Security," *Reuters*, May 8, 2020, www.reuters.com/article/us-japan-investment-mof/japan-tightens-rules-on-foreign-stakes-in-518-firms-citing-national-security-idUSKBN22K0Z0.

29. Shiro Armstrong and Shujiro Urata, "Japan First? Economic Security in a World of Uncertainty," Australia-Japan Research Centre (AJRC) Working Paper no. 01/2021, Crawford School of Public Policy, Australian National University, March 2021.

30. Tsuguhito Omagari and Yuki Sako, "New Japanese Foreign Investment Regulation Could Impact the Financial Services Industry and Undermine Japan's Corporate Governance Reform," K&L Gates LLP, December 9, 2019, www.jdsupra.com/legalnews/new-japanese-foreign-investment-53407/.

31. Mitsuhiro Kamiya and Akira Kumaki, "As Shareholder Activism Grows in Japan, New Amendment Places Limits on Foreign Investors," Skadden, Arps, Slate, Meagher & Flom LLP and Affiliates, January 21, 2020, www.skadden.com/insights/publications/2020/01/2020-insights/as-shareholder-activism-grows-in-japan.

32. Tatsushi Amano, "Japan's Economic Statecraft," Working paper, Strategic Japan 2022, Center for Strategic and International Studies, 2022, www.csis.org/programs/japan-chair/projects/strategic-japan.

33. Tomoo Marukawa, "Japan's High Technology Trade with China and Its Export Control," *Journal of East Asian Studies* 13, no. 3 (2013): 483–501.

34. "Japan Bans Huawei and Its Chinese Peers from Government Contracts," *Nikkei Asia*, December 10, 2018, https://asia.nikkei.com/Economy/Trade-war/Japan-bans-Huawei-and-its-Chinese-peers-from-government-contracts.

35. Tomoo Marukawa, "Export Restrictions in the Japan-China-U.S. Trilateral Relationship," *The Japanese Political Economy* 46, no. 2–3 (2020): 152–75.

36. Ministry of Economy, Trade, and Industry, Subcommittee on Security Export Control Policy, Trade Committee, Industrial Structure Council, "Interim Report (Overview)," October 8, 2019, www.meti.go.jp/english/policy/external_economy/trade_control/pdf/191008a.pdf; and Amano, "Japan's Economic Statecraft."

37. Gregory C. Allen and Emily Benson, "Clues to the U.S.-Dutch-Japanese Semiconductor Export Controls Deal Hiding in Plain Sight," Center for Strategic and International Studies, March 1, 2023, https://www.csis.org/analysis/clues-us-dutch-japanese-semiconductor-export-controls-deal-are-hiding-plain-sight.

38. "Japan to Limit Foreign Students' Access to Security-Linked Tech," *Nikkei Asia*, October 26, 2021, https://asia.nikkei.com/Politics/Japan-to-limit-foreign-students-access-to-security-linked-tech.

39. Gabriel Domínguez, "Japan, Long a Prime Target for Spying, Seeks to Improve Handling of Sensitive Information," *The Japan Times*, March 9, 2023, https://www.japantimes.co.jp/news/2023/03/09/national/economic-security-sensitive-info/.

40. Kristin Vekasi, "Politics, Markets, and Rare Commodities: Responses to Chinese Rare Earth Policy," *Japanese Journal of Political Science* 20, no. 1 (March 2019): 2–20.

41. Center for Strategic and International Studies, "Does China Pose a Threat to Global Rare Earth Supply Chains?" China Power Project, July 17, 2020, https://chinapower.csis.org/china-rare-earths/.

42. Ryosuke Hanafusa, "Japan to Pour Investment into Non-China Rare-Earth Projects," *Nikkei Asia*, February 15, 2020, https://asia.nikkei.com/Politics/International-relations/Japan-to-pour-investment-into-non-China-rare-earth-projects.

43. See Mireya Solís, "The Big Squeeze: Japanese Supply Chains and Great Power Competition," Joint U.S.-Korea Academic Studies, Korea Economic Institute of America (KEI), Washington, DC, July 30, 2021, 293–312, https://keia.org/publication/the-big-squeeze-japanese-supply-chains-and-great-power-competition/.

44. See Ministry of Economy, Trade, and Industry, "半導体、デジタル産業戦略" [Semiconductor and Digital Industries Strategy], June 2021, www.meti.go.jp/press/2021/06/20210604008/20210603008-1.pdf.

45. See "Japan to Subsidize TSMC's Kumamoto Plant by up to $3.5bn," *Nikkei Asia*, June 17, 2022, https://asia.nikkei.com/Business/Tech/Semiconductors/Japan-to-subsidize-TSMC-s-Kumamoto-plant-by-up-to-3.5bn.

46. See Cheng Ting-Fang and Lauly Li, "The Resilience Myth: Fatal Flaws in the Push to Secure Chip Supply Chains," *Financial Times*, August 4, 2022, https://www.ft.com/content/f76534bf-b501-4cbf-9a46-80be9feb670c. China's support goes beyond integrated circuit (IC) funds to include tax credits, support for the acquisition of foreign technology, and below-market equity investments. Some estimates put Chinese state support for semiconductors between 2015 and 2025 at $145 billion. See White House, "Building Resilient Supply Chains, Revitalizing American Manufacturing, and Fostering Broad-Based Growth," 100-Day Reviews under Ex. Order 14017, June 2021, www.whitehouse.gov/wp-content/uploads/2021/06/100-day-supply-chain-review-report.pdf?utm_source=sfmc%E2%80%8B&utm_medium=email%E2%80%8B&utm_campaign=20210610_Global_Manufacturing_Economic_Update_June_Members.

47. See Mireya Solís, "Toward a US-Japan Digital Alliance," Working Paper Vol. 1, Shaping the Pragmatic and Effective Strategy Toward China Project, Sasakawa Peace Foundation, October 2021, https://www.spf.org/iina/en/articles/mireya-solis_01.html.

48. Chad P. Bown and Kristin Dziczek, "Why US Allies Are Upset over Electric Vehicle Subsidies in the Inflation Reduction Act," Excerpts from the Trade Talks Podcast, Peterson Institute for International Economics, December 2, 2022, https://www.piie.com/blogs/realtime-economics/why-us-allies-are-upset-over-electric-vehicle-subsidies-inflation.

49. See Toshiya Takahashi, "Japan's Economic Security Bill a Balance between Business and the Bureaucracy," East Asia Forum, June 26, 2022, https:

//www.eastasiaforum.org/2022/06/26/japans-economic-security-bill-balances
-business-and-the-bureaucracy/.

50. See "Japan to Focus on Tech from 20 Fields as Part of Economic Security Drive," *The Japan Times*, July 20, 2022, www.japantimes.co.jp/news/2022/07 /20/business/economic-security-advanced-technology-sectors/.

51. Takayuki Kobayashi, Bill Emmott, and Robert Ward, "Japan's Economic Security Strategy," webinar, International Institute for Strategic Studies, May 12, 2022, https://www.iiss.org/events/2022/05/japans-economic-security -strategy.

SECTION 5

Geopolitics

CHAPTER 10

The Growing Pains of a Nascent Security Role

In the aftermath of World War II, Japan sought shelter under the U.S. nuclear umbrella and focused its energies on reconstruction and economic growth. The country's leaders renounced great power politics with a strict interpretation of the peace constitution allowing rearming exclusively for self-defense. Tokyo abstained from an overt regional security role, instead honing instruments of economic diplomacy. Japan's stunted security policy development paid off in the Cold War geometry but was found wanting as geopolitics shifted.

Japan's transition to the post–Cold War era in the 1990s was challenging. The postwar economic model and foreign policy doctrine were hobbled, forcing a reckoning over the country's future trajectory. Japan's diplomatic clout had centered on its unmatched economic dynamism and well-funded economic assistance programs. But the onset of slow growth and foreign aid budget cuts dimmed Japan's civilian power appeal. Conversely, one instrument in Japan's foreign policy toolkit that had deliberately remained dormant—an international role for the Self-Defense Forces (SDF)—was increasingly in demand.

Successive Japanese administrations passed bills authorizing a noncombatant SDF role in United Nations Peace Keeping Operations (PKO), anti-terror campaigns, and Iraq's reconstruction. These forays were mostly reactive, piecemeal, and frequently plagued by implementation difficulties. But they opened the door for Japan to craft a security role it had shunned for decades. The task of securing Japan grew more exacting with North Korea's nuclear weapons and missile advancements and a more powerful and assertive China. Japan's leadership instability, with its rapid turnover of prime ministers in the second half of the 2000s, raised questions about the country's ability to meet these security challenges.

RENOUNCING GREAT POWER POLITICS:
THE POSTWAR REBIRTH OF JAPAN

Japanese imperial ambitions resulted in the acquisition of colonies in Northeast Asia (Formosa in 1895 and Korea in 1910) during the Meiji era, ever-expanding military campaigns throughout the 1930s and first half of the 1940s in China (including the establishment of a puppet regime in Manchuria in 1932), and occupation of Southeast Asia and Pacific island nations (the Philippines, Malaya, French Indochina, Hong Kong, Singapore, and the Dutch East Indies, among others) during World War II. Japan's military expansionism inflicted enormous pain upon the region and brought the country to a path of self-destruction. The end of the global conflict saw Japan vanquished, with its economy and society in tatters and reeling from the unfathomable destructive power of the atomic bombs dropped by the United States on the cities of Hiroshima and Nagasaki.

Imperial Japan was no more. Its colonies and occupied territories were surrendered, as was the nation's own independence with the onset of a seven-year occupation by its erstwhile enemy, the United States (1945–1952). As Japan sought to rebuild, regain sovereignty, and reenter international society, it attempted fundamentally different solutions to its problems at home and abroad: democracy and civilian checks to stamp out the roots of militarism, and the abdication of the right to wage war.

The United States fundamentally assisted in the reorientation of the Japanese polity, not least because the occupation directives of democratization and demilitarization informed the American-drafted Constitution of 1946 (which to this day remains intact). That foundational document birthed postwar Japanese democracy with a substantive set of civil rights; ended imperial sovereignty and instead designated the emperor a symbol of the state; and adopted Article 9 to renounce the use of force to settle international disputes, giving way to the famous moniker of "peace constitution." In orchestrating this effort, General Douglas MacArthur, Supreme Commander of the Allied Powers, aimed to ensure that Japan would not rise again as a military foe and pushed for its disarmament. With quickly shifting geopolitics, however, American officials came to regret a few years later this decision and pressed Japan to acquire more robust defense capabilities.[1] Despite the American origins of the constitution,[2] Japanese agency has been fundamental to the transformation of Japan's security role. As Japan transformed into a representative democracy, the public and its elected representatives have shaped choices made on retaining and reinterpreting the strictures of Article 9 for the sake of advancing Japanese national interests.

Article 9 stipulates that "Aspiring sincerely to an international peace based on justice and order, the Japanese people forever renounce war as a sovereign right of the nation and the threat or use of force as means of settling international disputes." And to accomplish this aim, "land, sea, and air forces, as well as other war potential, will never be maintained. The right of belligerency of the state will not be recognized."[3] It is in this legal text that the origin of Japan's postwar security exceptionalism is to be found; but statesmanship, domestic contestation, and shifting international politics have been essential to Japan's reinvention of its security role while it has remained anchored to an unchanging constitutional text since 1947.

Prime Minister Yoshida Shigeru set the direction of postwar Japanese security policy with a strict reading of the constitutional constraints on the acquisition of military capabilities (which he came to define as permissible exclusively for self-defense purposes), the signing of an unequal alliance with the Americans to regain sovereignty (albeit not over all territory, since Okinawa was not returned until 1972), and the single-minded focus on economic recovery and the use of purely economic tools to rehabilitate Japan internationally.[4]

The Yoshida Doctrine signified Japan's deliberate abdication from great power politics. For Prime Minister Yoshida, the outsourcing of Japanese defense and the acceptance of a junior role in the alliance with the United States was a price worth paying to speed up Japan's economic recovery and to ensure its security in a world splitting apart into a rigid Cold War divide. This new strategic compass was not a complete rejection of power and military capability to protect Japan.[5] Far from it, Japan would be placed under the nuclear umbrella of the United States, host a large contingent of American troops on its soil, and establish its own Self-Defense Forces a few years after regaining independence. But the intent of Prime Minister Yoshida in establishing the SDF in 1954 was for it to be of limited size, to have a lessened role in security policy-making (the Japan Self Defense Agency was below ministerial level) with strict civilian controls, and to rule out overseas deployment of Japanese troops.[6] It was a bet to avoid abandonment (given the tight limits on Japanese power projection) and prevent entrapment into America's regional conflicts.

Emerging from World War II newly minted as a global power seeking to deter communist advances in different theaters, the United States established very different alliance systems in Europe and Asia. As Victor Cha has persuasively argued, the hub-and-spoke configuration for Asian alliances was driven by the United States' desire to exert control over its security partners and, in Japan's case, to facilitate its transition to a "status quo power supportive of American interests in the region."[7] Bilateral alliances were also a necessity given the strong distrust of Japan among countries in the region that had recently suffered the brunt of Japanese military aggression. Security cooperation with Japan was not an option for them, and they instead regarded the U.S.-Japan alliance as an insurance mechanism against future Japanese military adventurism.

The 1951 U.S.-Japan Security Treaty was a quid pro quo exchange of access to bases in Japanese territory for an implicit American defense guarantee. It placed Japan firmly on the side of the United States in the Cold War, including leverage to forestall an internal communist takeover. The defense pact rankled many for its provision authorizing American forces to quell internal riots. Indeed, Yoshida's political compromises over the terms of the alliance were far from universally accepted at home. Foreign policy emerged as a defining cleavage in postwar Japanese politics. On the left side of the political spectrum, the alliance with the United States and the creation of the SDF were considered illegitimate and contrary to the pacifist conviction of the public. And not all conservatives were prepared to toe the Yoshida line. Prominent Liberal Democratic Party (LDP) figures decried the asymmetrical terms of the alliance and the straitjacket on Japanese power projection, believed the attribution of war responsibility to be excessive, and yearned for more autonomy in charting Japan's international affairs.[8]

No figure was more influential among hawkish conservatives than Prime Minister Kishi Nobusuke, whose push to revise the terms of the alliance in 1960 generated the most severe political crisis of postwar Japan. The revised security treaty eliminated some of the most jarring inequities: the United States agreed to consult with Japan on the use of American troops in Japanese territory and the authority to intervene in domestic disturbances was scrapped. The renegotiation secured an explicit American commitment to come to the defense of Japan in case of armed attack (Article 5). But Japan had to acquiesce to references in Articles 4 and 6 to the significance of stability in the Far East and the possible need to mobilize American troops based in Japan to ensure it.[9] The ratification of the security pact in the Japanese Diet generated a political firestorm when the vote went ahead without the opposition present. Defining questions on foreign and domestic policy (the security alliance and respect of democratic rules) brought six million Japanese to the streets. While the revised security pact endured, the heavy-handed manner of its ratification cost Kishi his premiership.[10]

As this crisis subsided, the new equilibrium of the U.S.-Japan security partnership proved durable. A nonpunitive peace settlement and a less lopsided alliance, together with deepening economic and social ties, helped advance one of the most remarkable processes of historical reconciliation. Each country's recognition of the other shifted over time from one of bitter enemies to that of trusted allies. However, de facto U.S.-Japan defense cooperation remained largely underdeveloped during the Cold War era. There was little interoperability among their military forces, no clear demarcation of roles and missions among the allies, and stilted contingency planning to deal with potential regional crises. It was not until 1978 that the first U.S.-Japan Defense Cooperation Guidelines were adopted to make progress in some of these areas.[11] These guidelines would remain unrevised for almost twenty years.

Japan's regional security role was constrained. The 1951 San Francisco Peace Treaty had normalized Japan's relations with the forty-nine signatories but had not erased the trust deficit regarding Japan. Japan's relations with its closest geographical neighbors were the most fraught. Normalization of relations with South Korea had to wait until the mid-1960s and with Communist China until 1972. A peace treaty with the Soviet Union proved unattainable due to the Soviet refusal to return the Northern Islands grabbed in the closing days of World War II. Habits of security cooperation among the United States' Asian allies did not develop within the hub-and-spoke alliance system.

A stunted security role was also Japan's choice: Tokyo declined participation in regional security initiatives, concerned that a reassertion of a political role could trigger regional backlash.[12] Distrust about

Japan's regional intentions remained high, culminating in the riots that met Prime Minister Tanaka Kakuei's tour of Southeast Asia in 1974. Concerns over economic dominance and self-serving aid programs were tangible. The 1977 Fukuda Doctrine, spearheaded by Prime Minister Fukuda Takeo, sought to recalibrate Japan's relationship with the region by explicitly rejecting the role of military power and building a "heart-to-heart" relationship with the Association of Southeast Asian Nations (ASEAN) through more generous economic assistance and more balanced economic ties.[13]

The brakes applied to Japanese defense policy were ubiquitous. They came to include the three non-nuclear principles (to not possess, not produce, and not permit the introduction of nuclear weapons), a ban on weapon exports, and a self-imposed ceiling on defense expenditures at 1 percent of GDP.[14] Japanese statecraft aspired to the status of "civilian power," thereby seeking international influence only through economic and diplomatic means. But this trading nation was not a disarmed one. Far from it. In the waning days of the Cold War, Japan had the most advanced military among Asian countries.[15] After all, it seemed that Yoshida's insight had proven right: the day for Japan's rearmament would come once economic power grew.[16] And yet, the Yoshida Doctrine did not award Japanese policymakers a sure footing in the post–Cold War era. Japan's passive security role hindered its ability to navigate seismic changes in world affairs.

THE END OF THE COLD WAR: TRIAL AND ERROR IN JAPAN'S EMERGING SECURITY ROLE

Dramatic events such as the fall of the Berlin Wall in November 1989 and the dissolution of the Soviet Union in December 1991 led to the end of the bipolar international order. The dropout of the major Cold War foe compelled the United States and Japan to find a new purpose to their security bond, especially as the Americans expected Japan to make more meaningful contributions to collective security and to an emerging set of security challenges such as the war on terror.

Other vexing problems confronted Japanese policymakers. Beijing's violent crackdown on pro-democracy demonstrators at Tiananmen Square in June 1989 strained Japan's policy of economic engagement with China. In rebuilding Sino-Japanese ties, Tokyo had prioritized economic assistance, hoping that support of China's economic modernization objectives could facilitate progress in the task of historical reconciliation, facilitate access to the untapped Chinese market for Japanese companies, and incentivize a long-lasting Sino-Soviet split. China came to occupy pride of place in Japanese aid-giving, becoming the top recipient of official development assistance (ODA) loans. While Tokyo froze its economic assistance program in the aftermath of the Tiananmen Square massacre, it was the first to restart ODA loans to China a year later. In making this choice, Japanese officials were risking friction with the Western donor community and placing an uncertain bet that carrots would induce Beijing's restraint in internal and external affairs.[17]

The biggest foreign policy flop of the new era came early and hit hard: Japan's botched response to the 1991 Gulf War. When President Saddam Hussein's Iraq invaded Kuwait in 1990, the United States mobilized an international coalition to roll back the annexation and uphold the principle of prohibiting the use of force to redraw national borders. Japanese leaders declined to participate in the military operation, citing constitutional constraints, and instead made a $13 billion donation. Operation Desert Storm liberated Kuwait, but the crisis and its resolution underscored Japan's inability to heed the call for collective security. Its financial contribution was dismissed as mere "checkbook diplomacy," not even warranting an acknowledgment from the government of Kuwait when it thanked the international coalition that helped it regain its sovereignty. The new era placed Japan in unfamiliar territory. The limits of its economic-only diplomacy were evident, and Japanese officials had to grapple with what had remained taboo: an international security role for its Self-Defense Forces.

Peacekeeping

Upon cessation of hostilities, the Japan Self-Defense Forces joined an international minesweeping campaign in the Persian Gulf with the goal of restoring safe navigation to a critical sea lane. But Japanese diplomats understood more would be needed to avoid the country's marginalization from international peace efforts. They came to support the participation of Japanese SDF personnel in UN peacekeeping operations, both as a means to revitalize Japan's UN diplomacy (a few years later, Tokyo would announce its bid for a permanent seat at the Security Council), and to minimize domestic and international backlash to Japan's new international security role. The International Peace Cooperation Act (PKO Law) approved in 1992 constituted a significant milestone in Japan's security evolution, enabling for the first time the overseas deployment of Japanese troops in a noncombatant role and under the auspices of UN peacekeeping missions.[18]

However, the bill came with significant restrictions that limited the scope of Japan's contributions to peacekeeping missions. Japan's PKO participation would be contingent on satisfying five conditions: 1) A ceasefire agreement must be in place, 2) all parties must consent to the UN peacekeeping mission and specifically to Japan's participation, 3) the strict impartiality of the mission must be guaranteed, 4) if one of the above conditions was no longer met, Japan reserved the right to withdraw its participation, and 5) the use of weapons would be the minimum measure necessary to protect the lives of SDF personnel.[19] In the next few years, the PKO Law was revised on two occasions to enable faster deployments, allow for a limited expansion on the use of force in order to protect fellow peacekeepers and civilians under its care, and safeguard deployed equipment.[20]

Haltingly at first but more steadily later, Japan came to embrace peacekeeping as an important venue for its contributions to global stability. In the past three decades, more than ten thousand personnel from Japan have partaken in at least fourteen UN PKO missions across the globe.[21] Equally remarkable has been the shift in public opinion, which was steadfast against overseas SDF deployments (78 percent opposed in a 1990 poll) but grew very supportive of PKO missions over time, from 58.9 percent in favor in 1994 to almost 90 percent by 2012.[22]

Coalitions of the Willing

U.S.-Japan alliance managers had their hands full throughout the 1990s. Friction, misaligned priorities, and unmet expectations created strain in the bilateral relationship. A keen observer of U.S.-Japan ties, Funabashi Yoichi, worried about an alliance adrift. Bilateral tensions were running high on trade negotiations around "structural impediments" that hindered American firms' access to the Japanese market, and there was acrimony about numerical targets in a semiconductor trade agreement. The 1995 rape of a twelve-year-old Japanese girl by three U.S. servicemen in Okinawa triggered large-scale demonstrations that were fueled by the demand to bring the perpetrators to justice but also reflected deep-seated frustration with the disproportionate burden shouldered by Okinawa in hosting the majority of American bases in Japan. Coordination in responding to adverse regional security trends did not progress easily either. In 1994, the Japanese government was reluctant to go along with the American push for global sanctions against North Korea for its failure to allow international nuclear inspectors into the country.[23] The 1998 launch of a North Korean missile that flew over Japanese territory shook Japan's defense planners. This development drained Japan's support for the U.S.-brokered Agreed Framework, the purpose of which was to freeze North Korea's nuclear weapons program in exchange for two light-water nuclear reactors.[24] In response to the Taepodong-1 missile launch, the Japanese government froze its economic support to the Korean Energy Development Organization and only restarted it at the behest of the Americans.[25] North Korea's surreptitious nuclear and missile programs underscored the limits of close coordination among the allies.

Al-Qaeda's terrorist attacks against the United States on September 11, 2001, presented yet another test for U.S.-Japan relations. American strategic priorities changed swiftly as the war on terror became its most urgent task. U.S. policymakers responded by mobilizing coalitions of the willing to intervene militarily in Afghanistan in 2001 (where the Taliban regime was sheltering Al-Qaeda leader Osama bin Laden) and Iraq in 2003 (because the George W. Bush administration accused Saddam Hussein of developing weapons of mass destruction). Coming to the aid of the United States in the aftermath of 9/11 presented difficult questions for Japan. The Japanese government continued to rule out exercising its right to collective self-defense (i.e., to offer military support to an ally under attack) and the newly minted PKO bill did not contemplate deployments of Japanese troops outside of UN peacekeeping missions.

Prime Minister Koizumi Junichiro was nevertheless determined to make a strong show of solidarity with its U.S. ally and to avoid the policy paralysis that had botched Japan's response to the Persian Gulf War. He moved swiftly to ensure the protection of U.S. military personnel stationed in Japan and to explore options for SDF participation to support U.S. counterterrorism efforts. At record speed, the Diet approved in October 2001 the Anti-Terrorism Special Measures Law authorizing the Maritime Self-Defense Forces to partake in refueling operations in the Indian Ocean.[26] Japan eschewed a direct combat role in the war on terror, but the use of weapons by the SDF for defensive purposes was greenlighted, to protect not only itself but also U.S. and UK vessels involved in the Afghan mission. As Richard Samuels observes, this moved Japan closer to de facto collective self-defense.[27]

Japan's participation in the U.S. campaign in Iraq was harder because the war was controversial internationally and unpopular at home. Hence, the Koizumi administration carved out a role for the SDF in the rebuilding of Iraq post–Saddam Hussein. The Diet approved the Iraq Reconstruction and Humanitarian Assistance Special Measures Law in July 2003. Six hundred Japanese SDF members were sent to Iraq in 2004 to assist with the restoration of basic services through the reconstruction of roads, hospitals, and water treatment facilities. However, the pacification of Iraq was far from complete. Dispatched SDF personnel could not use weapons, so troops from other coalition countries (the Netherlands, United Kingdom, and Australia) had to protect the Japanese contingent. Japan's Iraq mission ended in 2006 with the public reluctant to extend Japan's participation for another year.[28] The Rebuild Iraq campaign showcased both a newfound will to have the Japanese military join coalitions of the willing but also underscored the tight restrictions on the use of force that set the SDF apart from its coalition partners. Koizumi's efforts to contribute to the anti-terrorism campaign, however, did pay off with a palpable improvement in U.S.-Japan relations topped by close personal ties between the leaders of both countries.

UNMET SECURITY CHALLENGES

Japanese strategic planners were keenly aware of the more exacting task of securing Japan in the new century. The North Korean nuclear and missile programs continued unabated and negotiations among the Six Parties (North Korea, South Korea, the United States, China, Russia, and Japan) to defuse the North Korean nuclear threat fizzled by 2009.[29] China's rapid growth enabled large defense expenditures that have surpassed Japan's since 2002 and contributed to a growing gap in military capabilities. In 2005, mass protests in China—fueled by unresolved historical grievances and Beijing's fanning of patriotic fervor—resulted in large-scale damage of Japanese property in China, incentivizing corporate Japan to diversify with "China+1" investment strategies. The ability of economic integration to serve as a ballast for China-Japan relations came under increasing strain.

The year 2010 marked China's dethronement of Japan as the second-largest economy in the world. It coincided with a nadir in bilateral relations due to territorial disputes. When the Japanese government arrested the captain of a Chinese trawler who had rammed a Japan Coast Guard vessel in the vicinity of the Senkaku Islands, China responded with an undeclared embargo on rare earth metals. Tensions erupted again two years later. The central government under Prime Minister Noda Yoshihiko purchased the islands in fall 2012 from their private Japanese owner to prevent nationalist Tokyo Governor Ishihara Shintaro from acquiring them. What the Japanese government saw as a prudent measure to forestall further friction the Chinese government interpreted as a unilateral change to the status quo. Ever since, the Chinese government has challenged Japan's administrative control of the islands with frequent naval and air incursions in the contiguous area of the Senkaku Islands. Consequently, "economic coercion" and "gray zone" tactics (pressure below the use of force) were added to the lexicon of Japanese contingency planning.

Concerns over America's global role and regional strategy contributed to Japan's disquiet. Protracted armed conflicts in the Middle East diverted America's attention away from Asia, and the onset of the Global Financial Crisis raised questions about U.S. stewardship of the world economy. Tokyo was alarmed by the apparent receptiveness of President Barack Obama's administration to the Chinese entreaty to bring forth a "new era of great power relations" and the countries' willingness to recognize each other's core interests in a joint U.S.-China statement in November 2009. Although the United States was not interested in a condominium with the Chinese, the anxiety in Japan about losing its special partnership with the United States was high.[30] Obama's announced pivot to Asia in 2011 helped ease this concern but raised further questions about the U.S. ability to deliver on the promised military and economic rebalance to Asia.

The security challenges were steep and Japan struggled to muster an effective response. Domestic politics played a large role. In the second half of the 2000s, Japan entered a period of political instability with six prime ministers in the same number of years. Long-term strategic planning was out of reach for these ephemeral administrations. While the LDP and Democratic Party of Japan (DPJ) sparred electorally, a broad understanding of the desirability of security reforms was discernable across party lines.[31] After Prime Minister Hatoyama Yukio's fiasco over the Futenma base relocation, subsequent DPJ leaders sought to advance foreign policy initiatives that would have deepened, not eroded, the U.S.-Japan alliance, including membership in the Trans-Pacific Partnership and, in particular, a reconsideration of the right to collective self-defense;[32] but they failed to deliver on these initiatives. Political dynamics in the post–Koizumi era—short prime minister tenures, deep intraparty divides, and a twisted Diet—afflicted both LDP and DPJ administrations, neutralizing the ability of elected leaders to be agents of change.

An indecisive Japan made for a poor strategic partner for the United States. Such was the stern message of the high-visibility Armitage-Nye report of August 2012 admonishing Japan to decide whether it wanted to remain a Tier 1 nation.[33]

NOTES

1. Kenneth Pyle, *The Making of Modern Japan*, 2nd ed. (Lexington, MA: D. C. Heath, 1996).

2. John W. Dower, *Embracing Defeat: Japan in the Wake of World War II* (New York: W. W. Norton and Company, 1999).

3. The Constitution of Japan, chapter 2, article 9, https://japan.kantei.go.jp/constitution_and_government_of_japan/constitution_e.html.

4. Pyle, *The Making of Modern Japan*.

5. Satoru Mori, "The New Security Legislation and Japanese Public Reaction," The Tokyo Foundation for Policy Research, December 2, 2015, www.tkfd.or.jp/en/research/detail.php?id=542.

6. Sheila A. Smith, *Japan Rearmed: The Politics of Military Power* (Cambridge, MA: Harvard University Press, 2019).

7. Victor Cha, *Powerplay: The Origins of the American Alliance System in Asia* (Princeton, NJ: Princeton University Press, 2018), 3, 5.

8. Richard J. Samuels, *Securing Japan: Tokyo's Grand Strategy and the Future of East Asia* (Ithaca, NY: Cornell University Press, 2007).

9. In a 1960 exchange of notes, the American government agreed to prior consultation with its Japanese counterpart in the case of mobilization of U.S. troops deployed in Japan to address a regional military contingency. See Adam Liff, "The U.S.-Japan Alliance and Taiwan," *Asia Policy* 17, no. 3 (July 2022): 139.

10. Tobias Harris, *The Iconoclast: Shinzo Abe and the New Japan* (London: Hurst Publishing, 2020).

11. Smith, *Japan Rearmed*, 44.

12. Paul Midford, *Overcoming Isolationism: Japan's Leadership in East Asian Security Multilateralism* (Stanford: Stanford University Press, 2020).

13. Corey Wallace, "Japan's Strategic Contrast: Continuing Influence Despite Relative Power Decline in Southeast Asia," *The Pacific Review* 32, no. 5 (2019): 863–97.

14. The three non-nuclear principles and the ban on weapon exports were both announced in 1967, and the self-imposed 1 percent of GDP limit on defense spending was first formally discussed in 1973 and was assumed as de facto policy but not officially adopted until 1976. See Ministry of Foreign Affairs of Japan, "Three Non-Nuclear Principles," www.mofa.go.jp/policy/un/disarmament/nnp/index.html; Ministry of Foreign Affairs of Japan, "Japan's Policies on the Control of Arms Exports," www.mofa.go.jp/policy/un/disarmament/policy/index.html; and John C. Wright, "The Persistent Power of 1 Percent," Forum Issue 4, Sasakawa Peace Foundation USA, Washington, DC, 2016, https://spfusa.org/wp-content/uploads/2016/09/1-percent-final.pdf.

15. Smith, *Japan Rearmed*, 52.

16. Kenneth Pyle, *The Japanese Question: Power and Purpose in a New Era* (Washington, DC: AEI Press, 1996), 26.

17. Mireya Solís, "China, Japan, and the Art of Economic Statecraft," Global China, The Brookings Institution, Washington, DC, February 2020, www.brookings.edu/research/china-japan-and-the-art-of-economic-statecraft/.

18. Peter Katzenstein and Nobuo Okawara, "Japan's National Security: Structures, Norms, and Policies," *International Security* 17, no. 4 (1993): 84–118.

19. See Ministry of Foreign Affairs of Japan, "Outline of Japan's International Peace Cooperation," May 14, 2015, www.mofa.go.jp/fp/ipc/page22e_000683.html.

20. Sheila A. Smith, *Japan Rearmed: The Politics of Military Power* (Cambridge, MA: Harvard University Press, 2019); and Kyoko Hatakeyama, "Japan's Peacekeeping Policy: Strategic Calculation or Internalization of an International Norm?" *The Pacific Review* 27, no. 5 (2014): 629–50.

21. Ministry of Foreign Affairs of Japan, "Japan's Contributions Based on the International Peace Cooperation Act," May 14, 2015, https://www.mofa.go.jp/fp/ipc/page22e_000684.html.

22. Opinion poll data cited in Hatakeyama, "Japan's Peacekeeping Policy," 636–37.

23. See David E. Sanger, "Tokyo Reluctant to Levy Sanctions on North Koreans," *The New York Times*, June 4, 1994, www.nytimes.com/1994/06/09/world/tokyo-reluctant-to-levy-sanctions-on-north-koreans.html.

24. Yoichi Funabashi, *Alliance Adrift* (Washington, DC: Council on Foreign Relations, 1999).

25. Hidekazu Sakai, "Continuity and Discontinuity of Japanese Foreign Policy towards North Korea: Freezing the Korea Energy Development Organization (KEDO) in 1998," in *Japanese Foreign Policy in Asia and the Pacific*, ed. Akitoshi Miyashita and Yoichiro Sato (New York: Palgrave Macmillan, 2001), 63–73.

26. Larry Wortzel, "Joining Forces against Terrorism: Japan's New Law Commits More than Words to U.S. Efforts," The Heritage Foundation, November 5, 2001, www.heritage.org/homeland-security/report/joining-forces-against-terrorism-japans-new-law-commits-more-thanwords-us.

27. Samuels, *Securing Japan*, 95–96.

28. Smith, *Japan Rearmed*, 81.

29. See Arms Control Association, "The Six-Party Talks at a Glance," January 2022, www.armscontrol.org/factsheets/6partytalks.

30. Michael J. Green, *By More than Providence: Grand Strategy and American Power in the Asia Pacific since 1783* (New York: Columbia University Press, 2017), 526–27.

31. Andrew Oros, *Japan's Security Renaissance: New Policies and Politics for the Twenty-First Century* (New York: Columbia University Press, 2017).

32. Michael J. Green, *Line of Advantage: Japan's Grand Strategy in the Era of Abe Shinzo* (New York: Columbia University Press, 2022), 88–90.

33. See Richard L. Armitage and Joseph S. Nye, "The U.S.-Japan Alliance: Anchoring Stability in Asia," *Report of the Center for Strategic and International Studies (CSIS) Japan Chair*, Washington, DC, August 2012), https://csis-website-prod.s3.amazonaws.com/s3fs-public/legacy_files/files/publication/120810_Armitage_USJapanAlliance_Web.pdf.

CHAPTER 11

A More Capable Japan

ASSESSING ABE'S LEGACY

Prime Minister Abe Shinzo delivered Japan a grand strategy.[1] His was a vision of a more capable Japan that could elevate its contributions to the U.S. alliance, balance relations with China by pushing back against its coercive activities without sacrificing the plentiful benefits of an economic exchange, and redraw the lines of economic and security cooperation across the vast Indo-Pacific area. Enhanced decision-making, new national security authorities, and diplomatic zeal were all essential components to the realization of this vision. The creation of the National Security Council (NSC) to provide a whole-of-government formulation of national strategy, the reinterpretation of the constitution to allow Japan the exercise of the UN-sanctioned right of collective self-defense under limited conditions, and the revival of the Quad, plus the launch of the Free and Open Indo-Pacific (FOIP) policy were important milestones.

An accounting of the late prime minister's foreign policy track record would have to include a strengthening of the U.S.-Japan alliance; the ability to steer cooperation among maritime democracies; a dedicated outreach to Southeast Asia, including capacity-building on maritime safety; and a blueprint for a rules-based order in the Indo-Pacific. While Abe ended the trend of diminishing defense budgets, his changes to Japan's security profile were less quantitative (a buffed-up military capability)

and more qualitative (making Japan a network power through the transformation of its security partnerships).

In some important ways, however, Abe stood in the way of his own
objectives. His ideological conservatism—on the peace constitution,
"comfort women," and the Yasukuni Shrine, for example—sowed distrust that made it difficult to advance his cause of constitutional reform
and stood in the way of repairing relations with Japan's neighbors.
Ultimately, Abe's foreign policy pragmatism loomed larger. He gave
up visits to the controversial shrine after 2013 and negotiated a "comfort women" agreement with South Korea in 2015. Abe's restraint in
his second term allowed him to avoid tying himself to a self-defeating
re-litigation of Japan's past and focus instead on increasing the country's influence to address the challenges of the present: China's bid for
regional hegemony, the inconstancy of U.S. foreign policy, and the risks
of a U.S.-China strategic rivalry that could go awry.

SECURITY REFORMS AND A DEEPER U.S.-JAPAN ALLIANCE

Changes to Japan's national security apparatus and strategy formulation took place at a fast clip with the establishment of the NSC, the
adoption of a State Secrets Law, and the release of Japan's first ever
National Security Strategy (NSS) within the first year of Abe's second
term in office. Coursing through these changes was the desire to create
whole-of-Japan decision-making that would benefit from an enhanced
intelligence capability to inform policy. By centralizing national security
decision-making at the NSC, the government could circumvent bureaucratic silos, which had stifled the sharing of classified information across
ministries.[2] At the core of the NSC is the four-minister meeting (prime
minister, foreign minister, defense minister, and chief cabinet secretary), which under the newly appointed National Security Advisor Yachi
Shotaro met frequently and for the first time offered top-down crisis
management and long-term strategic direction.

The State Secrets Law aimed to buttress the protection of classified
information to facilitate intelligence sharing with Japan's close security
partners, principally the United States. The bill allowed the government
to shelve sensitive information in designated areas for sixty years and
mandated jail penalties for public officials and reporters in case of unauthorized disclosures. Its enactment in early December 2013 generated
strong backlash in the Diet and among the public over concerns that the

veil of secrecy could reduce government transparency and accountability.[3] Although Abe weathered this political storm, it is indicative of the strong sensitivity in Japan to tightened security controls over information, given the abuse of the state intelligence apparatus during the World War II era.

With the release of the NSS in mid-December of that year, Prime Minister Abe honed his message on Japan's intended international role as a proactive contributor to peace. The NSS underscored the deteriorating regional environment, with North Korea's nuclear and missile programs and China's nontransparent military buildup, and made an indirect reference to the rise of coercive "gray zone" activities without directly calling out China. It identified three self-reinforcing strategic objectives: deterrence against an attack on Japan, a deepened alliance with the United States, and an improved global security environment anchored in the UN system. Just as Japan had acquired capacity for whole-of-government national security decision-making, the NSS pushed for a multidomain security approach to include sea, space, cyber, energy, and economic assistance policies.

The most significant security policy reform was the reinterpretation of Article 9 to recognize the right of collective self-defense under limited conditions through a Cabinet decision in July 2014, later codified into broader security legislation approved by the Diet in September 2015.[4] Abe had long advocated for the "normalization" of Japan—easing the strictures on the roles and missions of the Self-Defense Forces (SDF)—and in particular had raised the alarm that the outright rejection of the right of collective self-defense could hinder the alliance with the United States if Japan remained a bystander at a time of acute need for its partner. Abe revived the expert panel on security reform from his first term in office, which concluded that the extant government interpretation—recognizing only the right of self-defense—left Japan ill-prepared to face a deteriorating security environment. While the panel recommended the adoption of the full right of collective self-defense, Abe pushed for a limited reinterpretation to overcome the recalcitrance of his party's coalition partner Komeito and of bureaucrats providing legal counsel[5] at the Cabinet Office.[6] Three restrictive conditions were attached before the Government of Japan (GOJ) could use force to aid a close security partner under attack: Japan's existence must be at risk, there was no other way to address the present danger, and only the minimum amount of force would be utilized.

Besides the pathbreaking reinterpretation of collective self-defense, the new legislation allowed for SDF support activities (such as ship inspections and refuel operations, but no use of force) when "important influence situations" threaten to undermine Japan's security—provided armed conflict has not broken out. Other envisioned peacetime activities included asset protection missions for military vessels of close security partners. And to enhance the effectiveness of SDF participation in UN peacekeeping operations (PKOs), new authority was given to use weapons to protect civilian populations or fellow peacekeepers.[7] The two bills submitted to the Diet (Development of Peace and Security Legislation and International Peace Support) aimed to enhance the ability of the SDF to confront evolving challenges to Japan's security and avoid ad hoc decision-making during a crisis, while also reconfirming exclusively defense-oriented policy and democratic control by mandating Diet approval of SDF overseas deployments.

The overhaul of security legislation triggered a firestorm in the Diet and a public backlash, with the largest protests since the 1960 security treaty crisis.[8] Opponents of the bills denounced them as "war legislation," but the political crisis subsided. The right to a limited exercise of collective self-defense did not transform the U.S.-Japan alliance into a mutual defense pact, for Japan reserves the right to come to the defense of an ally only when it deems its own security is threatened.[9] But the security reforms deepened the U.S.-Japan security bond in new ways by enabling greater joint planning for contingencies, eliminating the geographical boundaries to allied security cooperation, and achieving greater interoperability in the revised 2015 U.S.-Japan defense guidelines through the adoption of an Allied Coordination Mechanism.[10]

While Abe invested heavily in the alliance, some of his security reforms were geared toward expanding Japan's strategic reach in the developing world through better coordination of foreign policy tools. In 2015, the government revised its Official Development Assistance (ODA) Charter to integrate aid-giving into its strategy of proactive pacifism. Japan for the first time drew a very explicit line connecting economic cooperation to its national interest, highlighting the contributions of ODA to peace, stability, and a rules-based order based on universal values. The revised ODA Charter allowed for assistance to foreign militaries to pursue noncombat activities such as disaster relief, rule of law enforcement, and the promotion of maritime safety.[11] Japan had come to embrace the need to employ all instruments of national power to secure an open, stable, and noncoercive regional order.

SHAPING THE INDO-PACIFIC

Long gone are the days when Japan avoided an overt political role in the region. Instead, Japanese foreign policy is increasingly geared toward a multilayered network of security and diplomatic partnerships to expand Japan's strategic space. These efforts have manifested in deeper cooperation among maritime democracies in the region, enhanced soft security cooperation with Southeast Asian nations, a regional blueprint for the Indo-Pacific, and a security diversification push through enhanced security and defense ties with both resident and nonresident powers.

Cooperation among Maritime Democracies:
The Quad 1.0

The origins of quadrilateral cooperation between the United States, Japan, Australia, and India go back to their coordinated relief operations in the aftermath of the devastating Indian Ocean tsunami of 2004. A few years later, Abe sought to revive this grouping by tapping on the countries' shared identity as seafaring democracies committed to protecting freedom of navigation and the rule of law. "The Quad" of liberal democracies was consistent with Abe's values-based foreign policy labeled the "arc of freedom and prosperity." Abe debuted the concept of deeper cooperation among regional maritime democracies in an August 2007 speech for the Indian Parliament, where he spoke of the confluence of the Indian and Pacific Oceans and the reasons for India and Japan to work together, with like-minded countries like the United States and Australia, to deliver freedom and prosperity to a broader Asia.[12] A tacit understanding among Quad participants was that China's military buildup and growing assertiveness were stressors for regional stability.

The Quad formally launched in spring 2007 and early activities included a maritime exercise (in which Singapore also took part). However, the first iteration of the Quad waned quickly, a casualty—as Tanvi Madan points out—of shifting domestic politics in each country and differences among them on how to reconcile their equities with China.[13] Concerns over alienating China and surrendering a beneficial economic relationship or cooperation to tackle other policy challenges (e.g., counterterrorism) limited the impetus for Quad collaboration.[14] The abrupt resignation in September 2007 of Prime Minister Abe, the Quad's staunchest advocate, was a blow. By early 2008, it was evident that the "arc of Asian democracies"[15] had reached a dead end when the Australian foreign minister shared with his Chinese counterpart that his country would not participate in further Quad meetings. While the lack of cohesion among Quad members was a major stumbling block, the initiative had encountered another serious hurdle: its lack of broad regional appeal. To the traditional suspicion in Southeast Asia of diplomatic initiatives that could eclipse ASEAN centrality, there were added worries about its lack of inclusivity (promoting cooperation among only a small group of democracies in the region) and perceived focus (pursuing security cooperation to balance against China's influence).[16]

Abe did not surrender the notion that a balancing coalition of maritime democracies was essential to Asia's peace and security. As he returned to office in December 2012, he called for an "Asian Security Diamond" composed of Japan, the United States, Australia, and India to act as "guardians of naval freedom" in order to prevent the South China Sea from becoming "Lake Beijing" and China effectively undermining Japan's administrative control of the East China Sea with its frequent trespasses.[17] And yet, the lessons of the Quad 1.0's demise provided a new compass for Japanese foreign policy, for the Abe administration came to advocate a regional blueprint that was more expansive, more inclusive, and multidimensional.

A Blueprint for Japanese Regional Leadership

The path to the Free and Open Indo-Pacific (FOIP) vision began with stepped-up diplomatic engagement with Southeast Asia. As recounted by the first National Security Advisor Yachi Shotaro, diplomatic tours by Prime Minister Abe, Deputy Prime Minister Aso Taro, and then Foreign Minister Kishida Fumio had covered most of Southeast Asia and Oceania in the first seven months of Abe's second term.[18] The prime minister launched the FOIP concept in his 2016 speech in Kenya at the Sixth Tokyo International Conference on African Development. Abe's desire to expand Japan's strategic horizons was evident in his remark that "Japan bears the responsibility of fostering the confluence of the Pacific and Indian Oceans and of Asia and Africa into a place that values freedom, the rule of law, and the market economy."[19] It was a bid for international leadership built on driving the benefits of connectivity while not excluding China, as Hosoya Yuichi points out.[20] The diplomatic push downplayed democracy promotion and instead emphasized the value of the rule of law in structuring relations among diverse countries, as well as the benefits of increasing options for economic and security cooperation to preserve freedom of choice.

Japan once more had recalibrated its regional strategy to encourage buy-in from Southeast Asia—just as it had forty years prior with the Fukuda Doctrine. But the package on offer was markedly different, for it went beyond deepened economic engagement to explicitly incorporate security and defense cooperation. In November 2016, Japan's Ministry of Defense issued its Vientiane Vision for defense cooperation with ASEAN. Building upon progress made since the 2000s, it encompassed a wide array of capacity-building efforts (intelligence, surveillance, reconnaissance, disaster relief, land mine clearance, transfers of defense equipment, educational exchanges, and multilateral joint training and exercises) to boost ASEAN nations' ability to safeguard their maritime and airspace security.[21] The aim was to construct a "soft security infrastructure," to borrow Corey Wallace's apt term,[22] rather than a hard balancing effort, given Japan's constraints and ASEAN's reluctance.

Japan's Indo-Pacific concept has caught on, with a growing set of countries using it as the organizing framework for their own regional strategy documents.[23] U.S. President Donald Trump's administration embraced the FOIP banner, although there were marked differences, since the American initiative lacked an economic engagement pillar and was explicitly anchored in strategic competition with China. Concerned the United States would ask the region to choose sides, ASEAN responded with its 2019 Indo-Pacific Outlook emphasizing inclusiveness, economic connectivity, and the role of regional platforms like the East Asia Summit, which are anchored on the ASEAN centrality principle.[24] Japan's own FOIP idea has evolved over time in order for the country to remain attuned to ASEAN's sensitivities: Japan agreed to relabel FOIP a "vision" and not a "strategy" and has embraced ASEAN centrality as a core guiding principle of FOIP.[25]

Bilateral and Minilateral Security Partnerships

Conditions for the revival of the Quad were more propitious. China's growing assertiveness in the decade since the demise of the first iteration of the Quad created much stronger incentives for the four democracies to reconvene in 2017. Border skirmishes with India, economic coercion and domestic political interference in Australia, the rejection of the Tribunal Award refuting Chinese expansive claims in the South China Sea, and transgressions into Japanese territorial waters, among other actions, heightened concerns about China's aims for the region. The second life of the Quad was built on a much stronger foundation since bilateral and trilateral ties among its members had deepened over the past decade. Japan's relationship with Australia and India made great strides during the first and second Abe administrations—part of a larger effort to cultivate new security partnerships,[26] as can be appreciated in Table 11.1.

China's reactions to the revived Quad have ranged from the dismissive (prognosticating its quick demise) to the alarmist (dubbing it an Asian NATO bent on encircling China). Both characterizations miss the mark. The Quad 2.0 is not a security pact with pledges of mutual defense but a mechanism that allows strategic coordination to preserve regional stability. Quadrilateral cooperation has matured through regular foreign ministers' and annual leaders' meetings since 2021 and a crisper formulation of the Quad's mandate as providing practical solutions to the region's problems. This has entailed the launch of working groups on COVID-19 vaccinations, infrastructure, climate change, supply chain resilience, and emerging technologies. The role of the Quad as a supplier of public goods has been well received in Southeast Asia. In a 2021 ISEAS-Yusof Ishak Institute survey, 59 percent of respondents deemed the strengthening of the Quad through practical cooperation a positive development for the region.[27]

While the Quad continues to evolve, Japan's FOIP initiatives on economic connectivity and security capacity-building positioned it well in Southeast Asia. Japan cinched the top score as the most trusted nation "to do the right thing to contribute to global peace, security, prosperity and governance" in ISEAS surveys of elite opinion in Southeast Asia[28] over the past four years.[29] Elite opinion in Southeast Asia sees the United States and China as exerting the greatest economic and strategic influence in the region, but trust toward the two great powers runs lower, especially for China.[30] In fact, respondents to the ISEAS survey see Japan as a "preferred and strategic partner" in the region to help ASEAN hedge against a China-U.S. strategic rivalry.[31]

Successes in deepening bilateral security partnerships and working in concert with democracies in the Indo-Pacific had one notable

Table 11.1. Japan's security diversification

Type of partnership	Australia	India	United Kingdom	France	Vietnam	Philippines	South Korea
Declaration strategic partnership	Yes, 2007 Elevated to Special Strategic Partnership in 2014	Yes, 2006 Elevated to Special Strategic and Global Partnership in 2015. Announced in 2015 the Japan and India Vision 2025 Special Strategic and Global Partnership Working Together for Peace and Prosperity of the Indo-Pacific Region and the World.	Yes 2017	Yes Elevated to Exceptional Partnership in 2013	Yes, 2009 Elevated to Extensive Strategic Partnership for Peace and Prosperity in Asia in 2014	Yes 2011	No
2+2 Consultative Mechanism	Yes 2007	Yes 2019	Yes 2015	Yes 2014	No	Yes April 2022	No
Acquisition & Cross-Service Agreement (ACSA)	Yes Signed 2010, effective 2013; new agreement effective 2017	Yes 2021	Yes 2017	Yes Signed 2018, effective 2019	No	No Possibility of ACSA discussed	No
Defense equipment & tech transfer agreements	Yes 2014	Yes 2016	Yes 2013	Yes Signed 2015, effective 2016	Yes 2021	Yes 2016	No

Type of partnership	Australia	India	United Kingdom	France	Vietnam	Philippines	South Korea
Information security agreements (ISA, GSOIA, GSOMIA)	Yes, Information Security Agreement (ISA)	Yes, military information security agreement	Yes, Information Security Agreement (ISA)	Yes, Information Security Agreement (ISA)	No	No	Yes, General Security of Military Information Agreement (GSOMIA)
	2012	2015	2014	2011			2016
Bilateral/ multilateral military exercises	Yes, regular bilat. exercises since 2009	Yes, bilat. exercises	Yes, bilat. exercises	Yes, bilat. exercises	Yes, bilat. exercises	Yes, bilat. exercises	No bilat. exercises
	Yes, multilat. exercises (e.g., Japan-US-Australia)	Yes, multilat. Exercises (e.g., Japan-India-U.S. and Quad Malabar exercises)	Yes, multilat. exercises (e.g., Australia-Japan-UK-US)	Yes, multilat. exercises (e.g., Japan-France-Australia-US, Japan-France-US, Japan-EU)	Yes, multilat. exercises	Yes, multilat. exercises (e.g., Japan-US-Philippines, Japan-US-India-Philippines)	Yes, multilat. exercises (e.g., Japan-US-ROK)
Visiting forces agreement	Yes Japan-Australia Reciprocal Access Agreement, 2022	No	Yes Japan-UK Reciprocal Access Agreement, 2023	No Possibility of Japan-France Reciprocal Access Agreement discussed	No	No Possibility of Japan-Philippines Reciprocal Access Agreement discussed	No

Sources: Wilhelm Vosse and Paul Midford, eds., *Japan's New Security Partnerships: Beyond the Security Alliance* (Manchester, UK: Manchester University Press, 2018); ministries in charge of foreign affairs and defense for Japan and above partner countries.

exemption: South Korea. The undeveloped security ties with this geo-graphically close neighbor stand out (see Table 11.1). Unresolved his-torical grievances over the sexual exploitation of Korean "comfort women" and forced labor during World War II, territorial disputes over the Takeshima/Dokdo Islands, and disagreements about the sincerity of Japanese apologies for atrocities committed during its colonization of the peninsula continue to cast a long shadow on Japan-Korea rela-tions. But contemporary domestic politics are essential to understanding current dynamics. South Korea's democratization has elevated victims' claims, whether they were granted compensation (workers) or not (women) in the 1965 treaty for the normalization of relations. Abe's past statements denying a direct role of the Japanese military in the "com-fort women" system and the inquiries during his second administration about the background of the 1993 Kono Statement of contrition (made by then Chief Cabinet Secretary Kono Yohei) sowed distrust.[32] Political polarization in South Korea, with one administration unraveling mile-stone agreements reached with Japan by the outgoing government, have prevented a lasting improvement in relations between the two countries.

Prime Minister Abe and South Korean President Park Geun-hye delivered an important breakthrough with the 2015 Comfort Women Agreement, whereby the Japanese government issued an apology and contributed 1 billion yen to a newly established foundation to com-pensate victims. President Moon Jae-in, however, hollowed out the agreement with the dismantling of the foundation in 2018.[33] Relations deteriorated further that fall with rulings from the South Korean Supreme Court awarding compensation for forced wartime labor and ordering the confiscation of some Japanese companies' assets based in South Korea. The pending liquidation of such assets is a red line for Tokyo, which regards this development as a violation of the normaliza-tion agreement that restored ties between both countries. Spillover into the economic and security realms has been effected through the mutual recission of preferred status on export controls after Japan tightened its regulations on the export of advanced chemicals to South Korea in July 2019. The South Korean government vacillated over terminating the military information-sharing agreement with Japan (it did not). There have been no winners from the current state of affairs, as Japan and South Korea have been unable to capitalize on shared interests as fellow democracies, allies of the United States, and advanced tech powers in an increasingly dangerous neighborhood.

THE CHINA QUESTION

China's rise to great power status has presented both economic opportunities and deep security challenges for Japan. The takeoff of the Chinese economy (aided by decades of Japanese economic assistance and hefty investments from Japanese corporations) and the pre-pandemic inflows of Chinese tourists have been important stimulants to Japanese economic growth and part and parcel of cost-minimization efforts in Japanese supply chains. China rose to become Japan's top trading partner, and Japan is also a top foreign investor in the Chinese market.[34]

As China's economic and military power steeply increased, so did its ambition to influence global and regional affairs. China has long been a beneficiary of the post–World War II multilateral system, so rather than eschewing it altogether, a major goal has been to increase its influence within it, as can be seen in campaigns to have greater sway over multiple UN bodies and the Bretton Woods institutions for trade, development, and finance. The quest for influence through the reform of international governance has also included institutional innovation, such as the establishment of the Asian Infrastructure Investment Bank (AIIB),[35] and stepped-up political and economic diplomacy, such as the establishment of groupings like BRICS (Brazil, Russia, India, China, and South Africa). But Chinese reformism has been accompanied by growing revisionism. Beijing has sought to undermine norms and regimes it sees as constraining its national power and prestige (U.S. alliances, freedom of navigation, protection of human rights, etc.),[36] and it has abandoned past caution to contradict the rules-based order more directly through its gray zone pressure tactics and economic coercion; unilateral claims over the sea, land, and airspace of its neighbors; and interference in their domestic political affairs.

China's campaign to become the dominant power in Asia could undermine important national interests of Japan. The establishment of a Chinese sphere of influence would marginalize the United States— Japan's security guarantor—from the regional order. Beijing's ability to project military power past the first island chain (extending from Japan's southwestern flank to Taiwan and the Philippines) and control strategic sea lines of communication in the East China Sea, South China Sea, and Indian Ocean would put Japan in a vulnerable position, both in defending itself and in sustaining vital economic activities.[37] As both economic magnet and security threat, China and the conundrums it presents play vividly in the minds of Japan's strategic planners.

As a frontline state, Japan has been cognizant of the destabilizing effects of how China has chosen to wield its power, especially against its neighbors. This wariness was evident even before U.S.-China relations turned decidedly more competitive. In an interview with *The Economist*, former Japanese ambassador to the United States Sasae Kenichiro noted that after flareups in tensions over the Senkaku Islands in 2010 and 2012, "We warned the U.S.: This is not a small compartmentalized issue between Japan and China, but a sign of a growing power in the region."[38] China's declaration in November 2013 of an Air Defense Identification Zone (ADIZ) over the East China Sea was a sign of further escalation that drew protests from the United States and Japan.[39] High-level Sino-Japanese political dialogue was effectively frozen for several years, and the two parties made slow progress toward devising a communication mechanism to prevent accidental clashes at sea and in the air, even though their vessels have been operating in close proximity. Such an agreement was only reached by mid-2018 but remained unimplemented.[40]

By then, a thaw in bilateral relations was palpable in other ways. Although neither China nor Japan were prepared to endorse each other's regional blueprints (FOIP and the Belt and Road Initiative), they agreed to promote business cooperation in third-country markets by signing fifty memoranda of understanding, which, though largely unimplemented, were representative of the countries' shared desire to stabilize relations.[41] Senior political visits resumed when Premier Li Keqiang traveled to Japan in May 2018 (the first visit by a Chinese premier in eight years), and Prime Minister Abe visited China the following fall (the first visit by a Japanese leader in seven years). Plans were made for a state visit by President Xi Jinping in 2020, but the COVID-19 pandemic intervened.

The improved climate for bilateral ties did not derive from a resolution of the territorial dispute. China's gray zone tactics challenging Japan's administrative control continued, as did Japan's efforts to boost the capabilities of its own coast guard and plan for the protection of remote islands. It did not reflect higher levels of trust. The Japanese public remains deeply skeptical of China's intentions, with 88 percent of Japanese reporting unfavorable views of China in 2021 (the highest out of the seventeen advanced economies surveyed that year).[42] Rather, the carefully orchestrated rapprochement harked back to the established practice of compartmentalizing the most vexing issues to prevent them from dominating the entire relationship. It was also aided by Beijing's more conciliatory approach as it contemplated an ever-expanding rift with the United States.

Ups and Downs of Allied Cooperation on the China Challenge

Despite the tactical rapprochement, China's military buildup and coercive diplomacy remain paramount concerns for Japan. In addressing them effectively, coordination with the United States is essential. The path toward U.S.-Japan coordination on the China challenge, however, has not been steady.

Throughout the second Abe administration, unease about the United States' ability to devise an effective Asia strategy and China policy was palpable. President Barack Obama's much-vaunted "pivot to Asia" largely failed to materialize when budget fights capped defense expenditures and a lame duck president was unable to secure a Trans-Pacific Partnership (TPP) ratification vote in a deeply polarized United States. Tokyo was not persuaded that the Obama administration was effective in curbing China's expansionism. In the aftermath of the Chinese ADIZ declaration over the East China Sea, the United States mounted an energetic response, including flying two B-52 bombers through the area, but its response to China's buildup of militarized outposts in the South China Sea appeared more tepid in light of China's strategic advances.[43] Widespread concern grew in Tokyo that the United States had failed to deter or punish China for its unilateral challenges to the status quo.[44]

With the election of Donald Trump in November 2016, American domestic politics loomed large over the future of Asia. The Trump presidency did not disrupt the U.S.-Japan relationship like it damaged many other U.S. strategic partnerships. The designation of China as a revisionist power in the 2017 National Security Strategy and the embrace of FOIP by the Trump administration were received positively in Tokyo as signs of greater resolve to counter China's revisionism and of Tokyo's influence in shaping its ally's Asia policy. To handle a mercurial American president, Prime Minister Abe invested heavily in personal diplomacy and touted Japanese investments and weapons purchases as tangible evidence of a more balanced relationship.

The Trump administration's "America First" foreign policy, however, reflected strains of unilateralism and isolationism that worked to Japan's detriment. The U.S. alliance system was weakened by Trump's actions: withdrawing from the TPP, harassing other allies and threatening to withdraw soldiers from South Korea and Germany due to bloated demands for expanded host nation contributions (a fourfold increase to cover costs of deployed U.S. troops in Japan's case), and imposing "national security" tariffs against allies and partners (including Japan). These actions also undercut American influence and prevented coordination among like-minded countries to compete against China.

How each ally grapples with the right mix of competition and collaboration has influenced their ability to coordinate on China policy. The Trump administration adopted a zero-sum framework of comprehensive competition with China with the intent of unilaterally curbing Chinese behavior over a wide swath of policy areas, and it increasingly defined the great power contest in ideological terms.[45] Abe sought to strengthen Japan's hand in competition with China, but he was keen to restore stability and opted for selective competition and cooperation. The Abe government strengthened its external balancing by deepening ties to the U.S. and like-minded countries and seeking to reduce economic overdependence on China. It devised proactive economic statecraft to compete with China in offering development finance and a different model for regional integration in Asia. At the same time, it sought to stabilize diplomatic relations with China to reduce friction and left room for cooperation in areas such as climate change and regional trade.[46] However, the competitive pull in the Japan-China relationship was more pronounced toward the end of Abe's tenure. China's record-breaking vessel incursions into the waters near the Senkaku Islands, intensifying pressure on Taiwan, crackdown on human rights in Hong Kong and Xinjiang, and mismanagement of the global COVID-19 pandemic that began with an outbreak in Wuhan put pressure on bilateral ties.

ENDURING BRAKES ON JAPAN'S SECURITY TRANSFORMATION

Abe's security reforms increased Japan's foreign policy capability by streamlining decision-making, improving intelligence sharing, and articulating whole-of-Japan national security objectives. The U.S.-Japan alliance deepened with landmark Japanese security legislation endorsing the right to collective self-defense under certain conditions, which enabled deeper strategic planning and interoperability. Japanese diplomatic initiatives, such as FOIP and the Quad, elevated Japan's international status, framed the regional strategies of other actors, and mobilized maritime democracies toward supplying regional public goods. Outreach to Southeast Asia was amplified with a soft security component, and Japan deepened its security ties with countries in the region and beyond. The second Abe administration's proactive economic statecraft and its role in a budding security network provided Japan some leverage vis-à-vis China, sparing it from the worst of China's "wolf warrior" diplomacy, as Professor He Yinan points out.[47]

Abe came short of accomplishing his most cherished goals, however: constitutional reform and a peace treaty with Russia.[48] The proposal to reform Article 9 that Abe championed in his second term was more modest, partly to accommodate the reluctance of coalition partner Komeito to accept more sweeping changes to security policy.[49] His proposed amendment was limited to adding language to make the constitutionality of the SDF explicit, but nonetheless opposition to amending the constitution grew because segments of the public distrusted his intentions.[50] Abe's assiduous courtship of Russian President Vladimir Putin and his reported willingness to accept the return of just two of the disputed northern Kuril Islands in order to conclude a peace treaty with Russia proved fruitless.[51]

In other areas of Japan's defense and security policy, there was remarkable continuity. Despite the continued deterioration of the security environment, Japan's defense expenditures flatlined for the past thirty years (see Figure 11.1). Abe did deliver gradual defense budget hikes, but within the historical norm of below 1 percent of GDP.[52] These modest increases were not enough to alter larger trends. China bypassed Japan on military expenditures in the early twenty-first century, and since then a yawning gap has opened between them. In the late 2000s, India also overtook Japan, and more recently South Korea has caught up with Japan. Importantly, none of these countries face the same constraints Japan does regarding criteria for use of force authorization, restrictions on the development of power projection capabilities, and limits to the types of overseas military operations that can be sanctioned. Security experts Jeffrey Hornung and Mike Mochizuki are spot on when they note that Japanese security exceptionalism is still alive *after* the Abe reforms.[53]

Figure 11.1. Military expenditure by country, 1990–2020 (constant 2019 million USD)

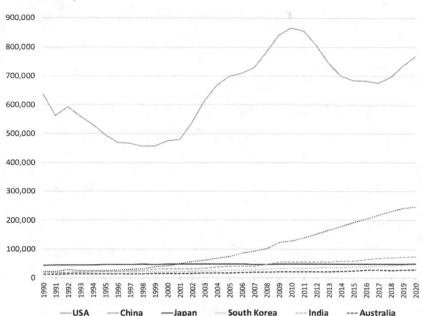

Source: Stockholm International Peace Research Institute (SIPRI), SIPRI Military Expenditure Database, accessed February 11, 2022, www.sipri.org/databases/milex.

The late Prime Minister Abe did transform Japanese foreign policy. It was during his second term that Japan was able to position itself as a strategic partner of the United States with a clear vision of the desirable regional order. Enhanced national security decision-making and the expanded network of economic and security partnerships crafted under Abe will serve his successors well.

NOTES

1. Michael J. Green offers an authoritative account of Japan's grand strategy under Abe. See Green, *Line of Advantage: Japan's Grand Strategy in the Era of Abe Shinzo* (New York: Columbia University Press, 2022).

2. Mayumi Fukushima and Richard J. Samuels, "Japan's National Security Council: Filling the Whole of Government?" *International Affairs* 94, no. 4 (2018): 773–90.

3. See Linda Sieg and Kiyoshi Takenaka, "Japan Enacts Strict State Secrets Law Despite Protests," *Reuters*, December 6, 2013, www.reuters.com/article/us-japan-secrets/japan-enacts-strict-state-secrets-law-despite-protests-idUSBRE9B50JT20131206.

4. In April 2014, the Japanese government lifted the ban on arms exports that had been in place since 1976 and had further restricted weapons sales based on the three principles issued in 1967 (no arms sales to communist nations, countries under UN sanctions, or countries involved in armed conflict). In lifting the prohibition, the Abe administration issued new guidelines to ensure weapons sales would be limited to trusted partners. The goals of the policy shift were to enhance the competitiveness of the Japanese defense industry through economies of scale, deepen U.S.-Japan cooperation through joint development and production of weapon systems, and expand Japan's influence in the world through military capacity-building efforts. See Shannon Dick and Hana Rudolph, "Japan Updates Arms Export Policy," The Stimson Center, April 24, 2014, www.stimson.org/2014/japan-updates-arms-export-policy-0/; and Martin Fackler, "Japan Ends Decades-Long Ban on Export of Weapons," *The New York Times*, April 1, 2014, www.nytimes.com/2014/04/02/world/asia/japan-ends-half-century-ban-on-weapons-exports.html.

5. The Cabinet Legislation Bureau offers legal counsel to the Cabinet and advises on the constitutionality of proposed bills.

6. Jeffrey W. Hornung, "Japan's 2015 Security Legislation: Change Rooted Firmly in Continuity," in *Routledge Handbook of Japanese Foreign Policy*, ed. Mary M. McCarthy (New York: Routledge, 2018), 22–40.

7. Satoru Mori, "The New Security Legislation and Japanese Public Reaction," Tokyo Foundation for Policy Research, December 2, 2015, www.tkfd.or.jp/en/research/detail.php?id=542; and Hitoshi Nasu, "Japan's 2015 Security Legislation: Challenges to Its Implementation Under International Law," *International Law Studies* 92, study no. 249 (2016): 249–80.

8. See Kiyoshi Takenaka, "Huge Protest in Tokyo Rail against PM Abe's Security Bills," *Reuters*, August 30, 2015, www.reuters.com/article/us-japan-politics-protest/huge-protest-in-tokyo-rails-against-pm-abes-security-bills-idUSKCN0QZ0C320150830.

9. Adam P. Liff, "Japan's Defense Policy: Abe the Evolutionary," *The Washington Quarterly* 38, no. 2 (2015): 79–99.

10. Green, *Line of Advantage*, 94, 104.

11. See Cabinet Office of Japan, "Cabinet Decision on the Development Cooperation Charter," February 10, 2015, www.mofa.go.jp/files/000067701.pdf.

12. See Shinzo Abe, "Confluence of the Two Seas," Speech to Parliament of the Republic of India, New Delhi, August 22, 2007, www.mofa.go.jp/region/asia-paci/pmv0708/speech-2.html.

13. Tanvi Madan, "India, the Indo-Pacific, and the Quad," in *Regional Perspectives on the Quadrilateral Dialogue and the Indo-Pacific*, ed. Scott W. Harold, Tanvi Madan, and Natalie Sambhi (Santa Monica, CA: RAND Corporation, 2020), 5–21, www.rand.org/pubs/conf_proceedings/CF414.html.

14. Kevin Rudd, "Why the Quad Alarms China: Its Success Poses a Major Threat to Beijing's Ambitions," *Foreign Affairs*, August 6, 2021; and Dhruva Jaishankar and Tanvi Madan, "How the Quad Can Match the Hype," *Foreign Affairs*, April 15, 2021.

15. As dubbed by Frank Ching, "'Asian Arc' Doomed without Australia," *The Japan Times*, February 22, 2008, www.japantimes.co.jp/opinion/2008/02 /22/commentary/asian-arc-doomed-without-australia/.

16. Yuichi Hosoya, "FOIP 2.0: The Evolution of Japan's Free and Open Indo-Pacific Strategy," *Asia-Pacific Review* 26, no. 1 (2019): 18–28.

17. See Shinzo Abe, "Asia's Democratic Security Diamond," Project Syndicate, December 27, 2012, www.project-syndicate.org/onpoint/a-strategic -alliance-for-japan-and-india-by-shinzo-abe.

18. See "Behind the New Abe Diplomacy: An Interview with Cabinet Advisor Yachi Shōtarō (Part One)," Nippon.com, August 8, 2013, www.nippon .com/en/currents/d00089/.

19. See Shinzo Abe, "Address by Prime Minister Shinzo Abe at the Opening Session of the Sixth Tokyo International Conference on African Development (TICAD VI)," Speech at the Kenyatta International Convention Centre, Nairobi, Kenya, August 27, 2016, www.mofa.go.jp/afr/af2/page4e_000496.html.

20. Hosoya, "FOIP 2.0."

21. See Ministry of Defense of Japan, "Vientiane Vision: Japan's Defense Cooperation Initiative with ASEAN," www.mod.go.jp/en/d_act/exc/ vientianevision/index.html.

22. Corey Wallace, "Japan's Strategic Contrast: Continuing Influence despite Relative Power Decline in Southeast Asia," *The Pacific Review* 32, no. 5 (2019): 863–97.

23. Parties that have issued Indo-Pacific strategies include India, France, Germany, the Netherlands, and the EU. See Darshana M. Baruah, "India in the Indo-Pacific: New Delhi's Theater of Opportunity," Carnegie Endowment for International Peace, Washington, DC, June 30, 2020), https:// carnegieendowment.org/2020/06/30/india-in-indo-pacific-new-delhi-s-theater -of-opportunity-pub-82205; and Girish Luthra, "An Assessment of the European Union's Indo-Pacific Strategy," Observer Research Foundation Issue Brief no. 504, November 10, 2021, www.orfonline.org/research/an-assessment-of -the-european-unions-indo-pacific-strategy/.

24. Jonathan Stromseth, "Don't Make Us Choose: Southeast Asia in the Throes of U.S.-China Rivalry," Report, The Brookings Institution, Washington, DC, October 2019, 14, www.brookings.edu/research/dont-make-us -choose-southeast-asia-in-the-throes-of-us-china-rivalry/.

25. Kei Koga, "Japan and Southeast Asia in the Indo-Pacific," in *Implementing the Indo-Pacific: Japan's Region Building Initiatives*, ed. Kyle Springer (Perth, Australia: Perth USAsia Centre, 2019), 24–37, perthusasia.edu.au/ events/past-conferences/defence-forum-2019/2019-indo-pacific-defence- conference-videos/keynotes-and-feature-presentations/pu-134-japan-book- web.aspx.

26. Wilhelm Vosse and Paul Midford, eds., *Japan's New Security Partnerships: Beyond the Security Alliance* (Manchester, UK: Manchester University Press, 2018).

27. Sharon Seah et al., "The State of Southeast Asia 2022 Survey Report," ISEAS-Yusof Ishak Institute, Asian Studies Centre, Singapore, 2022, 28, https://www.iseas.edu.sg/wp-content/uploads/2022/02/The-State-of-SEA-2022_FA_Digital_FINAL.pdf.

28. Japan's score decreased to 54.2 percent in 2022 from 68.2 percent in 2021, mostly due to a drop in Cambodian respondents' scores. See Seah et al., "The State of Southeast Asia 2022 Survey Report," 44.

29. ISEAS-Yusof Ishak Institute, "The State of Southeast Asia Survey," 2019–2022, www.iseas.edu.sg.

30. In 2022, the trust scores for the United States and China were 52.8 percent and 26.8 percent, respectively. See Seah et al., "The State of Southeast Asia 2022 Survey Report," 3.

31. Ibid., 33.

32. See "Japan's Abe Says Won't Alter 1993 Apology on 'Comfort Women,'" *Reuters*, March 13, 2014, www.reuters.com/article/us-japan-korea/japans-abe-says-wont-alter-1993-apology-on-comfort-women-idUSBREA2D04R20140314.

33. See "'Comfort Women': Japan and South Korea Hail Agreement," BBC, December 28, 2015, www.bbc.com/news/world-asia-35190464.

34. Qinchen Zhang, "Sectoral and Country-Origin Dynamics of FDI in China in 1997–2020," *The Chinese Economy* 56, no. 2 (2022): 89–103.

35. David Dollar, "Four Decades of Reforming China's International Economic Role," Paper presented at *Reform and Opening: Forty Years and Counting*, Center for the Study of Contemporary China, University of Pennsylvania, April 26–27, 2018.

36. Mira Rapp-Hooper et al., "Responding to China's Complicated Views on International Order," Alliance Policy Coordination Brief, Project on China Risk and China Opportunity for the U.S.-Japan Alliance, Carnegie Endowment for International Peace, Washington, DC, October 10, 2019, https://carnegieendowment.org/2019/10/10/responding-to-china-s-complicated-views-on-international-order-pub-80021.

37. Kurt M. Campbell and Rush Doshi, "How America Can Shore Up Asian Order: A Strategy for Restoring Balance and Legitimacy," *Foreign Affairs*, January 12, 2021, www.foreignaffairs.com/articles/united-states/2021-01-12/how-america-can-shore-asian-order; and Noboru Yamaguchi, "The Geostrategy of FOIP vs. BRI and the Role for Japan," Working paper no. 3, Shaping the Pragmatic and Effective Response to China Project, Sasakawa Peace Foundation, Tokyo, 2021, www.spf.org/iina/en/articles/yamaguchi_04.html.

38. Quoted in "How Japan Sees China," *The Economist*, January 1, 2022, www.economist.com/asia/2022/01/01/how-japan-sees-china.

39. Masafumi Iida, "China's Security Threats and Japan's Responses," in *Strategic Japan 2021: The Future of Japan-China Relations*, Center for Stra-

tegic and International Studies, Washington, DC, 2021, https://csis-website
-prod.s3.amazonaws.com/s3fs-public/210405_Iida_Security%20Issues.pdf
?Ag0IL6LQTTMb_HXsk3XJnIDMLazbE9Bg.

40. See "Japan and China Launch Defense Communication Mechanism to
Prevent Air and Sea Clashes," *The Japan Times*, June 8, 2018, www.japantimes
.co.jp/news/2018/06/08/national/politics-diplomacy/japan-china-launch
-defense-communication-mechanism-prevent-air-sea-clashes/.

41. Mireya Solís, "China, Japan, and the Art of Economic Statecraft,"
Global China, The Brookings Institution, Washington, February 2020, www
.brookings.edu/research/china-japan-and-the-art-of-economic-statecraft/.

42. Laura Silver, Kat Devlin, and Christine Huang, "Large Majorities Say
China Does Not Respect the Personal Freedom of Its People," Pew Research
Center, June 30, 2021, https://www.pewresearch.org/global/wp-content/
uploads/sites/2/2021/06/PG_2021.06.30_Global-Views-China_FINAL.pdf.

43. Ryan Hass, *Stronger: Adapting America's China Strategy in an Age of
Competitive Interdependence* (New Haven, CT: Yale University Press, 2021),
139, 141.

44. Satoru Mori, "U.S. Leadership in Maritime Asia: A Japanese Perspective
on the Rebalance and Beyond," in *China's Rise and Australia-Japan-U.S. Relations: Primacy and Leadership in East Asia*, ed. Michael Heazle and Andrew
O'Neil (Northampton, MA: Edward Elgar Publishing, 2018), 119–42.

45. Dollar, Hass, and Bader provide a good assessment of the maximalist
aims and limited accomplishments of the Trump administration's China policy.
See David Dollar, Ryan Hass, and Jeffrey A. Bader, "Assessing U.S.-China Relations 2 Years into the Trump Presidency," The Brookings Institution, January
15, 2019, www.brookings.edu/blog/order-from-chaos/2019/01/15/assessing-u
-s-china-relations-2-years-into-the-trump-presidency/.

46. Mireya Solís, "The Underappreciated Power: Japan after Abe," *Foreign
Affairs*, November/December 2020, www.foreignaffairs.com/articles/japan
/2020-10-13/underappreciated-power.

47. Yinan He, "The Japan Differential: China's Policy toward Japan during
the Trump Era," *Asia Policy* 17, no. 2 (2022): 99–123.

48. Adam P. Liff and Phillip Y. Lipscy, "Japan Transformed? The Foreign
Policy Legacy of the Abe Government," *Journal of Japanese Studies* 48, no. 1
(Winter 2022): 123–47.

49. Adam Liff and Ko Maeda, "Electoral Incentives, Policy Compromise,
and Coalition Durability: Japan's LDP-Komeito Government in a Mixed Electoral System," *Japanese Journal of Political Science* 20, no. 1 (2019): 53–73.

50. Kenneth Mori McElwain, "The Perils and Virtues of Constitutional
Flexibility: Japan's Constitution and the Liberal International Order," in *The
Crisis of Liberal Internationalism: Japan and the World Order*, ed. Yoichi
Funabashi and John Ikenberry (Washington, DC: Brookings Institution Press,
2020), 303–24.

51. See James D. J. Brown, "The High Price of a Two-Island Deal," *The Japan Times*, November 16, 2018, www.japantimes.co.jp/opinion/2018/11/16/commentary/japan-commentary/high-price-two-island-deal/.

52. Yuki Tatsumi, "Japanese Defence Spending at the Fiscal Crossroads," East Asia Forum, February 17, 2021, www.eastasiaforum.org/2021/02/17/japanese-defence-spending-at-the-fiscal-crossroads/.

53. Jeffrey W. Hornung and Mike M. Mochizuki, "Japan: Still an Exceptional U.S. Ally," *The Washington Quarterly* 39, no. 1 (Spring 2016): 95–116.

CHAPTER 12

Taming a Hobbesian World?

JAPAN'S SHARPER SECURITY CHOICES

In the post–Abe Shinzo era, there are no indications of Japan's strategic retreat. The opposite seems true. As the country faces a harsher international environment—war in Europe and a potential end to Asia's long peace (possibly through a Taiwan contingency)—rethinking Japan's defense architecture has gained greater urgency. National security debates are now front and center in Japanese elections and the public has not balked at plans for much larger defense budgets and the acquisition of military equipment that blurs the line between defensive and offensive capabilities.

This is a plastic moment as Japan revisits its National Security Strategy (NSS) and other defense and security strategy documents. Japan's strategic repositioning is shaped by heightened threat perception due to pressure coming from three fronts (China, Russia, and North Korea) and a deteriorating deterrence posture given the military buildup around its perimeter. Addressing these challenges will be critical to the U.S.-Japan alliance. In rolling out his "New Realism diplomacy," Prime Minister Kishida reconfirmed the centrality of the Free and Open Indo-Pacific (FOIP) vision and the Quad, but he has also expanded the reach of Japan's diplomacy by joining the G7 effort to oppose Russia's invasion of Ukraine through an unprecedented package of punishing sanctions.

Change is palpable, but so is continuity. The push for expanded military expenditures will be tempered by competing demands for COVID-19 relief and the agenda for socioeconomic revitalization. As Japan manages greater threats to peace in Asia and the fallout from conflict in Europe, the government's response will be bound by the high bar set for the activation of collective self-defense, the continued unofficial relationship with Taiwan, and the public's continued aversion to Japan's Self-Defense Forces' (SDF) combat operations abroad.

PERILOUS TIMES

The COVID-19 pandemic continues to wreak havoc, with lives lost and economies shattered, and has exposed the geopolitical fault lines preventing a coordinated international response to ease the public health crisis.[1] The domestic political trajectories of the great powers are of growing concern. The fate of American democracy is now in question as former U.S. President Donald Trump's failure to accept his defeat in the 2020 election encouraged a violent insurrection on January 6, 2021, at the Capitol to disrupt the peaceful transfer of power. In China, the foibles of one-man rule under President Xi Jinping are increasingly exposed and there is no tolerance for domestic dissent. Xi's prolonged zero-COVID policies and a disorganized reopening have imposed huge social and economic costs on China and threatened global growth. Under Xi, China has accelerated its pace of amassing a vast arsenal of nuclear, missile, and hypersonic weapons that could severely compromise the deterrence posture of the United States and its allies.[2]

Concerns over the arms race in the region are compounded by the growing threat from North Korea. In the course of 2022, North Korean leader Kim Jong-un's regime carried out upward of eighty-six missile tests—including launching a suspected intercontinental ballistic missile and one missile that flew over Japanese territory—and it appears ready to resume nuclear testing as well.[3] Closer Sino-Russian alignment, long a preoccupation of Japan's strategic planners, has become a more pressing reality. On February 4, 2022, these two powers issued a joint communiqué that advertised a friendship "with no limits" and support for each other's strategic goals in their respective neighborhoods, noting unity in opposing NATO enlargement, supporting Russia's proposals for binding security guarantees in Europe, rejecting the "formation of closed bloc structures and opposing camps in the Asia-Pacific region," and deeming the U.S. Indo-Pacific strategy a source of instability.[4] Russian President Vladimir Putin's unprovoked invasion of Ukraine three weeks later was informed by his deep-seated personal grievances over Russia's fortunes after the fall of the Soviet Union, his refusal to acknowledge full sovereign rights of former Soviet states, and his ambition to redraw the post–Cold War European order.[5]

THE LONG SHADOW OF UKRAINE IN EAST ASIA

Prime Minister Kishida's response to Russia's military aggression was energetic and unprecedented. He shelved Abe's Russia diplomacy. The limits of his predecessor's policy of diplomatic and economic engagement to facilitate an agreement on the territorial dispute and to help keep distance between Russia and China had become apparent long before Russian tanks crossed the Ukrainian border. This was underlined by the 2020 Russian constitutional amendment forbidding territorial concessions to foreign powers and the continued warming up of Sino-Russian relations that culminated in the February 2022 communiqué. In contrast to Japan's tepid response to the 2014 Russian annexation of Crimea, the Kishida administration strongly condemned Russia's aggression and fully partook in the international effort to impose punishing sanctions on a scale never seen before.

The Japanese government swiftly moved to freeze the assets of Putin and his associates, restrict transactions with Russia's central bank, exclude several Russian banks from the Society for Worldwide Financial Telecommunications (SWIFT) messaging system, prohibit new investments, strip Russia of its most favored nation (MFN) trading status, and impose stiff export controls on a large range of products, including high-tech components and machinery.[6] Citing energy security concerns, the Japanese government has decided against exiting the oil and liquified natural gas projects in Sakhalin, but has committed to a coal ban and phasing out oil imports from Russia. In addition to $800 million in humanitarian financial support for Ukraine in the first months of war, the Japanese government has taken two rare steps to aid Ukraine: sending nonlethal defense equipment to a country mired in a hot war, and welcoming refugees seeking to escape the conflict, with more than 1,300 Ukrainians accepted into Japan by mid-2022.[7] Significantly, the Japanese public supported Kishida's forward-leaning approach. A *Nikkei* poll in spring 2022 showed 60 percent approval of the government's response to the Ukraine crisis, while 44 percent of respondents deemed the sanctions appropriate and 42 percent thought they should be expanded.[8] Prime Minister Kishida's surprise visit to Kyiv in March 2023 to meet with President Zelensky marked a new milestone for contemporary Japan: the first trip of a prime minister to a war zone.

In mustering a robust response to Putin's full-scale invasion of Ukraine, Prime Minister Kishida drew a direct connection to safeguarding peace in the Indo-Pacific. Noting that "Ukraine may be East Asia tomorrow," Kishida urged a resolute stand against the use of force to unilaterally change the status quo, in order to maintain stability in the Taiwan Strait.[9] Due to China's raft of coercive measures (including live-fire military exercises surrounding Taiwan, cyberattacks, and import bans) to punish Taiwan for the August 2022 visit by U.S. Speaker of the House of Representatives Nancy Pelosi, there is deep concern that the timeline for a contingency plan for the Strait of Taiwan has accelerated. An end to Asia's long peace, especially as the risk of a Chinese military takeover of Taiwan grows, is top of mind for the U.S.-Japan alliance.

SHORING UP REGIONAL STABILITY

Under President Joe Biden, the United States has moved to repair alliances and create new venues for minilateral security and economic cooperation, such as the Australia-UK-U.S. nuclear-powered submarine deal (AUKUS)[10] and the Indo-Pacific Economic Framework (IPEF). The Biden administration has retained its Indo-Pacific focus even as it attends to the Ukraine crisis in Europe and has framed China as the pacing challenge for U.S. national security. Biden's Indo-Pacific strategy identifies as its central goal not to change China, but rather to influence the international environment in which it operates to curb its coercive practices.[11] This goal is only reachable through concerted effort among like-minded countries, and Japan has continued its ascent as America's most indispensable ally. Given its position in the first island chain, its role as host of the largest contingent of U.S. forces in the region, its technological sophistication, and its place at the center of the regional economic and security infrastructure, Japan is essential to the success of the United States' Asia strategy.

Abe's successors, Prime Ministers Suga and Kishida, have gone further in explicitly calling out China's disruptive behavior to the regional order and asserting the importance of stability in the Taiwan Strait in joint statements with the American president. Deterring China from using force to annex Taiwan—and defending the island if such a political decision were made—will test the mettle of the U.S.-Japan alliance. As China grows more powerful and assertive, the concern that it may attempt a military takeover of the island has intensified. Beijing has opted so far for a strategy of coercion without violence, notes Richard Bush, to undermine the confidence of the Taiwanese people in the ability of their government to secure their future.[12] But the coercion continues to intensify. While Taiwan's independence is Beijing's red line, the military option, especially if unprovoked by Taiwan, is a high-risk proposition for China, notwithstanding the dissipation of U.S. dominance. A modeling exercise by security policy scholar Michael O'Hanlon renders the outcome of a Chinese naval blockade as indeterminate.[13]

Calls in the United States to end the decades-long policy of strategic ambiguity (neither confirming nor denying a role in the defense of Taiwan) have grown. In Japan, some influential politicians and policymakers like the late Prime Minister Abe and former Defense Secretary (later special advisor to the prime minister) Kishi Nobuo have explicitly connected Taiwan's security to Japan's security.[14] But official policy in the United States and Japan is unchanged and the logic of strategic ambiguity remains strong, with both countries opting for a strategy of deterring China from using force to impose its will on Taiwan and discouraging Taiwan from proclaiming de jure independence that would likely trigger an armed conflict. Nevertheless, as the United States and Japan prepare for a possible Taiwan contingency, it is important to understand that their connections to the island are different, that for each of them the circumstances leading to a potential eventuality will play a large role in their response, and that much remains to be done by the allies to plan responses to different crisis scenarios.

As Adam Liff notes, Japan-Taiwan relations are deep and multidimensional, with strong people-to-people exchanges and robust economic ties, but security and defense ties are undeveloped. Japan does not have the equivalent of a Taiwan Relations Act, has never entered into a mutual defense agreement with Taiwan, and has not provided it with military equipment.[15] China's military choices will be a critical—but not the only—determinant of Japan's response. An attack on U.S. bases in Japan or in the Senkaku Islands would immediately lead to Japan's involvement under self-defense authorities. Additionally, U.S.-China military engagement in Japan's vicinity could be deemed by the Japanese government an important influence situation that requires an indirect role providing logistical and rear support as well as intelligence and surveillance, or it could be considered an existential threat to Japan, warranting the invocation of collective self-defense and a combat role for the SDF.[16] Given the high stakes of preserving the long peace and the unpredictability of kinetic war, buttressing deterrence and increasing the odds of different defense scenarios is of paramount importance to the U.S.-Japan alliance.

Another regional hotspot—the Korean Peninsula—is of growing concern. North Korea's reckless nuclear and missile programs constitute a major threat to regional stability and have provided a powerful incentive for deepened coordination among the United States, Japan, and South Korea. Upon the inauguration of South Korean President Yoon Suk-yeol in May 2022, the tempo of trilateral diplomacy grew markedly, spurred by the need to address the North Korean menace, but also driven by the priority attached by President Yoon to the improvement of relations with Japan as part of an Indo-Pacific tilt in the Republic of Korea's (ROK) foreign policy. In a noteworthy development, the United States, Japan, and South Korea announced a trilateral Indo-Pacific partnership on the sidelines of the November 2022 East Asia Summit in Phnom Penh. It highlighted the parties' common purpose in addressing key regional challenges: North Korea's nuclear and missile provocations, stability in the Taiwan Strait, and Chinese economic coercion.[17]

The vision for this trilateral partnership, however, cannot come to fruition in the absence of a Korea-Japan rapprochement. In a brave move, President Yoon announced in March 2023 a plan for an existing Korean foundation to make payments to forced labor victims with contributions from Korean firms, and with the expectation that Japanese firms might do so as well on a voluntary basis. The Japanese government struck a cautious note during the negotiations, offering an endorsement of past official statements of apology and stating it did not oppose voluntary contributions from Japan's private sector. A bilateral summit quickly materialized upon news of the forced labor compensation deal, marking the first such trip by a Korean leader to Japan in twelve years. Kishida and Yoon used their meeting to highlight the benefits that would come from a normalized bilateral relationship: a return of Japan-Korea shuttle diplomacy with regular visits from each country's leaders was announced; new dialogues to promote defense intelligence sharing and economic security were previewed, and the business federations from both countries pledged to promote youth exchanges. Additionally, Japan dropped the export control restrictions on semiconductor-grade chemicals, and the ROK withdrew its corresponding case from the WTO.

Yoon's wartime labor compensation package is not popular at home, however. An opinion poll showed that 56 percent of respondents oppose it, and the opposition party has accused the government of making unilateral concessions.[18] Bolder action from Japan—possibly through a joint statement on historical reconciliation and contributions from business groups (if not individual firms) to the foundation—would improve the chances of this historic deal taking root. It is here that Prime Minister Kishida has an opportunity to make a signal contribution to Japan's network diplomacy.

ON THE VERGE OF A SECURITY REVOLUTION?

Japan's defense architecture is front and center in the national political debate about the recalibration of the country's international role to meet the current geopolitical moment. Prime Minister Kishida, known as a foreign policy dove as a member of the liberal Kochikai faction (long associated with the Yoshida Doctrine tradition), surprised many with his tougher position on security policy in his bid for the prime ministership in fall 2021. As he debated the other Liberal Democratic Party (LDP) candidates vying for the top job, Kishida struck a different tone by conveying an openness to larger defense expenditures, the need for stronger missile defenses, and a willingness to entertain the acquisition of enemy base strike capabilities as options for Japan. After assuming office, Kishida rolled out his foreign policy vision, dubbed "realism diplomacy for a new era," in a late 2021 speech, which nevertheless had only a general action plan to protect universal values, secure Japan's peace and stability, and tackle global challenges.[19]

By the time Prime Minister Kishida delivered the keynote address at the June 2022 Shangri-La Dialogue, the message was both sterner and crisper. Noting the challenge at hand and Japan's special responsibilities, Kishida posited:

Can the rules-based international order we have built through hard work, dialogue, and consensus be upheld and the march of peace and prosperity continue? Or will we return to a lawless world where rules are ignored and broken, where unilateral changes to the status quo by force are unchallenged and accepted, and where the strong coerce the weak militarily or economically? That is the choice we have to make.[20]

Japan's 2022 review of its three core strategic documents—the National Security Strategy, the National Defense Strategy (formerly known as National Defense Program Guidelines), and the Mid-Term Defense Program—has taken place amid an unforeseen major war in Europe and ratcheted up tensions in the Indo-Pacific. Amid much greater global uncertainty, Japan has amplified its proactive foreign policy, inclusive of hard security arenas.[21] Many vectors are influencing Japan as it charts its strategic roadmap. For one, a reinterpretation of the China challenge is underway. While Tokyo desires stable bilateral relations with Beijing and the protection of its crucial economic relationship, the threat perception has grown more acute due to the intensification of China's coercive practices, and closer Sino-Russian coordination worries Japan's strategic planners. The focus on buttressing Japan's defense posture in the southwestern islands is increasingly viewed as insufficient in light of surmounting pressure north of Hokkaido and the deterioration of relations with Vladimir Putin's Russia. The Chinese and Russian pressure campaign against Japan has intensified, with high-visibility episodes including the circumnavigation of the Japanese archipelago by Russian and Chinese vessels in October 2021 and the appearance of Russian and Chinese strategic bombers near Japan at the time of the Quad summit in May 2022.

New horizons for Japan's networked security diplomacy are also part of Japan's updated security outlook. By articulating the interconnection of the liberal order across geographical spaces, Tokyo is well poised to strengthen ties with the EU and NATO (Kishida became the first Japanese leader to attend a NATO summit in summer 2022) while also maintaining its maritime security cooperation with Southeast Asia, a public goods agenda with the Quad, and closer defense and security ties with its strongest ally the United States and other strategic partners.

Prime Minister Kishida announced a relaunch of the FOIP strategy in a trip to India in March 2023. Concerned about the disparate responses from developing countries to Russia's aggression against Ukraine, the $75 billion dollar pledge for infrastructure and economic assistance to the Global South represents a doubling down on Japan's connectivity strategy—but this time with a larger reach in mind. The plan aims for a vast geographical expansion of the FOIP vision (to include Southeast and South Asia, Africa, the Middle East, and Latin America) with the goal of cementing its core principles (rule of law, respect for territorial borders, and freedom from coercion) and offering practical solutions to pressing issues such as food security, climate change, and debt sustainability. However, implementing this grander vision for FOIP is not without its challenges. Two come readily to mind: customizing the approach to meet the wide differences among countries and regions encapsulated under the broad Global South label, and ensuring ample resources to sustain a much larger level of ambition for Japan's connectivity efforts.[22]

Closer to home, Japan's physical proximity to growing stockpiles of ever-more-sophisticated nuclear weapons and missiles necessitates the government's strategic planning to focus on requisite investments to boost deterrence and improve defense capabilities across multiple domains, especially at a time of rapid shifts on the technological frontier.

As strategic debates deepened in Japan, two recommendations from the April 2022 report by the LDP's Research Commission on Security stood out: the adoption of counterstrike capabilities and a major increase in defense expenditures, keeping in mind NATO's "2 percent of GDP" reference point. A substantially larger defense budget would facilitate the modernization of Japan's SDF on multiple fronts, but the LDP commission emphasized a key signaling benefit as well, stating that "no country will help a country that is not prepared to defend itself, and a firm statement of Japan's resolve for its own self-defense will further strengthen the commitment to the defense of Japan by our ally, the United States" (author translation).[23] Larger defense outlays have been in the works. In late November 2021, the government approved an additional $6.8 billion for defense through the supplementary budget, which contributed to record-breaking total military spending.[24]

The redefinition of Japan's security posture has been forged by domestic political forces, not just geopolitical imperatives. It is clear the electoral calendar had an effect, since Prime Minister Kishida delayed the release of the national security documents to late 2022 to prevent clouding his party's chances in the Upper House summer election. With a strong showing for the ruling coalition at that electoral contest, Kishida gained a three-year window with no national elections during which he can focus on his domestic and foreign policy agendas. Coalition dynamics continue to influence the evolution of Japan's security policy, as the LDP's partner party Komeito has tempered some of the security reform proposals (e.g., nixed language that could hint at preventive or preemptive missile strike capabilities). Intra-LDP jockeying is an even larger force in the latest round of security policy reform. Before his tragic and sudden passing, former Prime Minister Abe led the largest LDP faction and was very outspoken in pushing further changes to Japan's security policy, highlighting Japan's stakes in Taiwan's security and urging debate on a nuclear sharing agreement with the U.S. to boost deterrence.[25] Kishida put the brakes on the latter idea right away, making the elimination of nuclear weapons a centerpiece of his foreign policy. Nevertheless, the void in the party left by Abe complicates Kishida's need to coordinate internally as the LDP advances major security reforms.

There are signs that some political constraints on Japanese security reform are easing. It is revealing that the LDP chose to include headline changes (hiking defense expenditures and developing counterstrike capabilities) in its election campaign manifestos *and* performed well at the polls in 2021 and 2022. When Kishida first rolled out his New Realism diplomacy, it was met with high levels of public support, with a 50–60 percent approval rating. It could well be that the messenger does matter, as Rob Fahey notes, since the public may be more receptive to proposals from the realist Kishida than from the culture warrior Abe.[26]

Recent polls suggest a shift in public opinion toward a more muscular defense outlook, but long-term trends have yet to be discerned. A June 2022 *Yomiuri Shimbun* poll, for example, showed 72 percent of respondents in favor of strengthening defense capabilities, while only 43 percent supported increasing military expenditures above 1 percent of GDP.[27] Public opinion on counterstrike capabilities is split (46 percent in favor and 46 percent against), and while discussing the nuclear option is no longer taboo, the public is decidedly against its pursuit (72 percent).[28] Significantly, public views have not changed in one other important dimension: an aversion to an overseas combat role for Japan's SDF. In a December 2020 survey by the Chicago Council of Global Affairs and the Japan Institute for International Affairs, 59 percent of Japanese respondents opposed the SDF fighting alongside the United States.[29]

Geopolitical exigencies and shifting domestic constraints shaped the National Security Strategy released on December 16, 2022. Noting that Japan's security environment is the most severe and complex since the end of World War II, the NSS points to ominous developments such as Russia's trampling of the general prohibition on the use of force and

China's attempts to change the status quo by force in the maritime and air domains in the East and South China Seas. China is identified as the "greatest strategic challenge" and requires Japan to call for responsible actions from Beijing. But Tokyo also seeks a stable relationship through enhanced security communication and cooperation in economic and people-to-people exchanges.[30]

The strategic document foresees a doubling down on Japan's network diplomacy. With a deepened U.S.-Japan alliance as an anchor, Tokyo is bent on augmenting its multilayered security and defense networks through agreements on information security, acquisition and cross-servicing, reciprocal troop access, and defense technology partnerships. To expedite defense equipment transfers and infrastructure development in counterpart nations, Japan will set a new cooperation mechanism separate from existing official development assistance programs.[31]

A redesigned defense architecture figures prominently in the strategic documents. Important milestones include the decision to acquire counterstrike capabilities and to abandon the self-imposed 1 percent of GDP ceiling on defense expenditures. These are bound to be transformational changes. By acquiring the capability to strike enemy bases, Japan is blurring the line between defensive and offensive weaponry, moving away from the traditional shield (Japan) and spear (U.S.) division of labor in the alliance.[32] This power projection capability is bound to spur a more integrated command and control strategy between the allies, not only because of requisite operational logistics (American intelligence and reconnaissance support will be essential to identifying targets given that Japan lags behind in these areas) but also due to the strategic consequences of a potential Japanese counterattack deep into Chinese or North Korean territories.[33]

The NSS pledges to raise Japan's defense spending to $318 billion, or 2 percent of its GDP, through 2027, thereby putting an end to the normative 1 percent ceiling. To meet this target, the GOJ plans to increase core defense spending by approximately 50 percent and to include line items that were previously not counted in the defense budget: Coast Guard operations, cyber capabilities, public infrastructure, and R&D.[34] To pay for a more robust defense budget, in late 2022 the ruling parties approved a plan for a $7.3 billion tax increase over the next five years. Broadly speaking, this plan anticipates a 4.5 percent hike in corporate taxes (with waivers for small enterprises), a 1 percent increase in the consumption tax (paired with a 1 percent reduction in the special Tohoku reconstruction tax), and a higher tobacco tax. Needless to say, additional taxes are not popular with the public and face dissent from Kishida's own party members, who were likely worried about the possible fallout so close to the unified local elections scheduled for spring 2023. In response, Prime Minister Kishida has pushed the implementation date to 2024[35] and hinted at the possibility of a future snap election to receive a public mandate ahead of the tax increase.

The perennial question in assessing Japan's security transformation is whether the country is prepared to cross the "normalization" threshold and take on a more traditional military role. Over the past decade Japan's security policy has been changing at a faster clip, and yet the answer to that question is still "not yet." The new counterstrike capabilities will remain wedded to the tight restrictions on the use of force overseas—Japan's survival must be at stake, no other means of response are available, and only the minimum necessary use of force will be employed. Moreover, Japanese public sentiment has not morphed abruptly from pacifism to realism. Hardened pragmatism seems a more adept descriptor of Japan's national mood as it reckons with a world of growing antagonism.

NOTES

1. Colin Kahl and Thomas Wright, *Aftershocks: Pandemic Politics and the End of the Old International Order* (New York: St. Martin's Press, 2021).

2. According to a Pentagon report from November 2021, China is poised to quadruple its arsenal to one thousand nuclear warheads by 2030. See Demetri Sevastopulo and Kathrin Hille, "China Tests New Space Capability with Hypersonic Missile," *Financial Times*, October 16, 2021, www.ft.com/content/ba0a3cde-719b-4040-93cb-a486e1f843fb; and Andrew F. Krepinevich Jr., "The New Nuclear Age: How China's Growing Nuclear Arsenal Threatens Deterrence," *Foreign Affairs*, May/June 2022, www.foreignaffairs.com/articles/china/2022-04-19/new-nuclear-age.

3. See Michelle Ye Hee Lee, "U.S. and South Korea Respond to North Korean Launch with 8 Missiles of Their Own," *Washington Post*, June 6, 2022, www.washingtonpost.com/world/2022/06/06/north-korea-ballistic-missile-us-south-korea/; and Choe Sang-hun, "North Korea Sees New Opportunities in 'Neo-Cold War,'" *The New York Times*, November 13, 2022, www.nytimes.com/2022/11/13/world/asia/north-korea-missile-tests.html.

4. See "Russia-China Joint Statement on International Relations, February 4, 2022," U.S.-China Institute, University of Southern California, February 4,

2022, https://china.usc.edu/russia-china-joint-statement-international-relations
-february-4-2022.

5. Angela Stent, "The Putin Doctrine: A Move on Ukraine Was Always
Part of the Plan," *Foreign Affairs*, January 27, 2022, www.foreignaffairs.com/
articles/ukraine/2022-01-27/putin-doctrine.

6. See Government of Japan, "Japan Stands with Ukraine," June 20, 2022,
https://japan.kantei.go.jp/ongoingtopics/pdf/jp_stands_with_ukraine_eng.pdf.

7. See Michelle Ye Hee Lee and Julia Mio Inuma, "Japan Has Always
Been Refugee-Averse. Then Ukraine Happened," *Washington Post*, June 21,
2022, www.washingtonpost.com/world/2022/06/21/japan-ukraine-refugees
-immigration/.

8. See Naoya Yoshino, "Getting Real: Kishida Marks 'New Era' in Diplomacy as Japan Looks Beyond Pacifism," *Nikkei Asia*, May 25, 2022, https://
asia.nikkei.com/Spotlight/The-Big-Story/Getting-real-Kishida-marks-new-era
-in-diplomacy-as-Japan-looks-beyond-pacifism.

9. See Robert Wright and Demetri Sevastopulo, "'Resolute' Ukraine Response
Vital to Deter China on Taiwan, Japan PM Says," *Financial Times*, May 5,
2022, https://www.ft.com/content/1850bba8-d2ea-48f6-9e33-763b008019b7.

10. Announced in September 2021, the AUKUS security and defense partnership will enable Australia to acquire nuclear powered submarines as a first
endeavor. Cyber security, AI, and quantum computing are additional areas of
future cooperation. See Tom Corben, Ashley Townshend, and Susannah Patton,
"What Is the AUKUS Partnership?" United States Studies Centre, September
16, 2021, www.ussc.edu.au/analysis/explainer-what-is-the-aukus-partnership.

11. The White House, "Indo-Pacific Strategy of the United States," National
Security Council, Executive Office of the President, Washington, DC, February
2022, www.whitehouse.gov/wp-content/uploads/2022/02/U.S.-Indo-Pacific
-Strategy.pdf.

12. Richard Bush, *Difficult Choices: Taiwan's Quest for Security and the
Good Life* (Washington, DC: Brookings Institution Press, 2021).

13. See Michael E. O'Hanlon, "Can China Take Taiwan? Why No One Re-
ally Knows," The Brookings Institution, August 2022, https://www.brookings
.edu/research/can-china-take-taiwan-why-no-one-really-knows/.

14. See Liam Gibson, "Abe Again Says Taiwan's Security Is Japan's Affair
and US Should Opt for 'Strategic Clarity,'" *Taiwan News*, February 27, 2022,
www.taiwannews.com.tw/en/news/4457017; and "Tokyo Says Taiwan Security Directly Connected to Japan—Bloomberg," *Reuters*, June 24, 2021, www
.reuters.com/article/japan-taiwan-china-security/tokyo-says-taiwan-security
-directly-connected-to-japan-bloomberg-idUSL3N2O64E5.

15. Adam P. Liff, "The U.S.-Japan Alliance and Taiwan," *Asia Policy* 17, no.
3 (July 2022): 125–60.

16. David Sacks, "Enhancing U.S.-Japan Coordination for a Taiwan Conflict," Discussion Paper, Council on Foreign Relations, January 2022, www
.cfr.org/report/enhancing-us-japan-coordination-taiwan-conflict; and Tetsuo
Kotani in "Japan and Asia's Security in 2022 with Kotani Tetsuo and Ueki

Chikako Kawakatsu," hosted by Robert Ward, *Japan Memo* podcast, Season 2, Episode 5, International Institute for Strategic Studies, June 7, 2022, www.iiss .org/blogs/podcast/2022/06/japan-and-asia-security-in-2022.

17. White House, "Phnom Penh Statement on U.S.-Japan-Republic of Korea Trilateral Partnership for the Indo-Pacific," November 13, 2022, www .whitehouse.gov/briefing-room/statements-releases/2022/11/13/phnom-penh -statement-on-trilateral-partnership-for-the-indo-pacific/.

18. Motoko Rich and Choe Sang-Hun, "Japan and South Korea Make Nice, but Can It Last?" *The New York Times*, March 17, 2023, https://www.nytimes .com/2023/03/17/world/asia/japn-south-korea-relations.html.

19. See Michitaka Kaiya, "Kishida's 'Realism' Foreign Policy Vision Put to Test by Russian Invasion," *The Japan News*, May 7, 2022, https://japannews .yomiuri.co.jp/politics/political-pulse/20220507-24286/.

20. See "Transcript: Japan PM Kishida's Speech at Shangri-La Dialogue," *Nikkei Asia*, June 11, 2022, https://asia.nikkei.com/Politics/International -relations/Indo-Pacific/Transcript-Japan-PM-Kishida-s-speech-at-Shangri-La -Dialogue.

21. I appreciate the feedback from an anonymous reviewer that helped me sharpen this point.

22. Jesse Johnson and Gabriel Dominguez, "With Renewed Push, Kishida Aims to Put His Own Stamp on Japan's Indo-Pacific Strategy," *The Japan Times*, March 21, 2023, https://www.japantimes.co.jp/news/2023/03/21/ national/politics-diplomacy/fumio-kishida-investment-foip-china/.

23. Liberal Democratic Party, "新たな国家安全保障戦略等の策定に向けた提言" [Proposal for Formulating a New National Security Strategy], April 26, 2022, https://www.jimin.jp/news/policy/203401.html.

24. Chieko Tsuneoka, "Japan Approves Extra Defense Spending and Sets a Record," *The Wall Street Journal*, November 26, 2021, www.wsj.com/articles/ japan-approves-extra-defense-spending-and-sets-a-record-11637916622.

25. See Jesse Johnson, "Japan Should Consider Hosting U.S. Nuclear Weapons, Abe Says," *The Japan Times*, February 27, 2022, www.japantimes.co .jp/news/2022/02/27/national/politics-diplomacy/shinzo-abe-japan-nuclear -weapons-taiwan/.

26. Rob Fahey, "Under Kishida, Japan's Security Reforms Gather Speed," *Tokyo Review*, June 6, 2022, www.tokyoreview.net/2022/06/under-kishida -japans-security-reforms-gather-speed/.

27. "2022年6月 電話全国世論調査 ^(質問と回答" [June 2022 National Telephone Opinion Poll: Questions and Responses], *Yomiuri Shimbun*, June 6, 2022, www.yomiuri.co.jp/election/yoron-chosa/20220605-OYT1T50163/.

28. Craig Kafura, "Does the Russia-Ukraine War Herald a New Era for Japan's Security Policy?" *The Diplomat*, May 16, 2022, https://thediplomat.com /2022/05/does-the-russia-ukraine-war-herald-a-new-era-for-japans-security -policy/.

29. Craig Kafura et al., "Strong Partners: Japanese and American Perceptions of the U.S. and the World," The Chicago Council of Global Affairs and Japan Institute for International Affairs, March 2022, 2, 9.

30. Cabinet Office of Japan, *National Security Strategy*, Tokyo, December 2022, https://www.cas.go.jp/jp/siryou/221216anzenhoshou/nss-e.pdf.

31. Ibid.

32. For a thorough analysis of the merits and demerits of the foreign territory strike debate in Japan, see Corey Wallace, "Japan and Foreign Territory Strike: Debate, Deterrence, and Defense Strength," *Journal of Global Strategic Studies* 1, no. 2 (2021): 30–78.

33. Christopher Johnstone, "Japan's Transformational National Security Strategy," Center for Strategic and International Studies, December 8, 2022, www.csis.org/analysis/japans-transformational-national-security-strategy.

34. "Japan Seeks to Raise 5-Year Defense Spending by 50 Percent," *Nikkei Asia*, December 5, 2022, https://asia.nikkei.com/Politics/Japan-seeks-to-raise-5-year-defense-spending-by-50.

35. "Tax Hike Plan for Defense Spending OK'ed, despite Lack of Schedule," *The Asahi Shimbun*, December 16, 2022, https://www.asahi.com/ajw/articles/14794229.

Conclusion

A Network Power in a Divided World

The seams of the world order are coming apart. The domestic malaise in many liberal democracies is evident as social inequality, political polarization, and populist upheaval undermine the institutions of representative democracy. In a broad expanse of the world, democratic decline is taking hold with authoritarianism on the rise. A large portion of the developing world is reeling from inequities in access to COVID-19 vaccines, food and commodity price hikes, protectionism in advanced markets, and debt insolvency. A technology revolution is transforming how societies, economies, and political systems operate. While globalization has lifted millions out of poverty, the weaponization of economic interdependence has made apparent the appeal of defensive economic measures and provided impetus for reshoring far-flung supply chains.

China and the United States increasingly view their relationship in zero-sum terms. China's nontransparent military buildup and acts of economic coercion have raised alarm about the possible consequences of a successful Chinese bid for regional primacy. The United States is increasingly consumed by hyper-partisanship, which has led to major foreign policy fluctuations, and has abdicated its traditional role as free trade champion. In the past, Asian economies thrived due to the stability of a U.S. security anchor encompassing multilateral organizations, as well as through the economic magnet of an opening China. Today, these conditions no longer hold, as China's economy stumbles due to its zero-COVID policy and disorganized reopening, the United States remains deeply divided, and multilateral cooperation is tested by growing discord. Asia's long peace grows more strained with rising tension in the East and South China Seas, North Korea's provocations, and the greater urgency of deterring conflict over Taiwan and preparing for a possible Taiwan contingency. Russia's revisionism has brought large-scale war to Europe and raised concerns about undeterred authoritarian powers using force to redraw international borders.

In this turbulent new world, Japan has emerged as an increasingly important ally for the United States. Sustaining a Free and Open Indo-Pacific, mobilizing maritime democracies to supply public goods in the region, and joint planning and training to strengthen regional deterrence are new milestones in the U.S.-Japan alliance. The alliance has become more multidimensional by including new lines of effort, such as boosting the resilience of supply chains, promoting science and technology cooperation, disseminating digital economy standards, and fleshing out novel tools for economic security purposes. In some areas, a reversal of roles in the region and beyond is in fact evident. It has been Japan, not the United States, which has brokered mega trade agreements, provided robust infrastructure financing to Asia-Pacific nations, and led the push to codify standards on data flows in the G7 and G20.

The greater scope and depth of the alliance is not just a response to a harsher international environment but also has much to do with Japan's own transformation. Because of the distance traveled, many of the old frames used to describe Japan's international role and its place in the alliance are a poor fit. Japan today is much more than the junior partner hosting U.S. military bases in exchange for shelter under the nuclear umbrella, or the passive actor that downplayed its regional political role and operated in the international trading system as a follower of rules set by others. Japan is no longer described as an unstoppable mercantilist juggernaut and host nation free rider. Nor does the image of a Japan in inexorable decline, sapped of regional influence and fading in importance to U.S. foreign policy, appear plausible. The predicted shift from "Japan bashing" to "Japan passing," as many assumed the country would sink into obscurity with an exhausted economic engine and unwieldy domestic politics, did not materialize.

However, the enormous obstacles Japan faces have not disappeared, including demographic contraction, energy dependence, and slow growth, to name a few. And while Japan's restrictions on the use of military power have eased, they remain the tightest among all U.S. allies with no desire from the public to soften the strictures on Japan

Self-Defense Forces combat missions. The interesting question, then, is how Japan was able to emerge from the lost decades, continue to operate within these sizable constraints, and find a way to articulate its most consequential grand strategy of the postwar era. In offering an account of Japan's underrated leadership, this book has underscored four major factors: 1) resilience to the populist wave (through globalization adjustment, social cohesion, and democratic stability); 2) enhanced political executive decision-making (due to institutional and administrative reforms coupled with periods of effective political management); 3) a strategy of all-out network diplomacy (crafting economic and security partnerships, clout through rulemaking); and 4) the premium placed on Japan's new leadership to sustain the international liberal system at a time of profound geopolitical uncertainty. These broad, sweeping vectors influenced one another, as can be gleaned from the themes woven together in this book's examination of the evolution of Japan's politics, political economy, and foreign policy.

CHANGE, NOT STAGNATION

Notwithstanding the image of stagnation, there has been palpable change across business, politics and policymaking, and diplomacy in ways that explain Japan's enduring economic influence and its ability to articulate more proactive domestic reforms and foreign policy agendas. On the economic front, Japan has struggled with protracted deflation, low productivity in several economic sectors, and a fragile and unequal recovery from various shocks. At the same time, business dynamism is evident in many areas. Japanese companies were pioneers in developing regional production networks, have specialized in the high-tech manufacturing of advanced materials and sophisticated equipment, and possess strongholds in key nodes of critical supply chains such as the semiconductor industry.

Behind the mantle of almost unbroken Liberal Democratic Party (LDP) rule, the political system has evolved in significant ways with electoral, political funding, and administrative reforms that transformed the nature of political competition, ushered in coalition governments, and enabled the emergence of strong executive power. The office of the prime minister acquired the power of policy initiative and execution and is no longer perennially overshadowed by iron triangles. The country's leaders can now rely on whole-of-government decision-making as they advance signature foreign economic policy initiatives (at the Trans-Pacific Partnership Headquarters) or devise and implement security and defense policies (in the National Security Council).

Facing a deteriorating security environment, Japan has seen substantial innovation in its foreign policy over the past decade. Many of the changes have been piecemeal and come with many strings attached, but they have deepened the security alliance with the United States (especially with the new interpretation of collective self-defense) and have placed Japan at the center of Indo-Pacific diplomacy. Japan's Free and Open Indo-Pacific (FOIP) concept has influenced how many nations inside and outside the region articulate their own regional strategies, and after a false start, the Quad made a comeback with summits between national leaders and a more robust cooperation agenda. This experience also taught Tokyo an important lesson: the need to ground its regional diplomacy in proactive diplomatic outreach to Southeast Asia based on tangible benefits such as infrastructure financing and maritime safety capacity-building.

China's civil-military fusion and ambitions to dominate advanced dual-use technologies, the sharp deterioration of U.S.-China relations, and the breakout of war in Europe through Russia's invasion of Ukraine continue to spur change in Japan's statecraft. Japan is at the forefront of efforts to devise a comprehensive approach to economic security, as it was the first country to appoint a specially designated minister with this portfolio, and these efforts will continue through the implementation of the new economic security bill passed in spring 2022. As discussed further on, this move presents Tokyo with complicated tradeoffs in recalibrating its relationship with China and balancing economic integration and national security. The response of Prime Minister Kishida Fumio's administration to the invasion of Ukraine broke new ground in Japan's foreign policy, putting an end to the previous policy of engagement with Russia; and Japan has joined international sanctions of unprecedented scope, including coordinated export controls to reduce Russia's access to advanced technology. As international politics shift, so have important coordinates of Japan's foreign policy through an evolving policy toolkit.

LESSONS FROM JAPAN

More and more, Japan seems less an outlier and more a bellwether for some of the complex policy challenges facing many advanced industrialized countries. The demographic cliff that will drastically curtail the share of the working-age population is no longer Japan's problem alone. In fact, scores of nations (including China) are already experiencing it. "Japanization" was a term coined to reflect a feared economic syndrome of stubborn deflation, stagnant growth, and low interest rates. Other industrialized nations have since experienced secular stagnation with demographic decline depressing demand and investment and building deflationary pressures.[1] Japan's macroeconomic challenges are no longer unique, making lessons learned from Japan more relevant. Case in point is monetary policy. Japan's tepid (at first) and full blown (later) experimentation with quantitative easing heavily influenced the policy choices of other central banks.

In the throes of the lost decades, Japan was a distant laggard from other Organization for Economic Co-operation and Development (OECD) nations in economic performance. However, the economy recovered from its banking crisis in the 1990s and overcame sharp downturns during the 2008 Global Financial Crisis and 2011 triple disaster. Through the 2010s, Japan's GDP per capita growth was on par with that of its OECD peers. But Japan has also caught up to the income inequality levels of other industrialized nations, even if the drivers of socioeconomic gaps are different.

Shared common problems and convergence in performance outcomes are not the only ways in which Japan's experience is more relevant. In some important dimensions, Japan has performed better than many of its peers. Japan's adjustment to economic globalization (with supply chain trade at the heart of its economic relationship with China), greater employment security, and more robust social safety nets has spared it the social backlash and protectionist surge experienced in countries like the United States. As the politics of the West have been roiled by a populist wave that has wounded the institutions of liberal democracy, Japan has exhibited democratic stability without steep social and political polarization. Hence, Japan has escaped the populist trap of hyper-partisanship, all-out attacks on the institutions of representative democracy, and weakened electoral integrity.

Japan is no longer the economic miracle to emulate nor the basket case of the industrialized world. It is a nation that has struggled on numerous fronts yet found a path through others. Japan's failures and successes provide both cautionary tales and constructive insights that speak directly to the experiences of a growing contingent of countries around the world.

A NETWORK POWER PAR EXCELLENCE

As the third largest economy with the ninth largest military budget in the world, Japan has sizable—but relatively diminishing—material capabilities. The most successful avenue for Tokyo to overcome resource constraints has been to establish networks and create new partnerships. Hence, at the heart of Japan's economic influence and diplomatic clout lies a connectivity strategy. Contrary to popular perception, Japan embraced economic globalization, doubling down on outward integration and supply chain development in the post-GFC period when many peer nations stalled in their globalization push. Through private investment, regional production networks, and public funding for infrastructure projects, Japan has become deeply embedded in the fabric of the Indo-Pacific economy. FOIP gained traction because it was propelled by tangible benefits: trade integration, infrastructure finance, foreign direct investment flows, plus capacity-building for maritime safety and defense equipment sales.

Japan now sits at the nexus of the two largest trade agreements in the region, the Comprehensive and Progressive TPP (CPTPP) and the Regional Comprehensive Economic Partnership (RCEP), and has a track record of disseminating economic standards across different forums. Tokyo embarked on a campaign to upgrade security partnerships with like-minded countries that generated substantive results. The relationship with Australia and India deepened markedly, Japan created strategic partnerships with Southeast Asian partners like Vietnam and the Philippines, and strengthened ties with European nations such as the UK and France. The Quad relaunched and consolidated. Japan leads with the largest number of defense dialogues in the Indo-Pacific and has been identified as the "quintessential smart power" by the Lowy Institute's Asia Power Index for its ability to leverage limited resources to maximize economic, diplomatic, and cultural influence.[2]

In myriad ways, Japan has been an active participant in rewiring the economic and security lines of cooperation in the Indo-Pacific, such as pushing for new trade agreements and expanding networks of bilateral and minilateral security cooperation. Nevertheless, acute geopolitical rifts, pandemic insularity, and the securitization of international economic relations have converged in the form of a profound stress test for Japan's connectivity statecraft.

ADJUSTING TO A FRACTURING WORLD

Japan has accomplished much since the lost decades set in and the nation's troubles piled up through demographic and energy shocks, volatile political leadership, and foreign policy equivocations. Yet, many critical problems remain unsolved and new challenges abound. At home, the government has yet to deliver a sustainable economic recovery that effectively tackles the sources of income inequality—chiefly inequities for non-regular workers and stagnant wages, among other factors. The revitalization of Japan's democracy through a more competitive party system and engaged citizenry is a key priority. So is delivering results in the grand plans for digital, green, and human capital transformations that are essential to Japan's future economic competitiveness and renewed social compact. In the post–Abe Shinzo era, key political tasks for the current and future administrations are to remain attuned to the demands of the public, restore public confidence in the aftermath of the Unification Church scandal, and avoid the politics of indecision that preclude effective governance.

Compounding geopolitical risks will test Japan in profound ways. With intensifying risks to peace in neighboring areas, including the Taiwan Strait, the U.S. alliance will remain the bedrock of Japan's security. But the allies have much work to do to strengthen deterrence given the regional arms race and more frequent instances of Chinese coercion that could escalate into conflict. There are threats to Japan's prosperity as well. Tokyo's connectivity strategy is at a crossroads, and there are two challenges at hand. First, the strict and protracted border closures implemented by the government during the COVID-19 pandemic were out of step with scientific guidelines and tracked poorly with the policies of G7 peers. They have hurt the country's international standing, frustrated attempts to ease the arrival of manual workers needed to address the labor crunch, and presented a formidable obstacle in the race to attract global talent essential to Japan's competitiveness. They are self-defeating since an inward-looking Japan cannot be a thriving Japan. Much is at stake, therefore, in how Japan manages its way back from the pandemic.

Second, state rivalry and technology competition have forced a reckoning in Japan's economic statecraft, which must strike a new balance between economic internationalism and national security. The greater risk of war in Asia and competition over dual-use technologies has increased the risks of overdependence on China. The pull for a stable Sino-Japanese relationship that diminishes the chances of conflict and preserves a beneficial economic relationship is still strong, but the path for cooperation is narrowing. As Tokyo fleshes out its economic security toolkit, it is eager to deepen coordination with its American ally, but the concern that the United States is mostly playing defense on globalization without a more ambitious economic engagement strategy persists.

The international economic order that Japan inhabits is in flux. The path ahead for Japan and many other countries is full of significant tradeoffs between openness and restrictions; multilateral commitments and unilateral security controls; and the use of economic instruments to pursue engagement and mutual dependence vs. hard-edged competition and risk minimization. It is not a world of deglobalization, for no one country can navigate the redrawn boundaries of economic interdependence and evolving geopolitical cleavages on its own and achieve its prosperity and security goals. Networks will be recalibrated, but they will continue to be a formidable asset. This makes Japan more, not less, relevant to what is yet to come.

NOTES

1. See Lawrence H. Summers, "Accepting the Reality of Secular Stagnation," *Finance & Development*, March 2020, www.imf.org/en/Publications/fandd/issues/2020/03/larry-summers-on-secular-stagnation.

2. See Lowy Institute, *Asia Power Index*, 2021 edition, https://power.lowyinstitute.org/power-gap/.

Acknowledgments

Writing this book has been a journey. As is often the case, the book I wrote was not the book I anticipated writing. And that process of discovery—of the story I increasingly felt compelled to tell in this volume—was of course exhilarating and frustrating. I could never have done this alone. I benefited from the support and wisdom of a community of scholars both inside and outside of Brookings. Alan Song at the Smith Richardson Foundation and Bruce Jones as then-Vice President of Foreign Policy at the Brookings Institution offered advice early on as I shaped and reshaped the research questions guiding this project. Suzanne Maloney, current Vice President of Foreign Policy at Brookings, offered all the support possible for my book-writing efforts and my role as director of the Center for East Asia Policy Studies. I owe a special debt of gratitude to my friend and colleague Michael O'Hanlon, who went beyond his duty as Director of Research in Foreign Policy at Brookings to offer great advice on the book's overall framing and provided detailed feedback for each chapter, which greatly improved my arguments. Mike always offers help with generosity of heart and a good dose of humor.

Scholars and public intellectuals whom I admire generously agreed to read chapters or the whole manuscript. I am grateful to Katada Saori, Adam Liff, Ulrike Schaede, and Funabashi Yoichi for their very valuable comments. Two anonymous reviewers provided very helpful feedback that helped me tighten the arguments. My dear mentor Richard Bush offered keen insights as I prepared my 2020 *Foreign Affairs* article "The

Underappreciated Power," which served as a guidepost for the book project. All remaining errors are, of course, mine.

My colleagues at the Center for East Asia Policy Studies (CEAP) at Brookings, Richard Bush, Ryan Hass, Bruce Jones, Patricia Kim, Tanvi Madan, Jonathan Stromseth, and Andrew Yeo, have helped me better understand the Indo-Pacific, thereby sharpening my understanding of Japan's role in this consequential region. Whether we are discussing regional developments during staff meetings, coming together to offer policy prescriptions for U.S. Indo-Pacific strategy, or traveling to the region and participating in panels and roundtables, I am frequently reminded of how fortunate I am to work with such brilliant and collegial folks.

I am indebted as well to Jennifer Mason, who early on provided research support for the book, and who in her capacity as Associate Director at CEAP does an outstanding job with all of the center's administrative tasks. With her characteristic efficiency, eye for detail, and good cheer, Jennifer made it possible for me to find the time and concentration required for book writing.

My deepest gratitude goes to Laura McGhee, Senior Research Assistant and Project Coordinator at CEAP. Laura has been my right hand in carrying out all the programmatic activity of the Philip Knight Chair in Japan Studies at Brookings and provided superb research assistance: tracking references, fact-checking, copyediting chapters, and composing scores of tables and figures. Laura's resourcefulness, standards of excellence, and coolness under pressure as impossible deadlines loomed were invaluable.

This book was generously funded by several research grants. I am very grateful to the Smith Richardson Foundation, the former Center for Global Partnership at the Japan Foundation, and the United States-Japan Foundation for their support of this research project. Brookings is committed to quality, independence, and impact, and this book and the support of these donors reflect this commitment.

This deep dive into Japan awarded me a precious intellectual opportunity: to broaden my horizons beyond my usual perch of foreign economic policy to better understand Japan's domestic evolution and transformed international role. It was with trepidation that I tackled new or less familiar topics for me such as immigration and demographics, political change and democratic resilience, security policy and hard power competition. This was an enormous learning opportunity—and undoubtedly a humbling one as I tried to make sense of the rich tapestry of forces influencing a country's path. While my understanding of these complex subjects remains incomplete, my ability to undertake deep and broad scholarly analysis of an evolving Japan would not have been possible without the foresight of Philip Knight in endowing a Japan Studies Chair at Brookings.

It is my family and friends, especially my daughters Natalia and Paola, who ultimately made these endeavors possible. Thank you for all the encouragement and for providing meaning outside of work—even though I work all the time!

This book is dedicated to the previous generation: my mother Mireya, and Joan and Edward Groobert. In their wisdom, generosity, and warmth, they are a tough act to follow, but I owe them a good try.

Index

About the Author

Mireya Solís is director of the Center for East Asia Policy Studies, Knight Chair in Japan Studies, and Senior Fellow in the Foreign Policy program at the Brookings Institution, where she specializes in Japanese foreign economic policy, international trade policy, and U.S. economic statecraft in Asia.